The hardships of Nomad life in the Wilderness. A Bedawin encampment

OLD TESTAMENT VOL. II

FROM MOSES TO ELISHA

Israel to the end of the Ninth Century B.C.

BY

L. ELLIOTT BINNS
D.D.

GREENWOOD PRESS, PUBLISHERS
WESTPORT, CONNECTICUT

Library of Congress Cataloging in Publication Data

Elliott-Binns, Leonard Elliott, 1885-
   From Moses to Elisha.

   Reprint of the 1929 ed. published at the Clarendon
Press, Oxford, which was issued as v. 2 of The Clarendon
Bible, Old Testament.
   Bibliography: p.
   Includes index.
   1. Bible. O.T. Historical books--Commentaries.
I. Title. II. Series: The Clarendon Bible ; v. 2
BS1205.E42 1979   222   78-10639
ISBN 0-313-21015-2

BS
1205
.E42
1979

This reprint has been authorized by the Oxford University
Press.

Reprinted in 1979 by Greenwood Press, Inc.
51 Riverside Avenue, Westport, CT 06880

Printed in the United States of America

10 9 8 7 6 5 4 3 2 1

EDITORS' PREFACE

THE first volume of *The Clarendon Bible* series to be published was part of the New Testament, Canon A. W. F. Blunt's Commentary on *The Acts of the Apostles*. Since the publication of that work we have considered the question of the Old Testament, and its place in our series. The inclusion of the Old Testament literature raised a number of difficult and perplexing problems. In these circumstances the General Editors requested *the Society for Old Testament Study* to be good enough to prepare a scheme. This has been done by Canon G. H. Box, with the assistance of other members of the Society, and the scheme is as follows :

Six volumes are to be devoted to the Old Testament literature, five of which will be concerned with the literature proper, and one with the external history. They have been grouped according to the following plan :

    I. Introductory. The external environment of ancient and post-exilic Israel, and its influence upon the development of Israel's religion.

    II. From the Exodus to the Fall of Samaria.

    III. The Decline and Fall of the Hebrew Kingdoms (down to the Fall of Jerusalem 586 B.C.).

    IV. Exile and Restoration (down to the end of the Persian Period).

    V. The later post-exilic Jewish Church (from the beginning of the Greek Period to the second century B.C.).

    VI. Final volume. This will deal with the prehistoric materials, the significance of myth and legend ; the general view of the History given in the documents, &c.

In this series Vol. I will be a manual of history ; Vols. II–V will deal with selected literature illustrating the period under review. In each book there will be a general introduction embracing about fifty pages, followed by a series of selected passages from the literature. *The text of these passages will not be printed*, but will be indicated in each case by reference to the R.V. ; but notes and explanations will be given on the passages. And there will be extended special notes on important points. Selected bibliographies will be printed in each volume, and maps and illustrations will be a feature.

The treatment of the Old Testament literature thus differs from the plan adopted in the case of the New Testament. But the general principles underlying the treatment are the same. The main idea is to set the books in their historic environment and to give a general constructive view of the development of the religion, with the aid afforded by modern critical and archaeological research. In particular, we desire to draw a clear line between what is historic and what is not strictly history ; and for this reason the beginnings of Israel's history and religion are traced from the Exodus : the consideration of the material found in Genesis is postponed till the final volume. We hope and believe that the series of volumes on the Old Testament which is now launched will provide a real discipline and preparation for those on the New Testament.

In conclusion, we may repeat what has already been said in the Preface to the New Testament volumes, which sufficiently sets forth the general aim of the whole series, both of the Old and New Testament :

' The problem of the teaching of Holy Scripture at the present time presents many difficulties. There is a large and growing class of persons who feel bound to recognize that the progress of archaeological and critical studies has made it impossible for them to read, and still more to teach, it precisely in the old way.

However strongly they may believe in inspiration, they cannot any longer set before their pupils, or take as the basis of their interpretation, the doctrine of the verbal inspiration of Holy Scripture. It is with the object of meeting the requirements not only of the elder pupils in public schools, their teachers, students in training colleges, and others engaged in education, but also of the clergy and the growing class of the general public, which we believe, takes an interest in Biblical studies, that the present series is projected.

' The writers will be responsible each for his own contribution only, and their interpretation is based upon the belief that the books of the Bible require to be placed in their historical context, so that, as far as possible, we may recover the sense which they bore when written. Any application of them must rest upon this ground. It is not the writer's intention to set out the latest notions of radical scholars—English or foreign—or even to describe the exact position at which the discussion of the various problems has arrived. The aim of the series is rather to put forward a constructive view of the books and their teaching, taking into consideration and welcoming results as to which there is a large measure of agreement among scholars. It is hoped to include a volume on the principles and logic of historical criticism.'

THOMAS OXON. ⎤
HERBERT WILD. ⎬ *General Editors.*
GEORGE H. BOX. ⎦

AUTHOR'S PREFACE

THE general purpose and scope of the series of Commentaries to which this volume belongs have been made clear by the Editors in their preface above : nothing further need therefore be furnished by way of explanation. It may, however, be as well to point out that in that preface the present volume is advertised as covering the period from the Exodus to the Fall of Samaria. As Dr. T. H. Robinson has already dealt with the latter event in Vol. III, *The Decline and Fall of the Hebrew Kingdoms*, in order to avoid unnecessary overlapping, I have brought my own commentary to an end with the death of Elisha. This is on other grounds a convenient terminus, for Elisha was the last of the great prophets before the rise of a new type with the coming of Amos.

The period which this volume covers is one of much importance since it includes the beginnings of the Hebrews as a nation and deals with the rise of the various institutions which gave to them their special character. In discussing the origins of laws and customs I have not hesitated to point out the primitive ideas and ideals which often lie behind them. The glory of Old Testament religion is that from low and superstitious beginnings it has been able to rise to such pure heights of spiritual attainment : to set forth its humble origins is therefore to do it no disservice.

In the spelling of proper names I have tried so far as is possible to preserve consistency ; to this end I have taken the forms given in *The Cambridge Ancient History* as a standard. In my references to other scholars and their works I have also endeavoured to use always the same wording. The enormous amount of ground covered by the volume has made it inconvenient

Author's Preface

to print any complete Bibliography. References have been given to further volumes on any points where space did not allow a full treatment and in the various standard commentaries on the separate books of the Old Testament lists of books will be found. Readers who may desire a Bibliography of Old Testament writings are recommended to obtain *A Scripture Bibliography* (Nesbit, 6*d*. net).

Finally, I wish to thank the general editors for reading through the contents of the following pages in both manuscript and proof. To Canon Box, in particular, I am indebted for several helpful suggestions and criticisms. I need hardly add that I have received every possible assistance from the officials of the Clarendon Press.

L. E. B.

GEDNEY VICARAGE, LINCS.

August 1929.

CONTENTS

LIST OF SELECTED PASSAGES xvii

LIST OF ILLUSTRATIONS xix

LIST OF MAPS xxi

INTRODUCTION

  A. Historical Background 1

    i. Egypt 1

    ii. Palestine in the Fourteenth Century B. C. 12

    iii. Assyria and Babylonia 21

    iv. Israel and Judah 27

  B. Israelite Religion to the end of the Ninth Century . . 45

    i. Early Hebrew Religion 45

    ii. The Wilderness Period 47

    iii. The period of Conquest and Settlement 49

    iv. From Solomon to Elisha 53

  C. The Biblical Sources for the Period 57

    i. Ancient Methods of Writing History 57

    ii. The Pentateuch (JE) 59

    iii. Joshua 62

    iv. Judges 63

    v. 1 and 2 Samuel 65

    vi. 1 and 2 Kings 66

  D. The Chronology of the Period 68

  E. Bibliography 72

NOTES TO SELECTED PASSAGES

The whole period from the Exodus to the death of Elisha can be conveniently divided up into four parts : I. Moses and the Exodus (Exod., Num., Deut.) ; II. The Settlement in Canaan (Josh., Judges, 1 Sam. 1–8) ; III. The United Kingdom (1 Sam. 9 to 1 Kings 11) ; and IV. The Divided Kingdom (1 Kings 12 to 2 Kings 13).

Principal Abbreviations 74

PART I. MOSES AND THE EXODUS

§ 1. The Early Life of Moses 75

  (a) Israel in Egypt (Exod. 1 ; Num. 11^5) 75

  (b) The Birth of Moses (Exod. 2$^{1-10}$) 77

  (c) The Flight to Midian (Exod. 2$^{11-22}$) 78

Contents

(d) The Call of Moses (Exod. 3^{1-12}) 81

(e) The Revelation of Jahveh (Exod. 3^{13-16}, 6^{2-9}) . . . 82

(f) The Three Signs (Exod. 4^{1-9}) 83

(g) Moses and Aaron (Exod. 4^{10-16}, $^{27-31}$) 84

(h) The Return to Egypt (Exod. 4^{18-26}) 85

§ 2. Moses and Pharaoh 87

(a) The First Plague : Water turned into Blood (Exod. 7^{14-25}) . 88

(b) The Second Plague : The Frogs (Exod. 8^{1-15}) . . . 88

(c) The Third and Fourth Plagues : Insects (Exod. 8^{16-32}) . 90

(d) The Fifth and Sixth Plagues : Murrain and Boils (Exod. 9^{1-12}) 91

(e) The Seventh Plague : the Hail (Exod. 9^{13-35}) . . . 92

(f) The Eighth Plague : the Locusts (Exod. 10^{1-20}) . . 92

(g) The Ninth Plague : the Great Darkness (Exod. 10^{21-29}) . 94

(h) The Institution of the Passover (Exod. 12^{1-28}) . . . 96

(i) The Tenth Plague : the Death of the Firstborn (Exod. 12^{29-36}) 98

(j) The Crossing of the Red Sea (Exod. $14-15^{21}$) . . . 99

§ 3. Israel at Sinai 101

(a) The Bitter Waters of Marah (Exod. 15^{22-26}) . . . 102

(b) The Revelation at Sinai (Exod. 19, 20^{18-21}) . . . 103

(c) The Covenant (Exod. 34) 104

(d) The Golden Calf (Exod. 32^{1-35}) 106

(e) The Divine Guidance (Exod. 23 ; Num. 10^{31-36}) . . 108

(f) The Tent of Meeting (Exod. 25^{1-9}, 29^{43-46}, 33^{5-11}) . . 108

(g) The Visit of Jethro (Exod. 18^{1-27} ; Num. 11^{24-30}) . . 109

(h) The Jealousy of Miriam (Num. 12^{1-15}) 110

§ 4. The Wanderings 111

(a) The Sending of the Spies (Num. 13) 111

(b) The Battle of Hormah (Num. 14^{40-45}, 21^{1-3}) . . . 113

(c) The Rebellion of Koran, Dathan, and Abiram (Num. 16^{1-35}) 114

(d) Manna and Quails (Exod. 16^{1-21}) 115

(e) Massah and Meribah (Exod. 17^{1-7} ; Num. 20^{2-13}) . . 116

(f) The Contest with Amalek (Exod. 17^{8-16}) 117

(g) The Brazen Serpent (Num. 21^{4-9}) 118

(h) The Conquest of the East Jordan Territory (Num. 21^{21-35}) . 119

(i) Balak sends for Balaam (Num. 22^{2-35}) 119

(j) Balaam blesses Israel (Num. 24^{1-13}) 120

(k) The Death of Moses (Num. 27^{12-23} ; Deut. 34^{1-6}) . . 122

PART II. THE SETTLEMENT IN CANAAN

§ 1. The Conquest of Canaan 123

(a) Joshua (Num. 27^{15-23} ; Deut. 3^{28}, $31^{14f.}$, ^{23}) . . . 123

(b) The Spies (Joshua 2) 124

Contents xiii

(c) The Crossing of the Jordan (Joshua 3⁹–4¹¹) . . . 125
(d) The Fall of Jericho (Joshua 5¹³–6²⁷) 126
(e) Achan's sin and its consequences (Joshua 7) . . . 128
(f) The Fall of Ai (Joshua 8¹⁻²⁹) 128
(g) The Ruse of the Gibeonites (Joshua 9³⁻²⁷) . . . 129
(h) The Battle of Gibeon (Joshua 10¹⁻²⁷) . . . 130
(i) The Defeat of Jabin (Joshua 11¹⁻⁹) 131
(j) Joshua's Farewell (Joshua 24) 132
(k) The Summary of the Conquest (Judges 1–2⁵) . . . 134

§ 2. The Rule of the Judges 136
(a) Othniel (Judges 3⁷⁻¹¹) 136
(b) Ehud (Judges 3¹²⁻³⁰) 137
(c) Deborah and Barak (Judges 4, 5) 138
(d) The Call of Gideon (Judges 6¹¹⁻³²) 141
(e) The Defeat of Midian (Judges 7) 142
(f) The Pursuit beyond Jordan (Judges 8⁴⁻²¹) . . . 143
(g) Abimelech's Rise (Judges 9¹⁻²¹) 144
(h) The End of Abimelech (Judges 9²²⁻⁵⁹) . . . 145
(i) Jephthah the Gileadite (Judges 11) 146
(j) Micah and his Image (Judges 17) 148
(k) The Trek of the Danites (Judges 18) 149

§ 3. The Struggle with the Philistines 150
(a) The Birth of Samson (Judges 13²⁻²⁵) 152
(b) Samson's Marriage (Judges 14) 153
(c) Samson's Exploits against the Philistines (Judges 15–16³) . 154
(d) Samson and Delilah (Judges 16⁴⁻³¹) 156
(e) The Birth of Samuel (1 Sam. 1) 159
(f) The Call of Samuel (1 Sam. 3) 160
(g) The Loss of the Ark (1 Sam. 4¹⁻¹¹) 161
(h) The Ark in the hands of the Philistines (1 Sam. 5) . 162
(i) The Return of the Ark (1 Sam. 6–7¹) . . . 164

PART III. THE UNITED KINGDOM

§ 1. The Rise and Decline of Saul 166
(a) The Choice of Saul (1 Sam. 9–10¹⁶) 166
(b) Saul's Opportunity (1 Sam. 11) 167
(c) Jonathan's Exploit and its Sequel (1 Sam. 14) . . 168
(d) The Rejection of Saul (1 Sam. 15) 169
(e) The Choice of Saul's successor (1 Sam. 16) . . 170
(f) David and Goliath (1 Sam. 17–18⁵) 172
(g) Saul's Jealousy (1 Sam. 18⁶⁻⁹, ²⁰⁻²⁸, 19¹⁻¹⁷) . . . 173
(h) David and Jonathan (1 Sam. 20¹⁻¹⁰, ¹⁸⁻³⁹) . . . 174

Contents

(i) David's Visit to Nob (1 Sam. 21$^{1-9}$, 22$^{6-23}$) . . . 174

(j) David spares Saul's life (1 Sam. 26) 175

(k) David at Gath (1 Sam. 21$^{10-15}$, 27) 176

(l) The Witch of En-dor (1 Sam. 28$^{3-25}$) 177

(m) The Death of Saul (1 Sam. 31 ; 2 Sam. 1$^{1-16}$) . . . 178

(n) David's Lament (2 Sam. 1$^{17-27}$) 178

§ 2. The Reign of David 179

(a) David at Hebron (2 Sam. 2) 179

(b) The treachery and death of Abner (2 Sam. 3$^{6-39}$) . . 180

(c) David becomes King of all Israel (2 Sam. 5) . . . 182

(d) The bringing up of the Ark (2 Sam. 6) . . . 183

(e) The Temple planned (2 Sam. 7$^{1-17}$) 184

(f) David's Sin (2 Sam. 11) 184

(g) David's Repentance (2 Sam. 12$^{1-25}$) . . . 185

(h) Absalom's Rebellion (2 Sam. 15) 186

(i) The Rival Counsellors (2 Sam. 16^{15}–17^{14}) . . . 187

(j) The Defeat and Death of Absalom (2 Sam. 18–19^8) . . 188

(k) The Revolt of Sheba (2 Sam. 20) 189

(l) The Story of Rizpah (2 Sam. 21$^{1-11}$) 190

(m) The Census (2 Sam. 24) 192

§ 3. The Reign of Solomon 193

(a) Adonijah or Solomon ? (1 Kings 1) 193

(b) David's last Charge (1 Kings 2$^{1-12}$) 194

(c) Solomon's Vengeance (1 Kings 2$^{13-46}$) . . . 195

(d) Solomon's Vision (1 Kings 3$^{4-28}$) 197

(e) Solomon and Hiram (1 Kings 5) 197

(f) Solomon's Buildings : (i) The Temple (1 Kings 6) . . 198

(g) Solomon's Buildings : (ii) The Palace (1 Kings 7$^{1-12}$) . . 202

(h) The Temple Furniture (1 Kings 7$^{13-51}$) . . . 202

(i) The Dedication of the Temple (1 Kings 8) . . . 204

(j) The Visit of the Queen of Sheba (1 Kings 10) . . 206

(k) Solomon's Adversaries (1 Kings 11$^{14-43}$) . . . 208

PART IV. THE DIVIDED KINGDOM

§ 1. The Schism 210

(a) The Breach between Judah and Israel (1 Kings 12$^{1-24}$) . 210

(b) The Religious Breach (1 Kings 12^{25}–13^{10}) . . . 211

(c) The Old Prophet (1 Kings 13$^{11-32}$) 212

(d) The Death of Abijah (1 Kings 14$^{1-18}$) . . . 213

(e) The Reign of Rehoboam (1 Kings 14^{21}–31) . . 214

(f) The Reign of Asa (1 Kings 15$^{9-24}$) 215

Contents

(g) The Reign of Omri (1 Kings 16²¹⁻²⁸) 216
(h) The Accession of Ahab (1 Kings 16²⁹⁻³⁴) 216

§ 2. The Ministry of Elijah 218
(a) The Great Drought (1 Kings 17¹⁻¹⁶) 218
(b) Elijah on Mount Carmel (1 Kings 18²⁰⁻⁴⁶) 219
(c) Elijah's Flight (1 Kings 19) 221
(d) Naboth and his Vineyard (1 Kings 21) 222
(e) Wars with Syria (1 Kings 20) 223
(f) The Death of Ahab (1 Kings 22¹⁻³⁸) 224
(g) Fire from Heaven (2 Kings 1²⁻¹⁸) 225
(h) The Passing of Elijah (2 Kings 2¹⁻¹⁸) 226

§ 3. The Ministry of Elisha 227
(a) War against Moab (2 Kings 3⁴⁻²⁷) 227
(b) The Shunammite and her Son (2 Kings 4⁸⁻³⁷) . . . 229
(c) The Healing of Naaman (2 Kings 5¹⁻¹⁹) 230
(d) Elisha and the Syrians (2 Kings 6⁸⁻²³) 231
(e) The Rise of Jehu (2 Kings 9¹⁻²⁶) 232
(f) The Death of Jezebel (2 Kings 9³⁰⁻³⁷) 233
(g) The Massacre of the Baal worshippers (2 Kings 10¹⁵⁻²⁷) . 234
(h) The Usurpation and Death of Athaliah (2 Kings 11¹⁻²⁰) . 235
(i) The Death and Burial of Elisha (2 Kings 13¹⁴⁻²¹) . . 235

APPENDIX. INSCRIPTIONS ILLUSTRATING OLD TESTAMENT EVENTS
1. The Assyrian Eponym List 237
2. The Tell el-Amarna Letters 237
3. The Stele of Merneptah, c. 1220 B.C. 237
4. The Moabite Stone 238
5. The Karkar Inscription of Shalmaneser III. 853 B.C. . . 240
6. The Black Obelisk of Shalmaneser III 242

INDEX OF PROPER NAMES 243
CHRONOLOGICAL TABLE . . . . . . *at end*

'The chariots of Israel and the horsemen thereof.' Elijah's ascent into heaven (2 Kings 2) represented on a panel of the doors of Santa Sabina, Rome. The carving is of the fifth century A.D.

LIST OF SELECTED PASSAGES

EXODUS.

1–2^{22} 75
3$^{1-16}$ 81
4$^{1-16}$ 83
4$^{18-26}$ 84
4$^{27-31}$ 84
6$^{2-9}$ 82
7^{14}–10 88
12$^{1-36}$ 96
14–15^{26} 98
16$^{1-21}$ 115
17 . . . 116, 117
18 109
19–20^{21} . . . 103
23 108
25$^{1-9}$ 108
29$^{43-46}$ . . . 108
32 106
33 108
34 104

NUMBERS.

10$^{31-36}$ . . . 108
11^{5} 75
11$^{24-30}$ . . . 109
12$^{1-15}$ . . . 110
13 111
14$^{40-45}$ . . . 113
16$^{1-35}$ . . . 114
20$^{2-13}$ . . . 116
21$^{1-3}$ . . . 113
21$^{4-9}$ . . . 118
21$^{21-35}$ . . . 119
22$^{2-35}$ . . . 119
24$^{1-13}$ . . . 120
27$^{12-23}$ . . . 122

DEUTERONOMY.

3^{28} 123
31$^{14f.,23}$ . . . 123
34$^{1-6}$ 122

JOSHUA.

2 124
3^{9}–4^{11} . . . 125
5^{13}–8^{29} . . . 126
9^{3}–10^{27} . . . 129
11$^{1-9}$ 131
24 132

JUDGES.

1–2^{5} 134
3$^{7-30}$ 136
4, 5 138
6$^{11-32}$ . . . 141
7 142
8$^{4-21}$ 143
9 144
11 146
13^{2}–16 . . . 152
17, 18 . . . 148

I SAMUEL.

1 159
3–4^{11} . . . 160
5–7^{1} 162
9–10^{16} . . . 166
11 167
14–18^{9} . . . 168
18$^{20-28}$ . . . 173
19$^{1-17}$ . . . 173
20$^{1-10}$ . . . 174
20$^{18-39}$ . . . 174
21$^{1-9}$ 174

List of Selected Passages

1 SAMUEL (*cont.*)

$21^{10\text{-}15}$	.	.	. 176
$22^{6\text{-}23}$.	.	.	. 174
26	.	.	. 175
27	.	.	. 176
$28^{3\text{-}25}$	.	.	. 177
31	.	.	. 178

2 SAMUEL.

1, 2	.	.	. 178
$3^{6\text{-}39}$	.	.	. 180
$5\text{-}7^{17}$.	.	.	. 182
$11\text{-}12^{25}$	.	.	. 184
15	.	.	. 186
$16^{15}\text{-}17^{14}$	.	.	. 187
$18\text{-}19^{8}$	.	.	. 188
$20\text{-}21^{11}$	.	.	. 189
24	.	.	. 192

1 KINGS.

1-2	.	.	. 193
$3^{4\text{-}28}$	.	.	. 197
5-8	.	.	. 197
10	.	.	. 206

1 KINGS (*cont.*)

$11^{14}\text{-}13^{32}$	.	.	. 208
$14^{1\text{-}18}$ . .	.	.	. 213
$14^{21\text{-}31}$	.	.	. 214
$15^{9\text{-}24}$.	.	.	. 215
$16^{21\text{-}28}$	.	.	. 216
$16^{29\text{-}34}$	.	.	. 216
$17^{1\text{-}16}$.	.	.	. 218
$18^{20}\text{-}19$	.	.	. 219
20	.	.	. 223
21	.	.	. 222
$22^{1\text{-}38}$	.	.	. 224

2 KINGS.

$1^{2}\text{-}2^{18}$	.	.	. 225
$3^{4\text{-}27}$	.	.	. 227
$4^{8\text{-}37}$	.	.	. 229
$5^{1\text{-}19}$	.	.	. 230
$6^{8\text{-}23}$	.	.	. 231
$9^{1\text{-}26}$	.	.	. 232
$9^{30\text{-}37}$.	.	.	. 233
$10^{15\text{-}27}$.	.	.	. 234
$11^{1\text{-}20}$.	.	.	. 235
$13^{14\text{-}21}$	.	.	. 235

LIST OF ILLUSTRATIONS

The hardships of Nomad life in the Wilderness. Photograph by Dr.
M. J. Rendall . . . . *Frontispiece*

Elijah's ascent into heaven represented on a panel of the doors of
Santa Sabina, Rome. Photograph, Alinari xvi

The Might of Egypt. W. Wrezinski, *Atlas zur altägyptischen Kulturge-
schichte* (Verlag J. C. Hinrichs'sche Buchhandlung, Leipzig) . 3

The Great Temple of Luxor built by Amenhotep III. Photograph by
Sir Alan Cobham 5

Ikhnaton and his wife, Nefertiti, worshipping Aton . . . 7

The buildings of Ramses II. Photograph, Metropolitan Museum of
Art, New York 9

A Tell el-Amarna Tablet. British Museum 13

The snows of Mt. Hermon seen from the Sea of Galilee. Photograph,
American Colony, Jerusalem 17

Looking down on the Dead Sea. Photograph, American Colony,
Jerusalem 19

Hittite soldiers. Photograph by D. G. Hogarth 23

Assyrians besieging a walled town. Photograph, Mansell . . 25

A Bedawin sheik and his tribesmen bringing down offerings to Egypt.
By permission of Egypt Exploration Society 29

A modern holy man of the East. Photograph by Mr. R. Gorbold . 39

A group of dervishes, from a drawing by a Persian artist of the
sixteenth century. By permission of Miss Jessie Beck . . 56

Tribute of 'Jehu of the land of Omri '. British Museum . . 69

A modern Egyptian brickmaker at work. Photograph by Gaddis and
Seif, Luxor, Egypt 77

Egyptian nobles hunting wildfowl in the reed banks of the Nile.
Photograph, Metropolitan Museum of Art, New York . . 79

A Palestinian shepherd leaning on his rod. Photograph by Mr.
J. P. G. Finch 85

1, A village on the banks of the Nile. Photograph by Mr. Percival
Hart ; 2, Water pouring through the Assuan Dam . . . 89

Egyptian Agriculture. Photograph, Metropolitan Museum of Art,
New York 93

A sand-storm sweeping over Khartoum. By permission of G. N.
Morhig, Khartoum 95

Pharaoh in his chariot pursuing his enemies. By permission of Dr.
Howard Carter and Metropolitan Museum of Art, New York . 99

The Cow-goddess Hathor, of Egypt. Cairo Museum . . . 107

List of Illustrations

Hebron to-day. Photograph, American Colony, Jerusalem . . 113

A relief from the Ishtar Gate of the temple of Marduk at Babylon. From R. Koldewey, *Das wiedererstehende Babylon*, 1925 (Verlag J. C. Hinrichs'sche Buchhandlung, Leipzig) 121

One of the panels from the gates of the Baptistry at Florence (by Ghiberti) showing, below, the Passage of Jordan and, above, the Fall of Jericho. Photograph, Brogi 127

Nāblūs 133

Eastern Keys 137

Heads of Philistines. By courtesy of Dr. H. R. Hall . . . 151

Samson and the lion. Photograph, Chaundy 155

The ' Boxer ' Vase from Hagia Triada. Photograph by G. Maraghiannie, Candia 157

Harvest in the East. Above, cutting ; below, carrying. Photographs by Mr. R. Gorbold 163

David and his harp. Bodleian MS. Douce 366 171

Part of the Davidic Walls at Jerusalem 181

A breach in the outer Jebusite Wall at Jerusalem 181

An Assyrian war-chariot. Photograph, Giraudon 185

The interior of the Dome of the Rock at Jerusalem. Photograph, American Colony, Jerusalem 191

An early representation of the Temple 199

A winged bull from Nineveh. British Museum 201

Phoenician metal-work. 203

A portable incense burner of Etruscan workmanship, found at Caere. Photograph, Alinari 205

A bas-relief from the Temple of Queen Hatshepsut at Deir-el-Bahari, showing the queen of the country of Punt bringing gifts. Cairo Museum 205

The storm-god Hadad. Photograph by D. G. Hogarth . . 207

A relief on the temple wall at Karnak commemorating Shishak's victory over Rehoboam. Photograph, American Colony, Jerusalem 214

The site of Sebastiyyeh. Photograph by Dr. M. J. Rendall . . 217

A mixed flock of sheep and goats watering at a stream of the Nahr Baradā. Photograph by Mr. J. P. G. Finch 231

Jezebel at the window. British Museum 233

Captives from Ḳarḳar. British Museum 239

The Black Obelisk of Shalmaneser III. British Museum . . 241

LIST OF MAPS

The Near East xxii

The Exodus xxiii

Palestine xxiv

Palestine as a centre of the Trade Routes of the East   20

Jerusalem . . . . . . *Back end-paper*

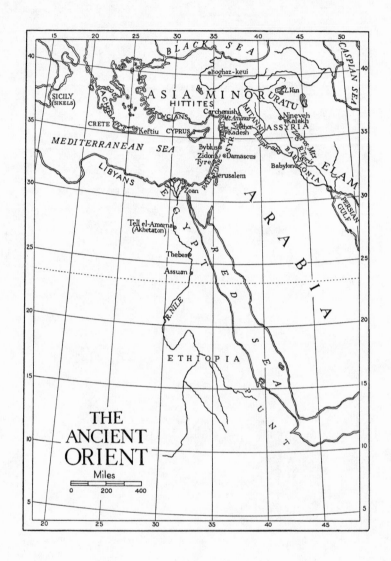

THE
ANCIENT
ORIENT

Miles

0   200   400

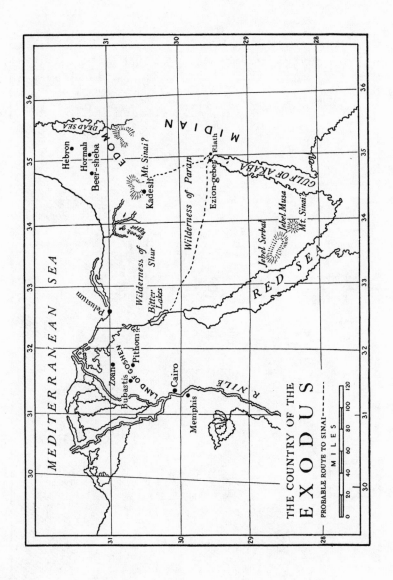

THE COUNTRY OF THE

EXODUS

PROBABLE ROUTE TO SINAI----

MILES

0   20   40   60   80   100   120

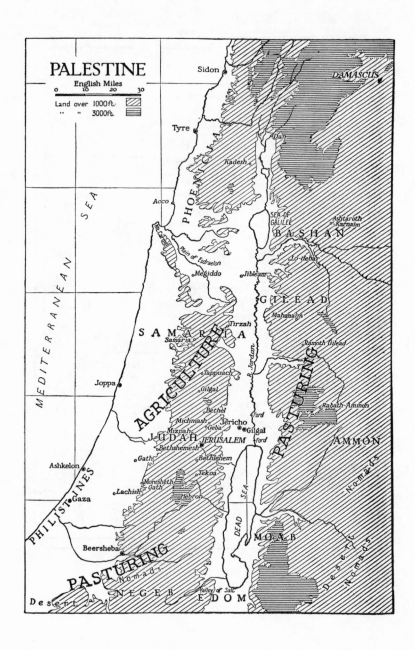

INTRODUCTION

A. HISTORICAL BACKGROUND OF THE PERIOD

IN order to understand any book or series of books which claim to deal with actual events it is necessary to know something of the circumstances in which they were produced and above all the background against which they arose. The labours of scholars, and in particular of archaeologists, enable us to reconstruct with considerable certainty the surroundings amidst which the Hebrew people originated and the influences which came to be exerted upon them.

i. *Egypt*

For the earlier part of our period Babylonia and Assyria lie in the background. The predominant world power is Egypt, although its supremacy is challenged more than once by the non-Semitic peoples of Asia Minor and North Syria whom we call the Hittites. After the death of Ramses III (1167 B.C.) its political importance gradually waned, but for ages it still remained what it had always been since history's dawn, the leader of the world in civilization and culture.

During the supremacy of the Hyksos, the mysterious enemy from the north who held Egypt in subjection for some two centuries, little was done to promote the nation's real mission; unless indeed the destruction of the nobility in the struggle, since it left the way open for a new type of political life, was a contribution to that end. It must not be forgotten, however, that these Asiatic conquerors were the first to bring the horse into the valley of the Nile.

Ahmose (c. 1580–1557 B.C.) was the ruler who expelled the invaders, and his reign marks the beginning of a new epoch; a period of some hundred and fifty years, during which the peaceful Egyptians were transformed by the inspiration of great leaders into a conquering army. On every side the enemies of the nation were driven back; Nubia was subdued, the encroaching Libyans from the west were pushed back, and in Syria the re-treating Hyksos were followed, and the arms of the Pharaoh made

2546·8   B

their victorious way to the waters of the Euphrates. Under the great conqueror Thutmose III (1501–1447 B.C.) even this frontier was crossed, and Egypt was now without a rival to challenge her complete supremacy in the civilized world. Under his grandson and namesake Thutmose IV (1420–1411) it began to be recognized that not by conquest alone could the empire be maintained, and the Pharaoh, by entering into an alliance with Artatama, king of Mitanni, began a new policy. It is possible that the rising power of the Hittites in Cappadocia had become threatening by this time, and that the two monarchs felt the need of reserving their strength to meet it.

To Thutmose succeeded his son, Amenhotep III (1411–1375), 'the most luxurious and splendid, as he was also the last, of the great Egyptian emperors'.[1] The trade and wealth of Egypt had increased beyond all expectation, each successive Pharaoh had tried to outstrip his predecessor in the magnificence of his buildings, and the whole land seemed to have a future of unbroken felicity. But all this display and luxury were undermining the strong and simple virtues upon which the empire had been built up ; foreign influences were crowding in, for good it is true as well as evil; and away in the distant north there was the threat, perhaps not yet fully recognized, of a new foe. The Hittite advance was slow, but its most alarming feature was the help which the invaders were receiving from the Pharaoh's own vassals. The measures which Amenhotep took to restore Egyptian prestige seemed, however, to meet the needs of the situation, and his last days were not disturbed by any anticipations of the coming storm.

There followed Amenhotep IV (1375–1358), the reformer and religious enthusiast. This amazing genius was the son of the late king and the low-born wife, whom, in defiance of tradition, he had taken to himself. She was a woman of great power and ability, and doubtless exercised much influence over her son. The latter, instead of spending his energies in restoring order in Palestine, where wandering tribes of Bedawin were combining with disloyal officials to destroy the last remnants of Egyptian supremacy, chose to play the part of a philosopher and religious reformer.

---

[1] Breasted, *Camb. Anct. Hist.* ii, p. 93.

The might of Egypt. Kneeling figures of conquered enemies. The black men are probably Nubians. Of the two bearded men clad in shirts, the first is probably a Mitanni, the second an Aramaean or Syrian. (Painting on a dado of a king's throne, Thebes. About 1375 B.C.)

In place of the multitude of gods worshipped by his predecessors Ikhnaton, as the king came to be called, wished to establish one supreme deity whom he named Aton, the solar-ray. This reform of religion was not at all to the liking of the Egyptian priesthood, the centre of whose power was the sanctuary of Amon at Thebes, and in order to destroy their influence Ikhnaton not only persecuted them but even went to the extreme measure of building a new capital, the famous Amarna, to give it its modern name. His labour was in vain; the resources, material and otherwise, of the priesthood were too strong, and when the Pharaoh sank into an early grave it was no long time before Thebes had regained its position and Amon was once more supreme. The new capital was left to fall into decay, and it was from its ruins that the Tell el-Amarna letters were recovered (see below, pp. 13 ff.).

But the time of Egypt's decay was not yet, and a period of fresh conquest still lay before her under the strong rule of the kings of the XIXth dynasty, who now came to the throne.[1] The first of these to make any really serious attempt to extend his influence into Syria was Seti I (1314–1292). He pushed as far north as the Orontes, and after fighting a battle with a Hittite force entered into negotiations with their king Mutallu(?) and as a consequence a treaty was made which brought the war to an end. Seti, like earlier kings, was a great builder, and the number of new temples which he erected and endowed added to the already dangerous power of the ecclesiastical leaders. To him succeeded Ramses II (1292–1225) who came to the throne by supplanting an elder brother. Warfare with the Hittites again broke out, and both sides, realizing the desperate nature of the struggle which was about to commence, strained every nerve to gather allies and to enrol mercenaries. A great battle was fought around Kadesh on the Orontes, the two armies were of vast size for the times, Ramses having not less than 20,000 men and his adversary about the same. The experienced Hittite was, however, more than a match for his eager young antagonist, and succeeded in dividing his forces in such a way that but for the intrepid valour of Ramses himself an over-

[1] 'The nineteenth dynasty represented the national reaction against the Asiatic faith of Khu-n-Aten and the government of the country by Asiatic officials.' Sayce, *Early Hist. of the Hebs.*, p. 158.

An air view of the great temple of Luxor built by Amenhotep III

whelming disaster must have overtaken the Egyptian army. In the end the Pharaoh fought his way out of the trap into which he had been enticed, and even enjoyed a triumphal entry into Thebes on his return home; but at best the campaign had been indecisive. Further campaigns seem, however, to have been more successful, though from a scarcity of records we do not know much as to their details; it is certain that Ramses marched his troops far north of Kadesh, whether in raids or in the way of permanent conquests is not clear. Some years of warfare were ended in 1272 by a lasting treaty made between Ramses and Hattushil, who had succeeded his brother Mutallu on the Hittite throne. The treaty was made on tolerably equal terms, but the growing power of Assyria must have made peace a matter of greater urgency to the Hittite ruler than to the Pharaoh. The treaty with Hattushil marks an epoch in the history of Egypt, it brings to a close a long period of fighting and expansion. But Egypt was still to be a pioneer in art and civilization.

Ramses II was not only a warrior, he was also a great organizer and builder. He evidently recognized that for the purpose of keeping in touch with Egyptian interests in Asia Thebes was inconvenient as the seat of the government; accordingly a new city was founded in the eastern Delta, not far from Pelusium, to which the Pharaoh gave his own name Per-Ramses, another 'store-city' was built not far from Bubastis, this he called Pithom (cf. Exod. 1¹¹). In addition vast sums were expended on the building or completion of temples—and in some cases the destroying of old monuments to provide material for the new—as well as in their endowment.

On the death of Ramses II his son Merneptah, who was already far advanced in years, succeeded to the throne and reigned for about ten years (1225–1215). Although he remained at peace with the Hittites, his reign was marked by much trouble in the Asiatic dominions of Egypt, brought about by the allies of the Hittites and perhaps fomented by them. The Pharaoh quickly invaded Palestine, and by severe and vigorous measures reduced it to obedience. Amongst the names of those thus roughly handled was a people named 'Israel', the first time the word is found in history. Meanwhile fresh trouble was arising in the Delta which

Ikhnaton and his wife Nefertiti worshipping Aton. A relief
in the Cairo Museum

was invaded by a large body of Libyans and other tribes. It is of interest to observe that several of these peoples allied with the Libyans were probably of European origin.[1] The invaders were met by the troops of Egypt before they had made much progress, and after the famous Egyptian archers had broken the Libyan ranks the chariots completed the victory and turned the battle into a massacre. This striking success brought much needed relief to Egypt on the west, just as the previous campaign had restored its prestige in the east.

Merneptah, like his father, was ambitious to be known as a great builder, and like his father he did not scruple to use the monuments of earlier sovereigns as a quarry from which to get a ready and almost inexhaustible supply of building material. To the student of the O. T. he is, however, most important as being probably the Pharaoh from whose rule the Hebrews escaped at the time of the Exodus. He was buried with his fathers at Thebes after a reign of much trouble and anxiety, especially for an aged man, during which the power of Egypt was maintained although with difficulty.[2]

After the death of Merneptah the country fell into anarchy. There were various claimants for the throne and none was able to establish his power over the whole realm. To add to the miseries of the situation famine broke out and the Libyans, perpetually hovering on the borders of the Delta, again began to force their way in, both as plunderers and as settlers.

The country was saved by the rise to power of Setnakht (c. 1200), who succeeded in overcoming his rivals and establishing sufficient control over affairs to hand on his rule to his son Ramses III, the founder of the XXth dynasty. Under this monarch the Egyptian military resources were re-organized in a great part upon the rather uncertain basis of foreign mercenaries. In 1194 the new organization was severely tested, for once again

---

[1] The Shekelesh were perhaps the Sikels of Sicily, the Ekwesh the Acheans. Other tribes were the Lycians and the Teresh, who were not improbably the mysterious Etruscans (Tyrsenians).

[2] It is sometimes stated that in his reign a Syrian obtained a position of power in Egypt much after the manner of Joseph in an earlier age. This statement 'is entirely without foundation and due to misunderstanding of the titles of Ben-'Ozen, the Syrian marshal of his court'. Breasted, Camb. Anct. Hist. ii, p. 169.

the Libyans invaded the Delta in great force, and in conjunction with them a numerous multitude advanced from Syria. Egypt was beset by land and by sea. But the resources of the Pharaoh proved equal to the occasion, and on both elements the Egyptians

The buildings of Ramses II. Front view of the great rock temple at Abu Simbel. The front, including the four colossal statues of Ramses II (each 65 ft. high), is carved in the living rock

were successful. The invaders from the north, however, still came on in great numbers, not so much by armies as by peoples; and in this period the last remnants of Hittite greatness seem to have been submerged beneath the continual waves of passing hordes. Again and again heavy fighting was necessary to save the Palestinian and Libyan borders from being crossed, and again and again Egypt came out of the contest victorious. Amongst the invaders who were thrust back were the Peleset (Pulesati), known to history as the Philistines (for the coming of the Philistines see below, pp. 150 f.).

Ramses III was followed by a series of monarchs bearing the same name, each enjoyed but a short period of government, and each had a desperate struggle to maintain himself. Meanwhile the real power was passing into the hands of the high priests of Amon, whose succession had become hereditary. The enormous endowments lavished upon the Temple by generations of Pharaohs had at last made it the wealthiest and most considerable power in the state, indeed it seemed to overshadow even the royal power itself.

The weakness in the central government soon manifested itself in Syria and Palestine. Within a generation of the death of Ramses III the might of Egypt beyond its eastern boundary had become a thing of memory only.[1] In the kingdom itself disunion, never far away under weak kings, was already showing itself, and a rival kingdom was established in the Delta under a noble of Tanis (Zoan), Nesubenebded to give him his native name, but who was known to the Greeks as Smendes. The last feeble Ramses of the XXth dynasty who still existed at Thebes under the shadow of the High Priest was at length quietly deposed, and the Priest stepped into his place somewhere about 1100 B.C.

Although Hrihor the High Priest might be recognized as ruler at Thebes and in southern Egypt, his title to the north was not so strong, and here another Pharaoh quickly seized his opportunity. At Tanis Smendes, as we have seen, had already founded the XXIst dynasty, and by the annalists he alone is regarded as a legitimate ruler. The relations between Tanis and Thebes are exceedingly obscure, sometimes one and sometimes the other seems to possess royal power. The priests of Thebes built a fortress at El-Hiba and so kept Upper Egypt fairly secure for themselves. The state of confusion came to an end when the Libyan mercenaries swept away the weaklings of both Tanis and Thebes and put on the throne Shishak of Bubastis, who founded the XXIInd dynasty in 947.

During this period the settlement of Canaan was being hurried

---

[1] An interesting light is thrown upon the state of the Syrian coast towns and of their contempt for Egypt by the travels of Wenamon, an Egyptian envoy who was sent to Byblus in the time of Ramses XII (XI) to obtain cedar for the priests of Amon.

on, and the early Hebrew monarchy was gradually establishing itself. The weak Pharaohs of the XXIst dynasty, about whom little is known beyond their names, were in no position to interfere. It is probable, however, that when David had driven out the Philistines the latter put themselves under Egyptian protection. If so David and his successor had too much work to do at home to trouble themselves about the matter so long as they were not attacked, and Egypt was too feeble to attempt any military aggression. Solomon, in the glory of his *parvenu* monarchy, was only too glad to take to wife a daughter of the ruling house of the ancient empire of Egypt; and her father gave as her dowry the troublesome town of Gezer. Apart from Solomon's desire to gain prestige from matrimonial alliance relations were likely to be friendly between him and Egypt because the latter depended very largely upon the goodwill of the Hebrew monarch for the carrying-on of their trade. Solomon, as H. R. Hall says, 'derived much of the power that made him able to talk as an equal to Egypt from his control of the trade-routes from Egypt to Babylonia and from the Red Sea to Syria—the lord of Gaza, of Eziongeber, and of Damascus was a powerful guarantor of peace and commerce'.[1]

Shishak (*c.* 947–*c.* 925), the founder of the new dynasty, was of Libyan descent. His name in Egyptian is *Sha-sha-n-k* and it is frequently, following the Assyrian vocalization, pronounced Sheshonk. His rise to power brought, though only for a time, a new spirit into the Egyptians and made them once again aggressive and dangerous to their neighbours. The nearest neighbour was Israel, and so it was upon Israel that the first blow fell. For some time Egypt had been the natural place of refuge for fugitives from Israel, as it remained to the very end (cf. Jer. 26[21], 43[7]). Amongst them, during the reign of Solomon, had been Jeroboam, an able- and forceful young man. On the death of Solomon, whose wisdom and prestige had kept the kingdom together in some semblance of power, Jeroboam returned and raised the standard of revolt among the northern tribes of Israel. There can be but little doubt that his enterprise was not merely connived at but also supported by Egypt.

Shishak was quick to seize his opportunity and to fall upon the

[1] *Camb. Anct. Hist.* iii, p. 256.

weak southern kingdom. Jerusalem was captured and the lavish offerings which Solomon had made to the Temple and the Palace went to swell the spoil of the Egyptians. On his return Shishak set up a vaunting inscription at Karnak, and no doubt felt himself the equal of Thutmose III or Ramses II. But this revival of former glories was but a feeble and transitory gleam, and Shishak himself did little more to extend it. He died probably in 925, a few years after his successful expedition. His son succeeded him, Osorkon I (c. 925–889). H. R. Hall thinks that he is really the mysterious Zerah the Ethiopian who invaded Judah and was defeated by Asa at Mareshah (2 Chron. 14^9 ff.). If this identification is correct the disastrous attack was the last attempt of Egypt to conquer Judah, and on its failure the Pharaohs of this dynasty seem to have settled quietly down into sleep and decay. There is an interesting possibility that they sent a contingent to help the allied Syrian kings who fought against Shalmaneser III at Ḳarḳar, for this monarch mentions a thousand men of Musri amongst his opponents. It is, however, much more probable that these were from Asia Minor than from Egypt. The later years of the XXIInd dynasty saw a fresh attempt of the Theban priesthood to recover its supremacy, and, as in the Tanite period, two rulers with very vague powers seem to have sat on rival thrones at the same time. The later Theban rulers were more fortunate, however, than the successors of Hrihor, for the annalists recognize them as legitimate sovereigns and name their dynasty the XXIIIrd.

ii. *Palestine in the Fourteenth Century B.C.*

In order to understand the history of the Israelite people, it is necessary to know something of the previous history of the land which they came to possess, and to realize the various influences by which they were affected after the Conquest.

The O. T. itself gives us some information as to the state of Palestine when the Israelites invaded it, but as this information was not written down till centuries afterwards, and as the ideas of later ages have been allowed to influence the writers, part of its value is taken from it. It is exceedingly fortunate, therefore, that we have much contemporary evidence for the state of Palestine in the pre-Exodus period.

Part of the evidence comes from the result of excavations which have been carried on at various sites, the most important of which are Tell el-Hesy (the ancient Lachish), Gezer, Taanach, and Tell el-Mutesellim (the ancient Megiddo).[1] Part is to be found in the tablets recently discovered at Boghaz-Kuei, the ancient Hittite capital in Asia Minor; but above all we are indebted to the contents of the tablets, some 300 in number, discovered at Tell el-Amarna, the site of the ruined city and palace of Amenhotep IV in Upper Egypt. The tablets form the state archives of the unhappy Pharaoh, and consist of letters, received by himself and his father, from a numerous and very varied series of correspondents. Included amongst them are kings of Babylon and of the Hittites, the governors of dependencies, Arab sheiks, and even a lady, who shows a very modern kind of interest in high politics. Our respect for the culture and civilization of the ancient

A Tell el-Amarna tablet

world cannot but be vastly increased by even a slight perusal of these most interesting epistles; for the mention in them of quite trivial affairs makes it evident that communication was as easy and as regular amongst them as it was in the modern world in the middle of the last century, before the invention of the telegraph and the increased use of the steam-engine. For the messengers, however, the matter was not quite so simple as for the correspondents, and

[1] For a good general account of the discoveries, see Driver, *Schweich Lectures*; and Macalister, *A Century of Excavation in Palestine*.

it would not take any great amount of imagination to picture to ourselves the bearers of some of these weighty missives in danger of sinking under the burden of the affairs of Babylon, in a literal and not a metaphorical sense.[1]

Many interesting and amusing sidelights of much value to the archaeologist and the general student are thrown on the life of the ancient world by these letters. For us they are mainly important for the immense service which they have rendered to Biblical scholarship by revealing so much of the conditions of Palestine before the Hebrew invasion.

Any one who is in any way familiar with the history of the Middle Ages can hardly fail to be struck, on looking through these letters, by the remarkable similarity which exists between the state of Palestine in the fourteenth century B.C. and that of Italy in the fourteenth century A.D. In each case the country was under the nominal rule of an absent suzerain, whilst the actual power was in the hands of a number of petty despots (cf. Joshua 2^2, 8^1, 9^1, $12^{9\ ff.}$) or of municipalities (cf. Joshua 9^{11}), ever ready to seize the opportunity of benefiting themselves at the expense of their neighbours. In further resemblance the whole land was overrun by bands of foreign mercenaries who were as willing to serve a city whilst its money lasted as to turn and join its enemies in sacking it when it was no longer able to pay their hire. The Pharaoh, like some of the emperors, cared but little for these things; so long as his tribute was duly collected and no great outrage against Egyptian rule was committed, the slaughter of a few Canaanites was a matter of little consequence.

The Canaanite cities, like those of Italy, were very wealthy, and the life of their citizens must have been exceedingly luxurious; we read in inscriptions of their chariots of silver and gold; and many gold and silver articles, inlaid tables, and other valuables are stated to have been taken by the Egyptians as spoil. It is quite possible that the Italian despots of the Middle Ages, who were famous as patrons of the fine arts, had their prototypes amongst the petty kings and governors of Canaan.

---

[1] The substance of this and the following paragraphs is taken from my booklet *Modern Discoveries and the Old Testament*, pp. 15 ff., No. 14 in 'Little Books on Religion' (S.P.C.K.).

One of the most interesting of these semi-independent local governors was Abdi-Khiba of Jerusalem. This personage had quarrelled with his mercenaries, and they had transferred their services to his rivals; the result was that Abdi-Khiba found himself in difficulty. His numerous letters to the Pharaoh do not seem to have met with much response, for the Egyptians were probably just as willing to have a mercenary chief as ruler of Jerusalem as a Canaanite prince. In addition, there seems to have been some considerable doubt about Abdi-Khiba's own loyalty. In the following letter he is defending himself against some charge of trying to become entirely independent:

'*To the king, my lord, my sun: thus* speaks *Abdi-Khiba thy servant. At the feet of the king, my lord, seven times and. seven times, have I fallen. Behold, the king, my lord, has put his name upon the East and upon the West. It is slander which they have heaped up against me. Behold I am not a prince, I am an officer of the king, behold I am a shepherd of the king. Neither my father nor my mother, but the strong arm of the king established me in the house of my father.*'

Another of his letters contains a very touching postscript:

'*To the scribe of the king says Abdi-Khiba thy servant. At your feet I fall. Bring these words clearly before the king, my lord: I am thy servant and thy son.*'

This postscript was doubtless accompanied by some more substantial expression of the writer's regard. Of the ultimate fate of Abdi-Khiba we have no information; one of his last letters is sufficiently gloomy:

'*The king no longer has any territory, the Habiru have wasted all the lands of the king. If the royal troops come this year the country will remain my lord, the king's, but if no troops come the territory of the king, my lord, is lost.*'

The general impression we gather of Palestine is that of a land full of disorder and insurrections, and internally weak. Here and there Egyptian fortresses and garrisons still existed, and sometimes a spasmodic effort would result in some restoration of order. Very prominent in the battles are bands of Aramaean nomads who are known as SA.GAZ (= robbers). In the time of Abdi-

Khiba, however, these nomads were known as the Habiru, a word which has a close linguistic connexion with Hebrew.

The Pharaohs of the new dynasty made some difference, and repeated invasions of Palestine and Syria restored Egyptian prestige. Both Seti and Ramses II in the age immediately before the Exodus carried out successful expeditions into Palestine, and it is interesting to notice that each of them makes mention of a certain people called the Asaru, a term equivalent to the Israelite tribe Asher. Merneptah, himself, in his ode of triumph, mentions a people of Israel amongst his victims.

But this revival of Egyptian supremacy in Palestine was not of long duration, for although Ramses III invaded the territory west and south of the Dead Sea, his successors were compelled to let slip their hold on the country.

According to the O. T. Palestine at the time of the first invasion was inhabited by a number of races. The two chief of these were the Canaanites and the Amorites, the former being the dwellers in the valleys and the latter in the mountains (Deut. 1⁷). In the lists of races which recur not infrequently (e. g. Joshua 11³, 24¹¹) mention is also made of the Perizzites, Hivites, Jebusites, and the Girgashites, of whom very little that is distinctive is known, as well as of the great nation of the Hittites, who come in rather strangely among their lesser brethren.[1]

The land of Palestine itself is of such importance in Hebrew history that some brief description of it is necessary.[2] The term Palestine is used rather loosely; in the wider use it includes the whole territory from Lebanon in the north to Edom in the south, and from the great desert to the Mediterranean. In the narrower usage the northern and southern limits are Dan and Beer-sheba, and the East Jordan territories are not included. This narrower country is about 140 miles long, some 90 miles wide in the south, and only 25 miles wide in the north; the whole area is about 6,000 square miles.

Palestine is not a rich land, it compares unfavourably with

[1] For the Hittites, see pp. 2 ff., above, and *Numbers* (West. Comm.), pp. 89 f.
[2] Kent has described it as 'the first chapter in God's great volume of revelation inscribed upon the history of the Hebrew people'. *Hist. of Heb. People*, i, p. 24.

Syria in this respect, and the fact that the sea-coast with its few ports was held by the Phoenicians and the Philistines during our period made the expansion of Israelite overseas trade impossible except during the brief years when Judah was in a position to occupy the Red Sea ports.

The snows of Mt. Hermon, seen from the Sea of Galilee

Some parts of Palestine were very fertile, especially the plain of Esdraelon and the luxuriant valley of the Jordan; in the latter the growth of vegetation is still remarkable. The greater part of it is and was barren, and intense efforts are required to gain its products, whilst scarcity is far from uncommon (cf. 2 Sam. 21¹, 1 Kings 17, 18). The chief fruits were grapes, olives, figs, and pomegranates (see Deut. 8⁸ and cf. Num. 13²³). There were a few large forests such as Lebanon and Carmel, but the fact that isolated terebinths are mentioned seems to show that trees were landmarks. In the same way there was a scarcity of rivers, the Jordan and the Kishon being the only considerable streams, though there were many springs and wells (Deut. 8⁷, 11¹¹). It is a mountainous country, and to its mountains it owes much of its rugged beauty.

There are great contrasts in the climate of Palestine due to the variety in its physical formation. The highest mountains in the land itself are not above 4,000 feet, but on the northern border the huge mass of Mount Hermon rises to more than 10,000 ft. From this height to the depths of the Jordan valley and the Dead Sea (some 1,300 ft. below sea-level) is a remarkable drop, and the difference in climate is equally remarkable. Kent has described these differences in striking language: 'A half-day's journey brings the traveller from the winter snows of Jerusalem to the tropical luxuriance of the Jordan valley, and another day of travel will introduce him to the barren wastes of the Arabian desert. From certain vantage-points one may see the columns of vapour rising from that great cauldron, the Dead Sea, and with almost the same glance behold the snowy heights of Mount Hermon. The temperate, tropical, and frigid zones are each represented. . . . Corresponding to these differences in climate are the contrasts in flora and fauna. The firs overshadow the palms. Here the wolf of the north contends with the leopard of the south over the carcass of the gazelle of the temperate zone. It is evident why the Bible is a book intelligible to people living in all climes, since the land which is its background is an epitome of the entire world.'[1]

As the training ground for a people destined by God to play a predominant part in the religious history of the world, no better land than that of Palestine could have been found, for it is at once secluded and yet not isolated. It is secluded because it lies off the great highways which connect Egypt with Mesopotamia; it is not isolated because these highways run close to its territory, and some of the less important actually cross it. The chief routes are as follows:

(1) From Egypt along the coast plain, by Mount Carmel to Phoenicia and the north.

(2) From Jerusalem to Jezreel and on to Damascus with connexions beyond.

[1] *Hist. of Heb. People*, i, pp. 23 f.

Looking down on the Dead Sea

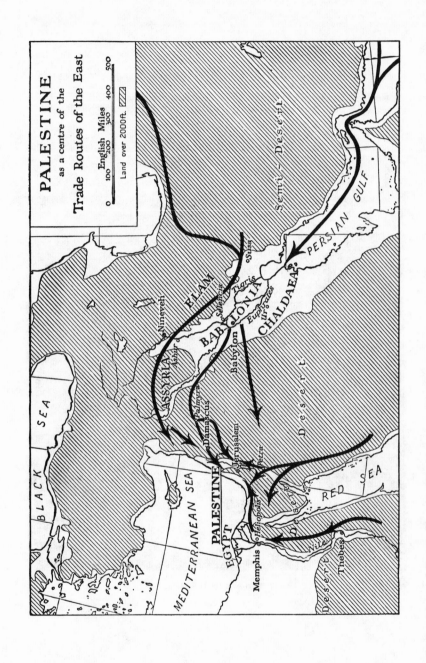

PALESTINE
as a centre of the
Trade Routes of the East

English Miles
0   100   200   300   400   500

Land over 2000ft.

BLACK SEA

MEDITERRANEAN SEA

PALESTINE

EGYPT

Memphis

Thebes

Nile

Desert

Desert

RED SEA

Heliopolis

Jerusalem

Damascus

Palmyra

Petra

ASSYRIA

Nineveh

Asshur

ELAM

Seleucia

Tigris

BABYLONIA

Babylon

Euphrates

Ur

CHALDAEA

Susa

Semú—Desert

Desert

PERSIAN GULF

(3) From Jericho to Beth-shan along the Jordan.

(4) East of the Jordan the road from Elath to Damascus.

Thus the dweller in Palestine was kept in close touch with all that was going on in the world around him as the passing caravans brought their news as well as their merchandise; but he was sufficiently secluded to prevent his own culture and ideas from being overwhelmed by foreign influences.

iii. *Assyria and Babylonia*

In the times immediately before our period Assyria and Babylonia were kept away from the north-east of Syria by the people known as the Mitanni, and from Palestine itself by the desert. Assyria was meanwhile improving her internal conditions, digging new wells, and erecting palaces. Externally, a policy of aggression led to struggles with Babylon, then under the Kassite dynasty. These encroachments were on the whole successful, although frequent outbreaks in Babylon and in Assyria itself rendered progress slower than otherwise it might have been.

The rise of the Hittites in the early part of the fourteenth century B.C. brought about the fall of the Mitanni to the great benefit of Assyria, who immediately seized upon part of their territories. Encouraged by this success Assyria made a further attempt upon Babylon, under Enlil-nirari (1368–1346), and was completely victorious. The collapse of the Mitanni had, however, brought Assyria face to face with the Hittites, and progress towards Syria was still held up. Another attack on the Kassites in the reign of Adad-nirari I (1305–1277), however, was once again successful. The great soldier and builder, Shalmaneser I (1276–1257), further consolidated the growing empire and extended it towards the north. Under his successor, Tukulti I (1256–1207), considerable progress was made in the north-west and successes were gained over the Hittites, whilst on the other border Babylon itself was captured. In the next century, however, the Moschi (Meshech of O. T.) seem to have overrun part of the Assyrian territories. Meanwhile Babylon was suffering from continual raids by the Elamites, culminating at last in 1169 by a movement sufficiently serious to overturn the whole dynasty. To the Kassites, who had ruled Babylon for nearly six centuries, succeeded the Pashe dynasty. This dynasty lasted only 132 years, but it included amongst its kings the great name of Nebuchadrezzar I (1146–1123). He was able to carry on a successful, though desperate, war with Elam, whom he finally defeated in a great dust-storm in which the opposing forces could hardly distinguish one another. The Elamites were glad to seek shelter in their mountains from the fierceness of their enemy and also from the unaccustomed heat. Against Assyria his good fortune failed him, and he met with complete defeat at the hands of Ashur-resh-ishi I (1127–1116), under whom the Assyrian power, after a period of decay, was once again lifting up its head.

Under the next monarch, Tiglath-pileser I (1115–1102), Assyria by one advance after another succeeded in overpowering all her neighbours. The Moschi were driven out of Mesopotamia and her arms were extended as far as the distant Mediterranean. The king claims that he took a ship of Arvad and sailed forth on the sea where he slew a dolphin. The power of Assyria was so threatening that even the Pharaoh of the time sent presents. But the death of Tiglath-pileser was also the signal for the loss of much of the conquered territory. Ashur-bel-kala (1092–1075) the son, though not the immediate successor of Tiglath-pileser I, erected certain statues in ' the land of the Amorites ', and lived on friendly terms with Babylon, but his reign came to an end by rebellion or intrigue, and it was followed by a long period of obscurity, decay, and internal trouble. About this time wave after wave of Aramaeans invaded Mesopotamia and even penetrated as far as Babylon. The tenth century found Assyria, if free from any immediate fear of invasion or conquest, yet ' reduced in territory, insecure in trade, exhausted by a long fight for existence'.

A new dynasty was founded by Ashur-rabi II (c. 1001), and it seems to have lasted some 200 years; but the various kings are little more than mere names. Ashur-rabi is notable for the setting up of an image of himself on Mount Amanus, but soon after this feat all connexion with the west was cut off by the capture of Mutkina by the Aramaeans and by their taking possession of Pitru (Pethor). The dynasty seems to have given itself to the improvement of the internal condition of Assyria and to the cultivation of trade.

Hittite soldiers. A slab from Carchemish, about 1000 B.C.

All these preparations helped to make possible the new period of expansion and aggression which began when Adad-nirari II (911–889) came to the throne. In a number of campaigns he restored the lost military prestige of Assyria and drove back her enemies on every side. He even succeeded in penetrating as far as the salt desert of modern Persia, a feat which was not to be rivalled for some two centuries. There was much fighting with Babylon, which had once again become a danger through the coming of the Chaldeans. This people had followed in the wake of other Semitic peoples and had established themselves at the head of the Persian Gulf. The Assyrian monarch was uniformly victorious in these contests, but Babylon was not finally subdued.

On the succession of Tukulti-Ninurta II (889–884) the reconquest of other of Assyria's lost dominions was undertaken and carried through. His brief reign saw the beginnings of the breaking down of the power of the Aramaeans which blocked the way to Syria and Palestine, and expansion in all directions. His son and successor, Ashur-nasir-pal II (884–859), took in hand the task of consolidating and organizing the conquests which previous monarchs had made. In his tenth campaign he crossed the Euphrates and received the submission of many Syrian and Phoenician princes. He was the real founder of the later Assyrian power in Syria and Palestine. Nearer home two enemies were threatening the peace and even the safety of the empire. To the east there was the newly arrived nation of the Medes, an Aryan people who had been pressing westward from the beginning of the century. The efforts of Assyria were mostly confined to keeping the Medes on the far side of the Zagros range. The other threat came from the Urartu, a powerful people living to the north of Lake Van, who about this time began to be aggressive. Ashur-nasir-pal made frequent raids into their country and thus succeeded in holding them back for the time.

Ashur-nasir-pal was not only a mighty warrior, but, like some of the great Egyptians, he was also an ambitious builder. Old cities and temples were restored by him; but his chief title to fame is the re-building of Kalakh (Nimrud), the ruined capital of Shalmaneser I. From his palace at Kalakh exceedingly important remains in the form of low reliefs have been brought to the

Assyrians besieging a walled town. A relief from Ashur-nasir-pal's palace at Nimrud

British Museum; in them we have the earliest examples of Assyrian art.

To him succeeded the famous Shalmaneser III (859–824). So great was the terror that had fallen upon the Aramaeans through the expeditions of Ashur-nasir-pal that his son had little to fear from them. The natural desire of Assyria to expand, however, caused him to lead a number of campaigns across the Euphrates. These were never entirely successful. In 853 a large Assyrian army was checked at Ḳarḳar by a confederation of Syrian kings, which included Ahab of Israel.[1] The allies managed to place in the field between sixty and seventy thousand men and a large number of chariots; the Assyrians claim to have inflicted immense losses upon them, none the less the action was not decisive in their favour. Another expedition was undertaken in 848 and again in 845, when a vast host of 120,000 men was led into Syria, but again without any decisive result being reached. At last in 841 Jehu of Israel and other princes paid tribute; but Hazael, the usurper on the throne of Damascus, faced the might of Assyria alone at a battle in Mount Hermon: he was badly defeated, losing 16,000 men,[2] but Damascus itself resisted all Shalmaneser's efforts to capture it. A later expedition in 837 was equally unsuccessful as far as Hazael was concerned, though he lost four cities and Tyre, Zidon, and Byblus paid tribute. To compensate for this lack of complete success in Syria, Shalmaneser made conquests to the north. By overcoming Cilicia he obtained control of the road into Asia Minor, a great achievement for both military and commercial purposes. In his dealings with the Medes and Urartu he was mostly content to remain on the defensive, as his father had been before him, discouraging their aggressions by frequent raids. In Babylon, however, he was much more successful than Ashur-nasir-pal had been, and obtained the recognition of Assyrian suzerainty. The last years of his life were clouded by family troubles, his son, Ashur-danin-pal, raising a revolt against him in 827. 'These last days did not', as Mr. Sidney Smith points out, 'obscure the glory of this vigorous monarch in the eyes of his successors; and his achievements must still be considered the basis of Assyrian imperial power. In the south he had established order

---

[1] See Appendix, p. 241.   [2] See Appendix, p. 242.

in Babylon; in the west he had reduced to absolute submission the whole of northern Syria; in the east he had deposed and set up kings in such a manner as to establish an Assyrian sphere of influence. In the north he had perceived that Assyrian control of the pass districts could not be secured until the Urartu had been attacked and defeated; and, though his campaigns in the southern districts of Urartu did not achieve this object, it is clear that trouble among the hill tribes was much less to be feared in his time than in that of his immediate predecessors.' [1]

The next king was Shamshi-Adad V (824–811). His first task was to restore peace at home, and having done this he had to recover the ground lost through the civil war. The internal dissensions were quelled by 820, but the whole of Assyrian influence especially in the west, was not regained during the lifetime of Shamshi-Adad. This task was successfully accomplished by his successor, Adad-nirari III (811–782). He was the last of the great kings of this period, and under his leadership the Assyrian arms were carried as far south as Philistia and Edom, whilst the stubborn Damascus was at length forced to submit. Nearer home further aggressions were made upon Babylon, but the Urartu were far from being subdued, and he left a grave danger to be encountered by his successors from this northern people. From the point of view of Israel, the downfall of Damascus was exceedingly important for it saved her in all probability from destruction (cf. 2 Kings 13[5]). The breaking down of her rival's power left Israel free to develop, and a short season of great prosperity was ushered in—only to be ended swiftly and tragically on the revival of Assyria under Tiglath-pileser III in 745.

iv. *Israel and Judah*

The story of the early years of the Israelite confederation of tribes is lost amidst legend and folk-lore. Until we reach the times of Saul and David, the writing of a really connected and authentic history is an impossibility. At the same time certain great events, and not a few striking personalities in the earlier period, stand out from amidst the general uncertainty. Few, I imagine, would be found to deny that some of the tribes were in Egypt, or that

[1] *Camb. Anct. Hist.* iii, p. 25.

a great leader, such as Moses, was responsible for giving form and cohesion to the many diverse elements of the new nation. The figures also of most of the judges and, in part at any rate, the deeds attributed to them, seem based on genuine reminiscences. Thus, whilst the general outlines of the story may be received with some amount of confidence, it is hard to sort out the details and to know what to accept as genuine tradition, what to reject as due to the imagination or the sense of fitness of a later age.

The rise of Israel makes a thrilling narrative. It is something much greater and more enlightening than it would have been had a mere chronicle, accurate to the minutest details, 'a skeleton map of events', been handed down to us. The narrative itself is a living thing, bearing traces in its features of the experiences through which it has come. What Nairne has written of the patriarchal period is true of the whole history: 'The presence of God is the genius of the story'.[1] In this section we trace out merely the secular side of the narrative, the flesh and bones of which the religious development is the living soul.

The history of Israel begins in Egypt, whither the ancestors of the tribes are said to have gone down in order to escape from famine in Canaan. Such action on the part of Bedawin is by no means uncommon, and as at the period of the migration Egypt was under the domination of the Hyksos, an Asiatic people, Semitic immigrants would presumably not have been unwelcome. In Exod. 22^{40} we are told that the people were in Egypt for 430 years, but since Moses and his contemporaries seem to have been the fourth generation only from Jacob there are grave difficulties in the way of accepting this statement literally. Hebrew tradition does, however, seem to suppose that all the people were in Egypt, though here it is necessary to remember that the writers of the O. T. frequently speak in a general way, disregarding exceptions. Also allowance must be made for the probability that in the long period which elapsed between the events themselves and the time when they were put into writing, traditions belonging to the different tribes which went to make up the later Israel, have been combined, and experiences, which originally befell parts of the people only, have been referred to the nation as a whole.

[1] *Everyman's Old Test.*, p. 2.

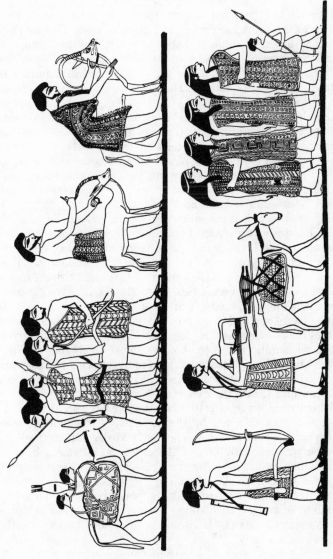

A Bedawi Sheik and his tribesmen bringing down offerings into Egypt. From a Benihasan tomb, *c. 1900 B.C.*

Egyptian history is not of great service in deciding what pro-
portion of the people sojourned in Egypt, or even whether they
were there at all. It seems probable, however, that the *Aperu* who
appear in inscriptions included Hebrews amongst them, for
Egyptians doubtless would not be at pains to distinguish one
Bedawin tribe from another. The *Aperu* are found in Egypt as
late as the time of Ramses IV (1172–1166), so that they can
scarcely be identified with the Hebrews, unless indeed some of them
failed to escape from Egypt at the time of the Exodus. A further
difficulty is that Merneptah refers to the Israelites in Canaan
about 1220 (see p. 6). It is possible that his inscription is, as
Wade suggests, 'a boastful account of the Exodus itself, considered as an *expulsion* of the Israelites',[1] or more probably that
'Israel' represents tribes who were either never in Egypt, or
having been there had moved out before the Exodus.[2]

The Exodus was preceded by a time of fierce oppression. The
expulsion of the Hyksos must have involved a change of policy
on the part of the rulers of Egypt towards their clients; but it is
not until the rise of the XIXth dynasty that real hardship seems
to have been inflicted on the Israelites. The XIXth dynasty arose
after the failure of Ikhnaton's attempt at reform in religion, and
its rulers were opposed to his pro-Asiatic policy. The harsh treatment of the Hebrews was, no doubt, part of a systematic attempt
to abolish Semitic influence. On the threat to Egypt from the
aggressions of the Hittites an even more rigorous effort was made
(cf. Exod. 1[10]) to control and keep down the aliens, and orders
were given for the destruction of all the male children.

Hebrew tradition records that Moses, the great hero of the race,
was saved from this fate by the ingenuity of his mother, who
having made an ark of papyrus floated her baby in it on the Nile.
Here he was found by one of the daughters of Pharaoh, who
adopted him as her son, and thus gave him the opportunity of
becoming learned 'in the wisdom of Egypt'.

An attempt to protect one of his oppressed countrymen led to
the killing of an Egyptian, and as the story became known Moses
had to fly to the desert. Here he was befriended by the priestly

---

[1] *O.T. Hist.*, p. 121, n. 2.
[2] See further discussion under *Chronology*, p. 68.

head of a tribe of Midianites, and, settling down amongst them, he married one of the chieftain's daughters. The call to rescue Israel from bondage came to him whilst in Midian, and with a fresh revelation of Jahveh, to whose sacred mountain he was led by his flock. Then came the return to Egypt, and the abandonment of the peaceful life of a shepherd for the anxious toil which awaits the revolutionary.

His efforts were from the first supported by his brother Aaron, though the earlier narratives make the latter play but a subordinate and indeed superfluous role in the drama. The elders of Israel, and the people themselves, received the promise of deliverance with hesitation, a hesitation which was hardly blameworthy and needed the working of signs to overcome it (Exod. $4^{1-9, 22-31}$). The overcoming of Pharaoh's opposition was more difficult. Time and again they failed to move him from his stubborn policy of refusing any period of absence, even a short one, to his slaves. At last, when a series of disasters to Egypt had culminated in a mysterious outbreak which slew the eldest sons, he was compelled to give way by his own panic-stricken subjects.

Israel, and the motley rabble which accompanied them, fled by night into the desert, and made their way by a gap between the frontier fortresses towards the sacred mountain of their new-found deity. Egypt, however, soon recovered from its panic, and a body of swiftly moving troops was sent after the fugitives. These were overtaken on the margin of a shallow piece of water into which they dashed as the one hope of escape. A strong wind had made a passage for them, and they succeeded in getting across in safety. The Egyptian chariots which followed were soon in difficulties in the soft ground, Jahveh taking off the wheels (Exod. 14^{25}), as the later writer with a vivid touch of true oriental exaggeration puts it, and the sea, flowing with renewed strength, they were overwhelmed and perished. This signal confirmation of the power of Jahveh and of His ability to help His people was never forgotten by the grateful nation, and it became the type and pattern of every other deliverance.

The people then pushed straight on to Sinai,[1] and there, to the

---

[1] For the arguments in support of this statement, see pp. 101 f.

accompaniment of one of those awe-inspiring theophanies, which Nairne has explained as 'sacramental tempests',[1] an alliance was made between Jahveh and Israel. This covenant was a unique thing in the history of religion because, as a great German scholar, Budde, has pointed out, its basis was ethical. Hitherto the God and the nation which worshipped Him were conceived of as being akin, or as having their fortunes bound up in some material way. Now Jahveh and Israel were linked together, not on a material basis (though that came in) or on one of kinship, but by entering into a moral and ethical relationship. It seems probable that Jahveh was originally the god worshipped by Jethro the Midianite, who as a descendant of Abraham may well have preserved amidst the freshness and freedom of desert life, the religion which his kinsmen lost amidst the temptations and oppressions of Egypt.

The site of Sinai is by no means fixed. The tradition which places it in what is now known as the Sinai peninsular goes no farther back than the third century of the Christian era. The geographical statements in O. T., for the most part, require some place nearer to Edom or to Kadesh; but the traditions are not in close agreement, and may well refer to different places. Further difficulty arises if Sinai and Horeb are, as seems essential, identified with one another. (For further discussion see Driver, *Exodus* (Camb. Bib.), pp. 186 ff.)

Between Sinai and the crossing of the Jordan at Jericho an indefinite period elapsed; the forty years or more of the traditional narrative is not of course intended to be an exact chronological statement. During this time the tribes wandered about the various stretches of wilderness in the neighbourhood of Kadesh, and underwent the experiences common to nomadic peoples—shortage of meat and of water; attacks from other Bedawin, whose camping-grounds may have been invaded, and all the murmurings and complaints against the leader inseparable from such hardships for a people, many of whom still sighed for the luxuries of Egypt.

Ingenious writers have tried to amalgamate the various tradi-

---

[1] 'All the theophanies in the Old Testament are sacramental tempests.' *Everyman's Old Test.*, p. 17.

tions which have been handed down concerning this period, and to arrange a number of stations visited by the people in due order of succession. These lists of stations, no doubt, contain much valuable information, and are probably based on ancient caravan routes. It is even possible to suggest plausible identifications with existing sites. But such identifications give us but little help, the important thing to notice is that during years of wandering, a generation which had been in bondage in Egypt died out, and a newer, fresher generation took its place; a generation better disciplined and of a more courageous spirit, and therefore fit to undertake the great task for which Jahveh had prepared them.

Soon after leaving Sinai and encamping at Kadesh an attempt was made to enter Canaan across its southern frontier. Twelve spies had been sent out, and all, with the exception of Caleb, brought back a discouraging report. The people broke out into murmurings and received punishment, whereupon they made an abortive expedition into Canaan and were defeated at Hormah.[1]

At the end of the term of wandering the people moved from Kadesh, and being unable to go through Edom they were compelled to march right round it. Their further progress was checked by Sihon, an Amorite king, who had seized part of Moab. A battle at Jahez placed Sihon's territories at the mercy of the advancing Israelites, and a further conflict ended in the defeat of Og, king of Bashan.[2] The country thus acquired was occupied by the tribes of Reuben and Gad, who were rich in cattle, but on condition that contingents from their tribes went with the rest of Israel to the conquest of the west Jordan territory.

Meanwhile the people of Moab had become alarmed, and Balak, their king, had sent for Balaam, a famous seer, to place Israel under a curse. His efforts were unavailing, in spite of several attempts, and in the end he confessed that his enchantments were powerless against a people blessed by Jahveh. The whole incident lets in a vivid light upon the invasion from the standpoint of those

---

[1] It is possible that an actual entry from the south was made by some of the tribes.

[2] So Deut. 3[1-11] records. It is difficult, however, to suppose that Israel went so far north at this time (cf. Judges 10[3 f.] also).

who suffered from it; it also has other interesting features, inasmuch as it shows us a non-Israelite seer who was apparently a believer in Jahveh.

In spite of all opposition the people swept up the east side of Jordan, neither curses nor enchantments keeping them back. But the leader who had encouraged them to make the effort necessary for escape from bondage, who had trained them in the desert, was not fated to bring them into the land of promise. He breathed out his patient yet passionate soul on one of the mountains of Moab with Canaan full in view below him. There he was buried in a hostile land, and even the place of his grave was kept secret, until finally it was lost from the minds of men.

Moses is one of the greatest names in history, and as in the case of other leaders—our own King Alfred, for example—many legends have gathered round his name. Some of these, no doubt, are true to fact, or contain a residuum of fact, many are the fruit of men's imagination as it played around the beloved dead. History knows him as the founder of the Israelite people and religion, religion knows him as the first forerunner of that prophet, greater than himself, whose Advent he dimly foresaw and welcomed.

Before his death Moses, by Jahveh's command, had nominated as his successor his own attendant, Joshua ben Nun. The choice was in many ways a happy one, for though Joshua had not Moses's power of organizing nor his prophetic gifts, the circumstances of the Israelites demanded a stern and efficient military leader, and Joshua was well fitted for such a position. In many ways he reminds us of Cromwell, a fanatical soldier with little interest in culture or beauty (much that is precious in Canaanite civilization must have been destroyed by him), moved by one thought only and blind to all else. His path of conquest through Canaan was marked by ruthless slaughter and neither age nor sex was spared. The picture of Joshua, however, is lacking in naturalness and owes much to the pens of later writers who desired to present their ideal of a religious soldier and of the resistless might of a consecrated army. In actual fact Joshua did not conquer the whole of Canaan, and the progress made was slow and by no means permanent. Nor was the sword the only factor. Alliances were entered into with communities, as, for example, the Gibeonites, and no doubt the union of Israelites and Canaanites was far from rare. Moreover, the nation did not fight as a single unit, even so late as the Song of Deborah Judah is not regarded as part of Israel.

The main outlines of Joshua's campaigns are as follows. Leaving the head-quarters at Shittim the army made a sudden and successful passage of the Jordan, no opposition being offered by the Canaanites. A base was established at Gilgal, not far from the strongly fortified city of Jericho, and from this base an attack was made on the great Canaanite fortress. Spies had already got into touch with a woman in the city named Rahab, and when the attack was delivered it was instantly successful; so much so that later ages believed that the very walls themselves fell down in order to admit the besiegers. A fearful massacre followed, in which none were spared except Rahab and her relations, and even the possessions of the men of Jericho were 'devoted'. Ai was the next objective and a small force was detached to capture it. Unfortunately it proved unequal to the task and was driven back, to the great dismay of the tribes. A deeper reason than mere insufficiency of numbers was sought by Joshua, and the disaster was declared to have arisen through the offence of a soldier named Achan who had taken spoil from amongst the things set apart for Jahveh in the capture of Jericho. Achan, together with his family, was put to death, and success instantly returned to the Israelite arms. Ai soon fell and its inhabitants were massacred, but on this occasion the people were allowed to loot the place. Bethel was next captured; as at Jericho a traitor was found in it, and another terrible scene of slaughter followed.

The ruthless policy of Joshua was successful inasmuch as four Canaanite cities in the neighbourhood submitted without opposition, indeed they beguiled the Israelite leader into an alliance. The principal of these new allies, the city of Gibeon, was immediately threatened by a confederation of other Amorite cities. Joshua was not the man to leave his friends in the lurch, and after a forced march he attacked their assailants. The men of Israel were completely successful and drove the Amorites down the Pass of Beth-horon. This battle carried with it the possession of Central Canaan. But though the Amorites were defeated in the field for the time, they were still in possession of impregnable fortified towns. One line of these fortresses with Jerusalem, Aijalon, and Gezer amongst them cut off the main part of Israel from the south; and another line of fortresses along the valley of Jezreel cut them off from their kinsmen in the north.

Joshua is said to have marched his army up as far as the Waters of Merom where a confederation of North Canaanite kings was defeated, but Israelite influence was never very strong to the north of the valley, even then Galilee was markedly gentile.

The seizure of the middle part of Canaan, however, was a great step towards the conquest of the whole land, and the military head-quarters seems to have been moved from Gilgal. The central sanctuary of the people was established at Shiloh, and the land divided up amongst the various tribes who made up the Israelite confederation.[1]

After Joshua came the period of the judges, and just as later thought has pictured Joshua as leading a united nation to a complete and final conquest of Canaan, so it has pictured the several judges as ruling the whole nation in due and orderly succession, from Othniel to Samuel.[2] A careful study of the O. T., however, reveals the fact that the authority possessed by each judge was only local, and that the Israelites found it as difficult as their Canaanite predecessors had done to establish any real union or cohesion during this period. Palestine, like Greece, is a land which tends naturally to the development of small communities, and the existence of the various Canaanite fortresses served to accentuate the lines of geographical division. Moreover, tribal jealousies aggravated the disunion, Ephraim in particular being a notable offender.

Thus the nation was weakened internally by jealousy and dissension, and at the same time it had to face external dangers.

---

[1] The survey and division of the land in Joshua 13–19 comes from P, and is an idealized account of what the writer thought should have taken place. Some division of the conquered territory probably did take place, and some had still to be conquered (cf. Judges 1).

[2] If the chronology of the period is in any way exact, some of the judges must have been contemporaries (see p. 70).

The Canaanites who survived, either behind the walls of their fortified towns, or mingled or even allied with the Israelites, were still threatening. From the desert, too, came Bedawin raiders who were not slow to attack a nomadic people attempting to find a permanent home. No settled policy on the part of Israel seems to have been followed in dealing with these different threats; temporary and local federations seem, however, to have been formed to meet particular dangers as they arose. The one link which bound the tribes together was their common faith in Jahveh, and it was in His name and to fight His battles that the most considerable gathering was made (Judges 5[23]).

The individual judges and their several exploits call for no comment here, save that attention may be drawn to the story of Abimelech and of his attempt, premature and unsuccessful as it was, to found a kingdom with the support of both the Israelite and the Canaanite elements in the land. The Samson stories, too, stand apart from the rest, being concerned with the almost non-Israelite tribe of Judah, and depicting the 'strong man' type of hero which was much more in accordance with Greek than with Hebrew ideals, the latter regarding craftiness as a much more admirable virtue (cf. Jacob and Esau).

The period of the judges is regarded by many scholars as one of degeneration in both politics and religion—and such indeed it was. None the less allowance must be made for the difficulties by which the nation was faced, for a time of transition and settlement is bound to be a time of peculiar temptations, a time when much that is good in the old is in danger of being lost or forgotten, and when novelties attract by their very newness. The unrest and lawlessness of the period 'when there was no king in Israel' prepared for the coming of the monarchy and the establishment of a settled rule and a central sanctuary.

The last of the judges was Samuel, and his rule seems to have been more widely recognized than that of his predecessors, and so he too prepared the way for the coming of the monarchy. Different traditions, however, in regard to Samuel have come down to us, and the real conditions of the period and even the mind of this great prophet cannot clearly be discerned.[1]

[1] See discussion of the sources, pp. 65 f.

In Samuel's early days the rise of a new danger had begun to threaten the very existence of the Israelites as an independent people. From their settlements on the coast the Philistines were gradually spreading east over the whole country, and they were no longer content with mere plundering raids, but seemed to be aiming at permanent conquests. A battle was fought at Eben-ezer in which the Israelites, in spite of the presence with them of the national palladium, the ark, were completely overthrown, and in their flight they abandoned even the ark itself. It is possible that the remarkable successes of the Philistines were due to the use of iron weapons, which they are thought by some to have been the first to introduce into Palestine (cf. I Sam. 13$^{19 \text{ ff.}}$).

The overwhelming danger which threatened the people drove them back on their God, and, as in the days of Deborah, an outburst of religious fanaticism drew the nation together. The most striking form in which this new enthusiasm manifested itself was in the rise of bands of prophets, the counterpart of the dervishes of Islam, who aroused and kept alive the national spirit and urged the people on to the Holy War. The book of Samuel tells us of a wonderful victory gained by the great prophetic leader; but this account can scarcely be accepted as historical, since it conflicts with the whole situation which called for the need of a king, and also with the predominant position of the Philistines even after the rise of Saul (13$^{3 \text{ ff.}}$, 14^{21}).

In their terror the people felt the need of some permanent leader around whom they could rally, and who would lead them forth like the kings of the nations around; a new Barak or Gideon, but one who would be able to hand on his authority to his successor. Such a leader was found in Saul the son of Kish, a Benjamite. He was chosen apparently by Samuel himself, and was a popular figure on account of his great stature. Some murmuring, however, seems to have taken place amongst the people, due perhaps to tribal jealousy, but the chance came to Saul to show his worthiness, and he did not fail to take it. The east Jordan town of Jabesh-gilead was besieged by Nahash, the king of Ammon, and so hard was the garrison pressed that they had agreed to a surrender, on degrading terms, unless help came within seven days. News was brought to Saul at Gibeah, and he

The rise of the prophets. A modern holy man of the East

immediately exercised his authority by summoning the people to follow him. A swift march enabled the army to surprise the Ammonite camp and a complete victory was gained.

Meanwhile the country was still, in part at any rate, under Philistine domination; and if the new king was completely to justify himself some great effort was needed to free the nation. The destruction of a Philistine garrison (or trophy) at Gibeah by Jonathan, the heroic son of the king, gave the signal for the rising. The Philistines were quickly on the move, and the army which Saul had gathered round him rapidly melted away as he retreated before them. With a remnant of only 600 followers he stood at bay at Gibeah. Once again Jonathan came to the fore, and by a sudden attack he brought confusion into the mixed host of the Philistines, amongst whom some Hebrews had been compelled to serve. The Israelites rallied and succeeded in driving out their foes for the time.

Other enemies besides Ammon and the Philistines were encountered by Saul during his reign, the most notable being the Amalekites. Doubtless these restless marauders had taken advantage of Israel's weakness to raid them incessantly. Saul adopted methods which in later times both Romans and Turks found the only course to pursue; he aimed at completely destroying their power. But in every case the flying Bedawin soon recovered themselves. Saul's expedition was noteworthy as it involved him in a bitter quarrel with Samuel. Some scholars think that the prophet was jealous of Saul's popularity and success, and sought means of undermining it.[1] Probably he had hoped to use Saul as an instrument of his own to serve prophetic ends and, finding him too stubborn, determined to find a more pliant successor. Nairne, who compares the rising of Israel against the Philistines to that of Italy against Austria, draws a parallel between Saul and Garibaldi on the one hand, and Samuel and the Pope on the other.[2]

The king, borne down by the burden of unequal war and in-

---

[1] Sayce says that Samuel 'would not conceal his mortification and hostility . . . (and) was not long in embodying his hostility in deeds'. *Early Hist. of the Hebs.*, p. 365.
[2] *Everyman's Old Test.*, pp. 46 ff.

ternal dissension, seems to have given way to terrible fits of
nervous depression. At length the tide of Philistine invasion
once more gathered force and the stormy life found peace at last
on the disastrous slopes of Mount Gilboa.

> Ye mountains of Gilboa,
> Let there be no dew nor rain upon you,
>> neither fields of offerings:
> For there the shield of the mighty was vilely cast away,
> The shield of Saul, not anointed with oil.

The successor whom Samuel had chosen was a young Bethle-
hemite, David by name. His early years are not clearly sketched
in the history, but in some way he was taken up by Saul, either
on account of his skill as a musician or because of his part in
slaying a Philistine champion named Goliath. Saul's brooding
soul, however, quickly became jealous of the brilliant young Jew;
and in spite of the efforts of Jonathan, who was drawn to David,
an open quarrel quickly broke out, and David was outlawed.
Part of his exile was spent in the country of Achish, king of Gath,
where he narrowly escaped being compelled to join the Philistine
host which invaded Israel. On the death of Saul David became
king of Judah or part of Israel (presumably as a Philistine vassal),
with his head-quarters at Hebron. The rest of the country was
under the nominal rule of Saul's eldest son Esh-baal (or Ishbosheth),
who was established at Mahanaim on the east of Jordan. The real
backbone of the Israelite kingdom, however, was Abner ben Ner,
and on his deserting Esh-baal for David (only to meet his death by
the treachery of Joab) the nation soon turned to Hebron for
a monarch for the whole people. David thus found himself, as the
reward of his craft and patience, the undisputed ruler of all Israel.

The work which Saul had failed to carry through was undertaken, with fresh hope and zeal, by the united nation under its
new monarch. As a result the Philistines were finally overcome,
and other nations were also defeated in warfare, mainly by the
skill of David's fierce commander-in-chief, Joab. The Jebusite
stronghold, Jerusalem, was stormed and turned into the national
capital; a happy choice since it had connexion with neither Judah
nor Israel.

The later years of David's life were clouded by domestic

troubles, which finally led to civil war; his favourite son Absalom, by playing on weaknesses in the nation, raised a party and attempted to dethrone his father. The rebellion, and the unsettlement which followed it, showed only too plainly that Israel and Judah were not yet welded together into a single people.

In spite of some serious lapses the career of David exhibits him as a man of fine character, especially when one remembers the very different moral standards of his time. Through his long life he was unswervingly loyal to Jahveh and amenable to His discipline. The example of his life of obedience must have had a profound influence on the religious life of Israel, especially as it concerned individuals.

David was succeeded by his illustrious son, Solomon. In this succession intrigue and plotting again played a prominent part, Solomon's rise being due to the influence of the harem which overcame the nominee of Joab and Abiathar. This reign was one of peace both internally, where the stern rule of a despot kept down any murmuring, and externally where exhaustion had for the time rendered Egypt and the powers of Mesopotamia of little account. This external peace was, however, giving the opportunity for the growth of Israel's most dangerous enemy of future years— the Aramaeans or Syrians. The internal peace was the means of vast developments of the Hebrew monarchy. Lavish building schemes were successfully carried through, and Solomon began to copy the barbarian splendour of other Oriental rulers. The combination of peace at home and abroad seemed at first to promise the growth of a new empire, but a narrow strip of territory like Palestine was insufficient to support such a structure, and the possibilities of wider conquests were once and for all removed when on the death of Solomon the kingdom was split in two by the rebellion of Jeroboam. None the less the reigns of David and Solomon loomed out through the sorrows and humiliations of the years that were to come as Israel's golden age.

In some ways Solomon reminds one of Henry VIII of England. He was a learned and cultivated monarch who began his reign with high ideals, but he was drawn down by the temptations of pride and lust. Like Henry, Solomon interfered decisively in the religious organization of his people, and his action in changing the priesthood placed the Church of Israel under the control of the monarch.[1] At the same time the prestige of Jahveh was much enhanced amongst the nations by the growing power of His chosen people.[2]

The burden of the glories of Solomon had fallen mainly upon the tribes of the north, and they had had the least benefit from them. On the succession of his son a determined effort was made to obtain release or at least some modification. Rehoboam, encouraged by a band of young and inexperienced courtiers, and rejecting the counsel of wiser heads, insisted on retaining all his father's rights, nay, he promised harsher demands. Israel turned away in disgust and the house of David never again recovered the sovereignty of the whole people. The northern tribes found a ruler in Jeroboam, a sagacious and energetic leader. By his religious measures he provided a substitute for the temple at Jerusalem, and thus made the breach not only political but ecclesiastical, though the god whom he gave to Israel was still Jahveh and no new deity.

The two kingdoms, Israel and Judah, continue side by side throughout the whole of our period. Judah remained ever faithful to the house of David, but upon the throne of Israel a succession of short-lived dynasties held precarious power from time to time. Israel was ever the predominant power and often Judah seems to have been in the position of a client state. Israel, moreover, was in close touch with foreign powers and for years had to carry on a life-and-death struggle with the Syrians, a struggle which was only ended by the downfall of the latter beneath the iron hand of Assyria. To the latter power Israel, which they called the land of Humri (= Omri), was well known amongst the Palestinian states, and Ahab was one of the allies who fought at Karkar in 853.[3]

The great names amongst the kings of Israel are few, perhaps because the writers of the O. T. were not sufficiently interested in them to preserve their doings. Jeroboam, the first monarch, was seemingly a person of power and force; Omri was sufficiently notable to give his name to the land; and Jehu, a fanatical follower

---

[1] See Sayce, *Early Hist. of the Hebs.*, p. 455.
[2] See Kent, *Hist. of Heb. People*, i, p. 206.
[3] See Appendix, p. 241.

of Jahveh against the Tyrian Baal, is perhaps worthy to stand beside them. For the O. T. writers the figure which commanded the most interest, and that of a sinister nature, was Ahab. Ahab was another Solomon intent on glorifying himself and his house by lavish building schemes. Like Solomon he was led astray by matrimonial alliances, and his wife, Jezebel, was to the prophets the very incarnation of all that was evil. The kingdom of Israel had owed its origin very largely to the action of the prophets, if one reads between the lines, who were perhaps anxious to free religion from the royal power and from the grip of an unreformed priesthood. But the kings of Israel were for the most part military adventurers with little care for ideals such as those of the prophets, and the breach gradually widened (1 Kings 14$^{1\,ff.}$, 16$^{1-4}$). When the influence of Jezebel became supreme in the councils of Ahab the battle was joined for a final struggle, and the prophetic ideals found in Elijah a worthy champion.

In their struggle against the house of Omri in the person of Ahab the prophets were greatly helped, it would seem, by the growing resentment of the people against acts of private tyranny and by the stirring of their ethical impulses. The story of Naboth and his vineyard is told at length, and its importance justifies such treatment. It is comparatively small acts of injustice such as this which move the hearts of a people against its rulers much more certainly than the exercise of despotic powers on a wider scale.

In Judah the current of affairs flowed on more peacefully and along more regular channels; as we saw above, the succession was never interrupted, save for the short intrusion of Athaliah. Two names only stand out in any prominence, Asa and Jehoshaphat. Each of their reigns was marked by great political and commercial activity, and at the same time by a revived interest in religion.

B. ISRAELITE RELIGION TO THE END OF THE NINTH CENTURY

To trace out the religious development of the people of Israel during a period of many hundred years with minute accuracy is not possible. Our sources of information are not contemporary, and often enough a story which apparently represents the religious conditions of an early period may be in its entirety the product of a later age which read back into the past the ideas of its own times. All that can be done is to try and present a broad view of the general development as far as it can be gathered from a critical study of the available authorities.

For convenience of treatment the whole period is divided up into lesser periods; but it should not be forgotten that these divisions are artificial to a great extent, and in different parts of Palestine different stages of development might be reached at different periods just as in India to-day. Contact with foreign influences would be more easy in big towns or near the trading routes than in remote villages, and consequently religious changes in the latter would lag behind the former, whilst on the contrary superstitions would linger. The countryside is notoriously slow to alter its religious convictions (cf. the word pagan which really means countryman). The southern peoples who had more of the Arab in them than the northern—the latter having large Canaanite elements—held purer and higher conceptions.

i. *Early Hebrew Religion*

Of Hebrew religion before Moses we have but little information. It was probably very similar to that of other Semitic peoples. In the nation of Israel as it is known after the settlement in Canaan many different elements were contained. It is probable that not all the tribes had been in Egypt, and some were less closely connected by race with the main body of Israel than others (the tribe of Judah in particular was very mixed), whilst Canaanite influences came in by alliance and inter-marriage.

The first religious ideas of the Hebrews were probably connected with the powers behind Nature. In all the various processes which resulted in harvest and in the increase of herds and flocks various supernatural beings were at work. Everywhere and at all times man was surrounded by spirits, and these spirits he could not afford to ignore. In most cases their presence was manifested in particular places such as trees and wells, and even in boulders; the tops of hills also were thought to be specially the homes of gods.

At such spots, and at others where a god had revealed himself by some manifestation of power, as by a lightning-stroke, altars were erected and some simple ritual was performed.[1] The sacrifices would be offered by the individual, or by the head of the family, 'a regular priesthood was a much later development', and beside the rude altar, pillars or stones (Exod. 34[13]; Judges 6[25]: cf. Exod. 24[4]), and perhaps roughly carved images would be set up. At stated intervals common feasts would be held; these feasts would mark the various stages of agricultural operations, such as the harvest or the vintage (Judges 9[27]).

It is by no means certain that Jahveh was known to Israel before the revelation to Moses. In J it is true He is represented as having been an object of worship from quite early times (Gen. 12[1]), but other writers held different views: cf. Joshua 24[2]; Gen. 35[2] (cf. 31[19]); Exod. 3[13 f.], 6[3]. If He were worshipped it would be by only a portion of the tribes who subsequently became Israel, perhaps indeed He was the god of Midian or of the Kenites.

In this early age no supreme deity was recognized; each tribe or city seems to have had its own deity whom it tended to regard as superior to the gods of other tribes whilst not denying the existence of the latter. Religion was largely based either on the fear of visitations or the desire for special benefits, but it had in it also much of rejoicing. The deity was regarded as in some sense the parent, perhaps even physically (Gen. 6[4]), of His worshippers.[2]

[1] On the persistence of sacred spots in Palestine, see S. A. Cook, *The Religion of Ancient Palestine*, pp. 18 ff. As he says: 'Religious practice is always conservative, and once a place has acquired a reputation for sanctity, it will retain its fame throughout political and even religious vicissitudes.'

[2] Cf. *Iliad*, xx. 215; *Aeneid*, vii. 220 f.

ii. *The Wilderness Period*

It is probable, as was suggested above, that by no means all of the tribes which were subsequently to call themselves by the name of Israel were in the wilderness together or even in Egypt. But the desert and its life had a marked effect on the life of the nation. In particular the work of Moses, which tradition placed there, was a predominant influence in moulding their future.

Moses is famous above all as the great lawgiver, and those laws which are considered to have the best claim to an early or Mosaic date have a strong religious tone. It is true that the chief interest of the nation is in the ritual side of religion; but in a primitive community, when religion has still much of the magical about it, the due performance of ritual is in the eyes of all the most important part of religion. The earliest code (Exod. $34^{17 ff.}$) is of this character, very simple and straightforward, but interested above all in ritual.[1] In the Mosaic legislation, and in every stratum of it, older material was contained; it was a kind of codifying of existing laws, or better perhaps customs, into a convenient and official form.

The ritual was very simple. An earthen altar, a loosely organized priesthood, not yet of any particular tribe or family (Exod. 24^5), and sacrifices offered for a variety of reasons. The revenue of the priesthood, although we have no definite information as to its amount or scale, would consist of dues from the worshippers. The work of the priest was by no means limited to officiating at the altar, he also acted as judge and as diviner.

The object of worship for the nation was Jahveh, the God who had revealed Himself to Moses on the sacred mount. Whether as some authorities think Jahveh had been known by name to the Fathers of the race, or whether He was then first disclosed, is a question which admits of no certain answer. At any rate, from Sinai onwards He was the sole legitimate deity for Israelite worship.

But although Jahveh was the only God for Israel, this did not mean that the gods of other races had for them no real existence. The first commandment in the Decalogue clearly recognizes that

[1] See p. 105, below.

other gods did exist, and that it was possible for the Israelite to transfer his allegiance to them. To do so would have been a grave offence against both god and nation, for the two were closely bound together.

That a covenant or agreement was made at Sinai is the testimony of Israel's early writers; and indeed it is far from unlikely that the origin of the nation was a confederation of desert tribes at Sinai under the protection of the God of Sinai. Jahveh, as the covenant god, was bound to fight for His people, and although the actual title ' Jahveh of Hosts' is not found in the Pentateuch the idea which gave force to the title is there fully developed. His presence was connected with particular places such as Sinai, or objects like the ark, but it was by no means limited to them.

Whether the Mosaic religion had in it some of those immoral features which made Canaanite religion so revolting to a more enlightened age is not certain; if they ever existed they have long since been obliterated from the records, though we find traces of such things in the later period (see below, pp. 110, 215). So far as we can see the religion of the desert, although it was fierce and sanguinary, was superior ethically to that of the surrounding peoples, and it contained within it the germs of moral and religious progress. This high character is usually held to be the result of the labours of one whom the Israelites regarded as amongst the earliest of their prophets, Moses himself. They further believed that his teaching originated not in his own mind, but that it was given him by Jahveh their God. Later ages see no reason for doubting the substantial accuracy of their belief. For whatever may have been ' the process by which Moses became possessed of the principles embodied in the Law, they may justly be regarded as derived from God if such derivation can be claimed for anything. The best warrant for the Divine commission with which he professed to be invested is the character of the work which he accomplished'.[1] This work was speedily to be tested on the entry into Canaan.

[1] Wade, *Old Testament History*, p. 164.

iii. *The period of Conquest and Settlement*

The characteristics of this period were strife and turmoil, everything was in a state of fluidity, and the religious ideas which had
been hammered out by the Israelites under their divinely guided
leader in the desert had to face the test, and that an exceedingly
severe one, of contact with the ideas of a higher civilization.
Moreover, the change of life which was necessitated by the trans-
forming of a pastoral people into an agricultural had its own
special temptations. Jahveh was a God of war, would He help
them in the processes of sowing and reaping? Would it not be
better to trust to the local Baals who from distant ages had been
lords of each little piece of territory, or could not some reverence
for them be combined with the worship of Jahveh?

The condition of Palestine when the Israelites invaded it has
already been described (see above, pp. 12 ff.). From a religious
point of view it shared in the primitive Semitic beliefs and
practices which marked the earlier stages of Israelite religion.

But whereas amongst the desert tribes there was little emphasis
on sexual elements in the worship; amongst the peoples of
Palestine they were probably present in large bulk. The leading
deity of the country was Hadad, the weather-god, who is named
Addu in the Tell el-Amarna Tablets and whose name was regarded
as being interchangeable with Baal.[1]

The settlement of Israel involved either the extermination of
the Canaanites or an amalgamation with them. It was the latter
process which actually took place, although subsequent writers
represented the matter otherwise, and we hear of alliances with
Canaanites both domestic and political. In this new community
what was to be the predominant religious influence? Sooner or
later religious unity must follow political unity, even if it does
not, as in the case of our Saxon forefathers, actually precede it.
Now religious unity may be established in different ways. The
deity of the one race may be enforced upon the other, or the two
may go on side by side. In the former case, although the name

---

[1] 'The interchange of Baal and Addu in certain names in the Amarna
letters shows that Addu could naturally be called Baal, and to the Egyptians he was apparently *the* Baal.' S. A. Cook, *Rel. of Anct. Pal.*, p. 89.

of the deity who survives may be that of the conquerors, it is almost inevitable that his characteristics and the method of worshipping him will have been modified by those belonging to his defeated rival.

In the case of Jahveh and Baal there appears to have been such a modification, at least in the popular mind. Jahveh was actually called Baal,[1] and the prophets were continually at war against the tendency to confuse Him with the Canaanite deity. The original conceptions of two closely related Semitic peoples must have been so much alike that religious unity arrived at by compromise was an obvious and easy course. The testimony of the archaeologist supports the theory that such compromises took place, for his labours have revealed no violent gap in the evolution of religious customs and practices—a reliable clue to the ideas which lie behind them—from the pre-Exodus age to times much later. As S. A. Cook puts it: 'the external (archaeological) evidence does not reveal that hiatus which would have ensued had there been a dislocation of earlier conditions by invading Israelite tribes; earlier forms are simply developed, the evolution is a progressive one'.[2] What are the limits of this period of settlement and conquest? Various answers, such as the establishment of the monarchy, might be given to this question, but for our purpose perhaps the close of the reign of David is the best terminal point. The boundaries were then fixed, and the last Canaanite fortress had then been reduced. Moreover the reign of Solomon marks the beginning of a new epoch, both politically and religiously, more clearly than that of Saul, who was hardly king of Israel at all, and whose rule and methods were largely a continuation of those of the judges.

In spite of much admixture of Canaanite ideas Jahveh was still the God of Israel, the leader of its armies in battle (Judges 5[23]; 1 Sam. 18[17], 25[28]). As in the wilderness period His presence was closely linked with the symbol of the ark and its coming could be regarded as His coming. As a rule the ark was kept in a tent

[1] Cf. the names Esh-baal (see p. 180) and Meri(b)baal, and see Hos. 2[16].
[2] *Rel. of Anct. Pal.*, p. 115. At the same time there was a real breakdown of culture following the Israelite settlement: see Macalister, *A Century of Excavation in Pal.*, pp. 238 f.

(2 Sam. $7^{6\ f.}$), but the dwelling at Shiloh seems to have been a more substantial structure (1 Sam. $1^{7,\ 9}$, 3^3). But although Jahveh was regarded as the God of Israel He was, again as in the desert period, not the only existing deity. To the average Israelite the gods of the surrounding nations were just as real as Jahveh, though he secretly hoped they were not as powerful (Judges 11^{24}), and each was the proper object of worship in his own land (1 Sam. 26^{19}).[1]

There is no trace yet of an elaborately organized priesthood. Different sanctuaries seem to be ministered to by different families, but the Aaronic priesthood, afterwards to be supreme in Israel, can hardly be traced through the period with any certainty. Eleazar followed Aaron (Num. $20^{25\ ff.}$) and to him succeeded Phinehas (Judges 20^{28}), then the succession is lost. Eli was probably descended from Ithamar (cf. 1 Sam. 22^2, 14^3, with 1 Chron. 24^3: and see Josephus *Antiq.* V. xi. 5). Professional priests or Levites appear as wandering about the country (Judges 17^7, 19^1), and their ministry seems to be regarded as more desirable than that of other folk (Judges 17^{13}), although there is no trace of any monopoly of the priesthood, indeed Samuel, or David, or David's sons (2 Sam. 8^{18}), young men of the people, as in earlier times, were considered quite qualified to offer sacrifices (Exod. 24^5; cf. also 2 Sam. 20^{26}).

The number of sanctuaries seems to have been considerable, and they appear to have been scattered about the face of the land from Dan (Laish) in the far north (Judges 18^{30}) downwards. Amongst the most famous were Beth-el, Gilgal, Mizpah, Ramah, Nob, and Gibeon.

We have but little information on the subject of the revenues of the priesthood. They were entitled to a part of flesh-offerings but under certain restrictions (1 Sam. $2^{13\ ff.}$), and no doubt took their part in sacrificial meals. Various kinds of offerings are alluded to mostly in the books of Samuel. The sacrifices known as burnt offerings, peace offerings, and meal offerings were already well known, and the custom of pouring out libations to God was by no means uncommon (see 1 Sam. 1^{24}, 7^6, 10^3, 2 Sam. 23^{16}). The

[1] 'When the gods reign like feudal princes over their principalities their sphere is limited and other districts or kingdoms belong to other gods.' S. A. Cook, *op. cit.*, p. 69.

custom of making vows appears also to have been frequent, although the two instances recorded in Judges 11[30 f.] (Jephthah's daughter), and 2 Sam. 15[7] (Saul's vow) seem to emphasize the foolishness of making them too rashly.

Of the machinery and furniture of the religion we have some knowledge though it is by no means detailed. The mysterious Ephod—which sometimes appears to be a linen garment (1 Sam. 14[40ff.], LXX) and at others can be best explained as an image (Judges 8[23]; 1 Sam. 21[9]), and which was regarded with sufficient veneration as to make it worth stealing—was used in some way for divining as were the Urim and Thummim (see 1 Sam. 14[40 ff.], LXX). All these like the Teraphim are by no means understood. The Teraphim seem to have been some kind of idol in human form (cf. 1 Sam. 19[13]) perhaps for this reason they were forbidden (1 Sam. 15[23]).

Alongside the priest, whose main care was the service of the sanctuary and the giving of judicial decisions either by means of the sacred lot or otherwise, stood the prophet from whom he was not sharply distinguished. A leader like Samuel, although probably not a priest by profession, and certainly not by birth according to later requirements, yet exercised priestly functions.

The conception of prophecy current in this period of Israel's religious development was primitive, and the prophet himself was not always regarded with particular respect. Two names for the office are found in actual use—the seer (*Hozeh* or *Ro'eh*), and the prophet proper (*Nabi*).

The seer, as the name itself shows, had special insight into the things of God and could also look into the future. His methods were quiet and orderly, and, if Samuel is a typical seer, he occupied a position of social importance and was respected by his fellow citizens.

The prophet was much more akin to the modern dervish. He frequently fell into wild estatic fits and even deliberately induced them (2 Kings 3[15]). According to the statement in 1 Sam. 9[9], the prophet gradually drove out the Seer, but at the same time he took over some of his characteristics, such as 'second-sight' (2 Kings 6[17]). The prophets were not held in high reputation, and in later times Amos repudiated any connexion with them (Amos

7^{14}). But in spite of their strange and, to our minds, unhealthy methods, these early prophets represented a real stage in the divine dealing with Israel, for it was to Jahveh that they pointed men and it was to His service that their lives were devoted.

The prophets as a body were thus fanatically devoted to the service of Jahveh; they were also fanatically devoted to Israel, and indeed played no small part in arousing and keeping active the patriotic spirit of the nation—Deborah and Samuel are obvious examples of this side of the prophetic activity. The movement was propagated by the gathering round each great leader of a number of disciples, or sons, to use the Semitic term. These bands of prophets often gave way to wild fanatical out-bursts which were liable to draw to them easily excited souls. The rest of the people seem to have regarded them with a certain measure of contempt not unmixed with that superstitious rever-ence which in the East is still paid to madmen.

Religion in this period had not yet begun to exercise much influence upon morals, the standard of which was exceedingly low (cf. Judges 8^{31}, $14^{1 \, f.}$, 16^1). The evidence for this comes mainly from deeds not deliberate statements: Jael, Gideon, Samson are all guilty of actions of either treachery or violence which revolt the conscience of Christians; by their contemporaries, and even by a later age, such deeds were taken as a matter of course.

iv. *From Solomon to Elisha*

As we have already seen the reign of Solomon marked the beginning of an epoch in Israelite history religiously as well as politically. The change from David to Solomon is from the open-air life of an Arab chief to the artificial atmosphere of an Oriental despot. Religiously Solomon carried out the designs of his father, unless our records misrepresent the development of events. For David having secured a political centre for his kingdom in the newly conquered Jebusite stronghold at Jerusalem conceived the idea of building there a sanctuary to the nation's God. No doubt at first the glorification of the royal state by the erection of a magnificent private chapel was a weighty motive, but gradually the whole religious life of the people began to turn to Jerusalem and its temple as the special dwelling of Jahveh. The local sanctuaries were still maintained (1 Kings 3²), but with declining glory, and in order to restore their prestige and to attract clients they seem to have encouraged Canaanite customs of a sexual character, especially in the northern kingdom after the schism.

With David the internal settlement of the affairs of the nation was for the time achieved, and his successor could look abroad and feel that he might begin to develop relations with foreign powers. The making of alliances, however, involved in many cases marriages by one contracting party with the daughter or some near relation of the other; thus Solomon's many wives no doubt can best be explained. They brought with them foreign luxuries and foreign gods, and the wise monarch was himself led astray by them. The struggle of the prophetic party was to be not only with Canaanite survivals, but also with foreign customs and religious ideas.

Then came the breach between the two kingdoms, a political breach which was accompanied by a religious schism. Strangely enough no new God was adopted by either of the two divisions of the tribes of Israel, but in Jerusalem and Beth-el alike it was Jahveh who was claimed as the God of the nation. In order to prevent his subjects resorting to the attractions at Jerusalem Jeroboam, the first sovereign of North Israel, made lavish gifts to the two great sanctuaries at Beth-el and Dan where we are told that he erected two calves of gold (1 Kings 12²⁶ ᶠᶠ·). Further he organized a new priesthood chosen from among non-Levites, so the later writer said, though it is doubtful if the custom of restricting the priesthood to the tribe of Levi had become absolute by the time of Jeroboam. It is true that the chief among the priesthood would have been attracted to the royal shrine, and so Jeroboam would be compelled to choose his clergy from men of lower standard. In Jerusalem, as well as at Beth-el and Dan, material representations of the deity were still allowed to remain; that is if the brazen serpent, supposed to have come down from the days of Moses, worshipped there until the time of Isaiah (2 Kings 18⁴), was a representation of Jahveh. One great change Solomon had made in the priesthood: he had deposed Abiathar and placed Zadok in his stead, thus transferring the ecclesiastical power from one family to another.

The great interest of the period, subsequent to the time of Solomon, both political and religious, lies in the northern kingdom. As Israel was stronger and wealthier than Judah so was its religious life more vigorous, though by no means so pure. The fact that it lay nearer to outside influences made also a considerable difference. The great struggle between the faith of Jahveh and that of the Syrian Baal was really decided in the north by the work of the Gileadite prophet Elijah.

Elijah is one of the most living and attractive characters of the Old Testament, and even his failings make him more human and more lovable. He was a prophet from the desert, and it was the old pure faith of the desert that he came to revive among a people led away by foreign luxury and foreign cults. His was a direct and simple mind; and his methods were equally direct and simple, by a later age they might be called ruthless. He saw one thing clearly and gave all his powers to it. Jahveh or Baal was to be the God of the people. He asked no question about details of ritual, about the worship of the calf which later prophets found so obnoxious; bigger things were at stake and he concentrated on them. That is why it is unsafe to base any argument as to the lawfulness of the altars on the one erected or rebuilt by him at Mount Carmel. Like the earlier prophets with whom he stood in a direct line of succession he was a patriot and a fanatic, and he did his work in a thorough manner. His influence with the nation was in consequence immense, and to the end of its days he was the prophet who was to reappear and to restore all things.

After Elijah came a figure of very different stature and very different methods—his own disciple Elisha. Elisha had been snatched away from his farm and his family by the stern call of the older prophet (1 Kings 19[19]) in a scene described with few details, but with intense dramatic force. When Elijah disappeared from among men, as suddenly as he had appeared, all recognized in Elisha his successor.

Elisha was a man of the court, not of the desert; he lived with his fellows, and was known amongst them; he did not startle them by sudden violent comings and goings. But his methods, if not so drastic as those of his master, were equally thorough. As a prophet he suffers from being overshadowed by Elijah, indeed, one is never sure how far stories about Elijah have not been transferred to him by popular tradition. He is nearer in some

A wandering band of Muhammadan dervishes, from a drawing
by a Persian artist of the sixteenth century

ways to the later prophets, though even he, like some modern dervish, made use of music in order to bring on the prophetic frenzy (2 Kings 3^{15}).

C. THE BIBLICAL SOURCES FOR THE PERIOD

i. *Ancient Methods of Writing History*

Those who approach the study of O.T. with some knowledge of modern historians and their methods are bound to be deceived and disappointed if the records are viewed simply as literature. Ancient historians, including those who wrote the books of the O.T., had very little idea of criticism, they accepted much that was told them without sifting the true from the false, they had a strong sense of what would fit in well with their subject matter and illuminate and adorn it, but only a weak critical ability. History was not written for its own sake, but to serve some purpose which was considered of greater importance. To the Hebrew history was only significant as showing forth God's revelation of Himself through the medium of the experiences of the chosen people. We must remember that the Jewish writers did not claim to write 'history' at all, there are no 'historical' books in the Hebrew bible; although we use the term of certain compositions even books like Joshua, Judges, Samuel, and Kings are classed with the Prophets; they are not so much records of events as an interpretation of them. Hence it follows that what was of value from a religious point of view received much attention, what was merely of secular importance was hardly mentioned. A good illustration of this tendency can be found in the treatment of the reign of Omri. According to outside sources of information he was one of the greatest of all the Israelite kings, but the writer of I Kings 16 dismisses him with only a few verses, simply because he signified little for the religious development of the nation.

Again, to contrast ancient and modern methods of writing history, the modern historian, after mastering his sources, reproduces them in a continuous narrative making use of his own words, or if he wishes to give the exact phrases used in his authority he quotes them in a footnote or between inverted commas. Such methods were unknown in ancient times. To take a case outside the O.T.—I do this merely to show that such methods were the accepted literary custom of the times, not merely the peculiarity of the Biblical writers—Herodotus only refers to 'older historians when he wished to correct or contradict them . . . more frequently he silently incorporates their statements and words without mentioning them by name. . . . Reviewers did not exist in his day, nor were marks of quotation or even footnotes as yet invented, and Herodotus might therefore plead that, although he quoted freely without acknowledgement, he was not in any real sense a plagiarist. He only acted like other Greek writers of his time.' [1]

Another process which was continually going on was in a sense the reverse of this, for by it, instead of writers making unacknowledged borrowings from one another, they made unauthorized additions to a work already in existence. This method of historical writing continued right down into the Middle Ages, and the Chronicles of the various monastic houses were continually being enriched so that the original would almost have disappeared altogether did we not possess other versions of it.[2]

We are not then to look upon the so-called historical books of the O. T. in the same way as we should on a great modern historical work like Stubbs's *Constitutional History of England*, or Creighton's *History of the Papacy*, as being the product of a single critical mind; but as containing matter derived from various ages, simply collected together, often without much attempt at arrangement, and sometimes with contradictions left for the reader to account for as best he can.[3]

For the whole of the period covered by the present volume, from the exodus from Egypt up to the death of Elisha, we possess no contemporary authorities; the age of the written prophets has not yet begun. Much, however, of the matter is early, and in the

[1] Sayce, *The Egypt of the Hebs. and Herodotos*, pp. 176 f.
[2] Some very apt illustrations of the methods of medieval historians as serving to illustrate O. T. writings will be found in Carpenter and Harford Battersby, *The Composition of the Hexateuch*, pp. 5 ff.
[3] In regard to such inconsistencies Nairne has pointed out that the author 'had accounts of action and judgements of character before him which contradicted one another. He conceived it his duty to decide what was the real course of events; and this he did on the whole with fair mastery; but he has been honest enough to leave certain discrepancies. We ask, for instance, when and how David first entered Saul's service, and we get no clear answer from the historian's double account. This is his confession that he cannot clear everything up.' *The Faith of the Old Testament*, p. 19.

best sense reliable as giving an account, true in its main outlines, of what actually occurred. The different stages within the period itself have different records upon which they are based, and these have different value as historical sources. We will now proceed to describe them and endeavour to assess their value.

ii. *The Pentateuch (JE)*

The earliest of our records consists of the last four books of the Pentateuch, as the five law books are usually called, Exodus, Leviticus, Numbers, and Deuteronomy. These deal with the life story of Moses and the fortunes of the Israelites from the oppression in Egypt up to the time when they encamped on the east of Jordan before attempting the entry into the Promised Land.

A tradition of great antiquity has ascribed the authorship of the whole Pentateuch, commonly called the Five Books of Moses, to Moses. A study of the books themselves, however, reveals no trace of any claim to their having been written by the great deliverer; on the contrary, since Moses is always referred to in the third person and even his death is described (Deut. $34^{5\,ff.}$), they can hardly as a whole have come from his pen. Robertson, who is claimed as a conservative scholar, concludes that 'the books of the Pentateuch, like the historical books which follow them, are anonymous. The book of Genesis gives no hint of its authorship, neither does the book of Leviticus; and the few passages found in the other books which speak of Moses writing such and such things "in a book" will be discovered on examination to refer to certain specific things. Indeed, the very fact of such expressions occurring within the books may even be taken as a presumption that it was not he who wrote the whole'.[1]

The mere fact that Moses appears in the third person in the Pentateuch does not in itself make his authorship impossible, for similar cases have been known elsewhere. Nor need the account of his death stand in the way, for it could quite justly be regarded as an appendix, added in order to complete the life story of the great lawgiver and leader. Jewish tradition varies in its attitude to this account, some writers like Philo and Josephus, unwilling to allow any criticism of the Mosaic authorship, state that he wrote the

[1] *The Early Religion of Israel*, p. 44.

record of his death by anticipation,[1] others more reasonably suppose that Joshua was responsible for it.[2]

The traditional authorship of the Pentateuch must therefore be given up if we are really to understand and to study the books as historical documents. This does not mean that the whole of the matter contained in them is later than Moses, some is probably earlier, some is contemporary, whilst some is much later. The simplest way of accounting for the rise of the tradition of the Mosaic authorship is to suppose that an original nucleus did actually come from him and that succeeding ages made additions to this nucleus still preserving the original name.

A careful examination of the Pentateuch, especially if it be conducted in the original Hebrew, almost inevitably suggests that whoever gave the final form to the books and whenever this stage of their development was reached, many documents or oral traditions were combined in them; and further that these traditions, whether oral or written, had their origins amongst people of different points of view and living in widely separated generations. It will perhaps be well to give a few instances of narratives or incidents which appear more than once in the story and also of some which seem definitely to disagree the one with the other. The call of Moses is twice given (Exod. $3^{2 ff.}$ and $6^{2 ff.}$), as is the story of the quails (Exod. 16 and Num. 11), and that of the striking of the rock (Exod. $17^{1 ff.}$ and Num. 20^{1-13}). It may be that such incidents did actually occur more than once, a possible explanation also of the two-fold appointment of Moses' coadjutors (Exod. $18^{21 ff.}$, and Num. $11^{14 ff.}$), but such repetitions are so frequent and so similar in detail that some other explanation seems to be necessary. Furthermore, in certain of these repetitions the subject would seem to be considered from an entirely different standpoint. Examples of this are to be found in the matter of the speaking powers of Moses (cf. Exod. $4^{10 ff.}$ with $8^{9 f.}$, $26^{f.}$, &c.); the agent, by whom the wonders were wrought, in Exod. $7^{8, 20}$, $8^{5, 16}$, 9^{8}, 12^{1} (all P), this agent is

---

[1] Philo, *Vit. Mos.* iii. 39; Josephus, *Antiq.* IV. viii. 48. In the Medieval Chronicles it is not uncommon for the writers to be represented as recording their own deaths; one very naïve illustration of this custom may suffice: 'I Lodovico Boncente Monaldeschi was born in Orvieto . . . in 1327 . . . and lived to the age of 115 . . . and died of old age' (see Muratori, xii, p. 529).

[2] See the famous passage in the Talmud, *Baba Bathra*, 14 *b*.

Aaron, in Exod. 7^{14}, $8^{1, 20}$, $9^{1, 13, 22}$, $10^{1, 12, 21}$ (all JE) it is Moses; in Exod. 16^{31} the manna tasted like wafers made with honey, in Num. 11^8 like fresh oil; in Ex. $38^{25 \text{ f.}}$ the census has already taken place, but according to Num. 1 it was still to be made. Other instances of different traditions may be found in the name of Moses' father-in-law, and also in the name of the Sacred Mountain (Sinai in J and P; Horeb in D and E).

That the Pentateuch was made up of different documents or sources would be admitted I think by all schools of critics; the difficulty arises when the attempt is made to arrange these various sources into groups and to trace their origins. The system which in broad outline has been accepted by the large majority of scholars in recent years is that generally associated with the name of Wellhausen. This system would divide up the Pentateuchal sources into four main groups known for convenience sake as J, E, D, and P. There is in addition a smaller source known as the Law of Holiness (H) which underlies Lev. 17–26, traces of whose influence can be found here and there in the rest of the Pentateuch.

These various sources come from widely different dates. The most recent of them is that known as P, or the Priestly source. As this source did not reach its final form until the post-exilic period and as its writers regarded all past history from the point of view of their own day and interpreted it accordingly, its value for our purposes is not great; it does undoubtedly, however, contain many early traditions. So, too, the source known as D, or the Deuteronomic source, comes from a time later than the death of Elisha. Most scholars regard it as belonging to the time of Josiah; the law-book discovered in the temple being held to be substantially our present Deuteronomy: see Robinson, *The Decline and Fall of the Hebrew Kingdoms* pp. 239 ff. Other critics would put it later still. In any case it cannot rank as a first-class source for our period.

The two sources which are our chief authorities are those known as J and E. The names are derived from the different names used for the deity before Exod. 3^{15}: J, or the Jahvistic source, uses the personal name Jehovah (or Jahveh); whilst E, or the Elohistic source, uses Elohim, which is the Hebrew word for 'God' in a plural form. Both sources contain very early traditions concerning the people of Israel. J, which comes from Judah, is perhaps slightly the older; whilst E, which belongs to the northern part of the country, is in the main a little later. The approximate dates are 850 and 750 B.C. respectively.[1]

iii. *Joshua*

The book makes no claim to having been written by Joshua himself, and indeed the statement in 24^{26} that 'Joshua wrote these words' (i.e. $24^{2\,ff.}$) tells against it for had the whole book come from him there would surely have been no need to emphasize his authorship of one particular passage.

Joshua is grouped by some critics with the five books of the Law to form the Hexateuch, but the tradition of the five books or Pentateuch is so strong that it seems unnatural to add another. It is true, as critics contend, that the sources of the Pentateuch (J, E, D, P), can be traced into Joshua; cf. the presence in it of a number of contradictions or doublets; cf. 8^9 with 8^{12}, $11^{21\,f.}$, with $15^{13\,ff.}$, 23^8, with 24^{14}. But they can also be traced beyond, so that it is better to preserve the traditional grouping.[2]

The book naturally divides up into two equal parts 1–12, the story of the conquest; 13–24 the apportionment of Canaan and Joshua's farewell charges to the people.

The second part of the book is derived almost entirely from P or D, and does not therefore concern us, save that 24 (the second of Joshua's farewell speeches) is from JE. In the earlier chapters (1–12), J and E form the main constituents, though a Deuteronomic editor seems to have worked over their contributions before they were finally combined with P. The debt due to J and E severally is a matter upon which scholars are greatly at variance; some think that J is only occasionally used, others find traces of the source throughout. One thing is certain, as Sellin

---

[1] Fuller treatment of the many questions which arise concerning these sources, the methods by which they have been distinguished, and also the different theories which are held concerning them will be found in Simpson, *Pentateuchal Criticism*, Chapman, *Introd. to Pentateuch* (Camb. Bib.), and Carpenter and Harford Battersby, *The Composition of the Hexateuch*. See also the Introductions of Driver and of Sellin.

[2] For a fuller discussion, see the present writer's *Numbers* (West. Comm.), pp. xviii f.

points out in his *Introduction to O.T.*, p. 98, two different conceptions of the conquest appeared in the original, before it was taken over by the Deuteronomic editor. One conception he attributes to J 'according to which the division of the land took place before the invasion, the various tribes acted by groups or individually, and it was not at first found possible to drive out the Canaanites from the cities to the plains; cf. 13^{13}, 15^{13-19}, 16^{10}, $17^{11-13, \ 16-18}$, 19^{47} (Joshua is known to it, though he has not the same prominence as in the other, 17^{16-18}; cf. Judges 1^{22b} original text; 2^{23})'. According to E, says Sellin, Joshua 'plays the part almost of a second Moses, at the head of the Tribes, overthrows with the aid of Divine Miracles, in the course of seven years (14^{10}; cf. Deut. 2^{14}), the twelve Kings of the Amorites (24^{12}), and thus, in the main (14^{12}; cf. Judges 3^1), has in that period taken possession of the whole country'. Sellin would further suggest that in E itself two strands of narrative had been combined—but this subject is too complicated to be pursued farther and reference must be made to his volume already cited.

iv. *Judges*

The book of Judges, in its present form, divides up quite obviously into three unequal parts: (*a*) an Introduction telling of the seizure of Canaan by the various Israelite tribes (1^1–2^5); (*b*) the main section dealing with the actual stories of the judges (2^6–16^{31}); (*c*) an Appendix containing a number of stories illustrating the supposed conditions of the age (17–21).

(*a*) The matter contained in this short introductory section mostly appears to be duplicated by small fragments in Joshua, e.g. 13^{13}, $15^{13-19, \ 63}$, 16^{10}, 17^{11-13} (all J). It is important for the admission that the original conquest was far from complete. It seems to come from J; the passages from Joshua noted above suggest this, as well as the prominence given to Judah.

(*b*) The main bulk of the book, as we now have it, has been worked over by a Deuteronomic editor. His work breathes a much more deeply religious spirit than that of the ancient narratives; indeed, his main purpose is not to teach history but religion. To this end the stories have been fitted into a fixed outline, by no means an unusual method of preserving ancient records, and the object of the framework is to point the moral. The succession of events is described—the forsaking of Jahveh, His consequent anger, the deliverance unto the hands of an enemy, the cry of penitence, and then the coming of a deliverer (cf. 2^{11-16}, 3^{7-9}, &c.). In the original narratives matter of the most diverse kind had been included; this becomes clear when any attempt to estimate its religious value is made: Barak and Gideon on one side are in striking contrast with Jephthah and Samson on the other. Occasional speeches have been inserted after the accepted manner of Thucydides and other ancient historians.

The material which the editor used probably came from oral traditions preserved in the different tribes, and some scholars find it possible to divide it up into two distinct groups corresponding to the J and E of the Pentateuch. One interesting fact in connexion with this early material should not be overlooked— the survival of a double account, poetry and prose, of the defeat of Sisera (4 and 5).

The stories originally concerned the tribe or collection of tribes to which they had reference, and the jurisdiction of any particular judge was limited to his own particular group and its connexions; no doubt some of the judges were contemporaries. The effect of the editorial revision is to give a chronological succession of rulers of all Israel with wide powers. Perhaps the book as it left the hand of this Deuteronomic editor lacked the story of Abimelech (9) and those of the lesser judges (3^{31}, 10^{1-5}, 12^{8-15}). If so it then told the histories of the six great judges: Othniel, Ehud, Barak, with whom Deborah must be coupled, Gideon, Jephthah, and Samson.

(c) The Appendix divides into two sections: 17–18 which seems to reflect a very primitive state of society, and 19–21 the last two chapters of which contain late ideas and much that seems to be purely imaginary. Hatred of the house of Saul may have inspired the narrative of the outrage at Gibeah.

v. *1 and 2 Samuel*

The books which bear the name of Samuel quite obviously did not come from his pen since he himself died (1 Sam. 25) long before the close of the period to which the books refer. In the Greek version of O.T. the books are named 1 and 2 Kings.

The sources of information available for the composition of the books were many and various. The editor and the compilers have drawn upon official records of the court, the memories of eye-witnesses—in some cases at least—and legends and traditions, some of them very ancient. As in the case of the Pentateuch not a little of the material consists of duplicate accounts of the same event. The most obvious instance of this is in the matter of the origin of the monarchy; in 1 Sam. 9^{1-10}, $11^{1-11, 15}$, 16 Samuel is in favour of the idea, and does all he can to support the king, in 1 Sam. 8, 10 $^{17-25a}$, 12 the people demand a king and Samuel submits to them. Other examples are the different versions of David's first acquaintance with Saul (16^{14-23} and 17^{12-58}), and the sparing of Saul's life (24 and 26). Most of these duplications occur in the section 1 Sam. 7–2 Sam. 1 which deals with the life of Saul, and they seem to represent two distinct traditions. The earlier is favourable to the monarchy as represented by its first king; it is vivid and full of small details. This source goes as far as 2 Sam. 20, and the suggestion has been made that it came originally from Abiathar, the priest of Nob. Its standpoint, and even its language, suggests connexions with J of the Pentateuch. A later strand of narrative holds the monarchy as unpleasing to God, and the first monarch no rightful ruler. This strand ends at 2 Sam 1 and has affinities with E. Its attitude to David is favourable since he is willing to act under the direction of the prophets.

Included amongst the sources was probably a history of the ark, from which 1 Sam. $4^{1b}-7^1$ was taken, as well as separate biographies of Samuel, of Saul, and of David. At some period an editor of the Deuteronomic School made contributions to the book, and the ingenious suggestion has been made that he wrote 2 Sam. 8 as a summary of 9–20 which in the interests of space he omitted from his edition.

The books are exceedingly valuable as preserving many ancient beliefs and practices; such as early ideas of prophecy (1 Sam. 9^{6-9}, 10^{10-13}), the belief that Jahveh could only be worshipped in His own land (1 Sam. 26^{19}), the effects of *taboo* (1 Sam. 14^{36-45}; 2 Sam. $6^{6\,f.}$), the requirements of blood-revenge (2 Sam. 21), the evil of a census (2 Sam. 24), and small and incidental details like the lamp (1 Sam. 3^3), the teraphim (1 Sam. 19^{13}) and the contest between the ark and Dagon (1 Sam. 5).

vi.   *1 and 2 Kings*

The book as a whole (for a single book it really is) comes from a date not earlier than the middle of the Babylonian Captivity, since events which then occurred are recorded in it. The book, however, must have existed in a shorter form before this period (cf. 1 Kings 8^8 and 9^{21} which suggest a pre-exilic date), and as in the case of modern histories from time to time it received supplements to bring it up to date.

The main sources upon which it was based are acknowledged in the book itself. They were a Life of Solomon (1 Kings 11^{41}), a History of the Kings of Israel (1 Kings 14^{19}) and a History of the Kings of Judah (1 Kings 14^{29}). These records, especially the Histories of the two series of Kings, would be kept by an official specially appointed for the purpose as was the custom in every oriental court. In addition, the Court History of David was used for 1 Kings 1–2 and many smaller sources supplemented the official chronicles. The standpoint of the book is, however, that of its final editor who was a member of the Deuteronomic School. This standpoint can be seen at once by the judgements passed on the various kings. Every king of Judah, with the shining exceptions of Hezekiah and Josiah, is condemned because he offered sacrifices at the high places, and every king of Israel for following the sin of Jeroboam. The fortune, good or bad, of the monarch is declared to have depended on his practice in these matters.

A large use seems to have been made of temple records and lives of the prophets, especially of the two great outstanding figures of Elijah and Elisha.

The literary difficulties in the way of the editor were not slight since he had to tell the story of the two kingdoms, Judah and Israel, side by side; an awkward business which is apt even in

fiction to make the movement drag (cf. Charles Dickens' *Bleak House*
where alternate chapters are given up to the fortunes of different
sets of characters). In order to bring the two kingdoms into
relation with one another the editor has adopted a chronological
formula which serves as a framework for the whole history
(cf. the similar framework in Judges). A full formula is that in
1 Kings 15[9 f.] 'in the twentieth year of Jeroboam king of Israel
began Asa to reign over Judah. And forty and one years reigned
he in Jerusalem; and his mother's name was Maacah the daughter
of Abishalom'. In recording the corresponding kings of Israel no
mention is made of their mothers, a slight thing but indicating
the greater interest taken by the editor in Judah (in Chronicles
the interest in Judah is absolutely predominant). The record of
each reign is closed by a formula telling of the death of the king
and of the fate of his body, an exceedingly important thing for
an Oriental.

D. THE CHRONOLOGY OF THE PERIOD

For nearly the whole of the period from the exodus to the death of Elisha there is little or nothing which can be considered reliable as a basis for chronological reckoning. The O. T. records themselves, before the book of Kings, contain few definite statements, and any references to outside nations from which possible clues might have been obtained are so vague as to be useless for the purpose. As an example the reference to the Egyptian rulers as Pharaoh, without any personal name, may be given.

Many of the statements of time are obviously artificial and therefore unreliable, especially when they have been supplied by an editor and do not form part of the original narrative. In the book of Kings, where elaborate synchronisms are made between the kings of Judah and Israel, errors seem to have crept in, and the two lists between the dates of the death of Solomon and the Fall of Samaria give 165 years for the kings of Judah, but only 144 years for their contemporaries in Israel. Various attempts to explain this difference have not met with complete acceptance.

The length of the sojourn of the Hebrews in Egypt is quite uncertain since both the date of their arrival and of their departure are unknown. If the O. T. writers had but preserved the names of the Egyptian Pharaohs under whom various events happened it would have been possible to date the exodus; as it is, different dates have been suggested and the whole subject is a matter for dispute. To give more than a bare outline of the evidence in favour of the various theories would occupy a larger amount of space than can here be afforded. Four main theories have been advanced which would place the exodus each at a different time. (a) *The expulsion of the Hyksos* (c. 1580 B.C.). This was the opinion of Josephus, and it is held by no less a scholar than H. R. Hall; see *The People and the Book*, p. 3. According to this theory the Pharaoh 'who knew not Joseph' was Ahmose I and his famous daughter Hatshepsut, perhaps, the protector of Moses. (b) *The Age of the Amarna Letters* (c. 1450–1370 B.C.). By this theory the oppressor is Thutmose III and the exodus took place in the reign of his successor, Amenhotep II. Much influential support has been

Tribute of 'Jehu of the land of Omri'. A relief from the black obelisk of Shalmaneser III (see p. 242)

given to this date by which the Hebrews invading Canaan can be connected with the Ḥabiru of the Letters. (*c*) *The period of the XIXth dynasty* (*c*. 1225). This may be called the traditional date, with Ramses II as the Pharaoh of the oppression and Merneptah as the Pharaoh of the exodus. The majority of scholars probably still support it. (*d*) Another suggested date is *a period in the XXth dynasty*. Personally, I am prepared to believe that there were a number of invasions by tribes who afterwards were absorbed in the Hebrew confederation. S. A. Cook says of these various theories: 'Each of the groups has points in its favour, but deals so drastically with the biblical evidence that should any one of them be justified (through fresh external evidence) the very secondary character of the biblical narratives will only be more unmistakable.' [1]   The evidence for the different theories has been collected by J. W. Jack, *The Date of the Exodus*.

We come next to the period of the settlement for which we have to rely on the book of Judges. This contains an elaborate chronological scheme covering the whole book, and making a total of 410 years. But the time which elapsed between the exodus and the beginning of the Temple buildings was according to I Kings 6[1] only 480 years. This allows a bare seventy years for the wilderness wanderings, for Eli, Samuel, Saul, and David. The solution seems to be (apart from the obvious artificiality of many of the figures—note the recurring forty years and multiples of forty) that many of the judges were rulers not in succession nor over all Israel, but were contemporaries.

When we reach the period of the kings a much greater measure of certainty is attainable, and synchronisms with events in Assyrian history make it possible to test the accuracy of the biblical figures and, if need be, to correct them by the more careful Assyrian records.[2] In our period there are two important events recorded in Assyrian history which concern Israelite rulers: these are the Battle of Ḳarḳar 853 B.C., in which Ahab took part, and the payment of tribute by Jehu to Shalmaneser III in 841. Between

---

[1] *Camb. Anct. Hist.* ii, p. 356, n. 2.

[2] The Assyrian records preserved exact chronological data. As in Athens and Rome each year was named from a special official and the lists of these officials have been preserved, in many cases in several copies, so that their accuracy is almost beyond question. See Appendix, p. 237.

these two events a period of twelve years only elapsed according to the Assyrian records. But in O.T. there are no less than fourteen years between the last year of Ahab and the first of Jehu, that is if Ahaziah reigned two years and Jehoram twelve. It is just possible that the years of these last two kings are merely approximate and that 853 was the closing year of Ahab and 841 the opening year of Jehu's reign. The former possibility is, however, difficult, for how are we to reconcile it with the accounts of Ahab's death fighting against the Syrians, who in the same year were his allies against Assyria. The later period of the kings contains several much more serious chronological difficulties, but as these lie outside the period of the present volume reference may be made for them to Robinson, *The Decline and Fall, &c.*, p. 230.

E. BIBLIOGRAPHY

The number of books which have been written on this period is so considerable that only a selection can be given, and those mainly such as will be found useful in meeting the needs of schools.

General Books on O.T.

A very stimulating book is Nairne's *Everyman's History of the Old Testament*. There is a good *Short Introduction to the Old Testament* by Box; other more advanced volumes are the Introductions of Driver, of Gray, and of Sellin. There are also many Old Testament Histories of which perhaps the best is Wade. Articles in the various Dictionaries of the Bible are very helpful, such as those in Hastings, and the *Encyclopaedia Biblica*.

The Pentateuch

Simpson's *Pentateuchal Criticism* is the best introduction, though Chapman (Camb. Bible) is also good. More advanced students should use Carpenter and Harford Battersby *The Composition of the Hexateuch*.

Commentaries. The chief series are the International Critical Commentary (I.C.C.), The Cambridge Bible for Schools and Colleges (Camb. Bib.), The Cambridge R.V. for Schools (Camb. R.V.), The Century Bible (Cent. Bib.), and The Westminster Commentary (West. Comm.). There are also the single-volume Commentaries of Dummelow, of Peake, and the New Commentary published by S.P.C.K.

EXODUS. McNeile (West. Comm.), Driver (Camb. Bib.), Bennett (Cent. Bib.), Binns (Camb. R.V.).

LEVITICUS. Chapman and Streane (Camb. Bib.), Kennedy (Cent. Bib.).

NUMBERS. Gray (I.C.C.), McNeile (Camb. Bib.), Kennedy (Cent. Bib.), Binns (West. Comm.).

DEUTERONOMY. Driver (I.C.C.), G. A. Smith (Camb. Bib.), H. W. Robinson (Cent. Bib.).

JOSHUA. Cooke (Camb. Bib.), H. W. Robinson (Cent. Bib.).

JUDGES. Moore (I.C.C.), Cooke (Camb. Bib.), Thatcher (Cent. Bib.), Lanchester (Camb. R.V.), Burney *The Book of Judges*.

1 and 2 SAMUEL. H. P. Smith (I.C.C.), Kirkpatrick (Camb. Bib.), Kennedy (Cent. Bib.).

1 KINGS. Barnes (Camb. Bib.), Skinner (Cent. Bib.).

2 KINGS. Barnes (Camb. Bib.), Skinner (Cent. Bib.), Box (Camb. R.V.).

NOTES TO SELECTED PASSAGES

PRINCIPAL ABBREVIATIONS

Camb. Bib.	The Cambridge Bible for Schools and Colleges.
Camb. R.V.	The Cambridge Revised Version for Schools.
Cent. Bib.	The Century Bible.
cf.	compare.
D	The Deuteronomic Source of the Pentateuch.
E	The Elohistic Source.
Enc. Bib.	*The Encyclopaedia Biblica.*
H.D.B.	Hastings's *Dictionary of the Bible*.
I.C.C.	The International Critical Commentary.
J	The Jahvistic Source of the Pentateuch.
LXX	The Septuagint Version.[1]
mg.	margin.
P	The Priestly Source of the Pentateuch.
P.C.	Peake's one-volume Commentary.
P.E.F.Q.S.	The Palestine Exploration Fund Quarterly Statement.
Syr.	The Syriac Version.[2]
Vg.	The Vulgate (Latin) Version.
West. Comm.	The Westminster Commentaries.

[1] This is a translation of O. T. into Greek. It was made in Egypt and, according to tradition, by seventy elders—hence the name.

[2] This version was probably made in the first century A. D.

PART I

THIS part of our period covers the lifetime and activities of Moses.
It is divided up into four sections as follows:

(1) The Early life of Moses.
(2) Moses and Pharaoh.
(3) Israel at Sinai.
(4) The Wanderings.

The sources of information upon which we depend for our
knowledge of the history of the period are the books of the
Pentateuch (omitting Genesis which is too early) and in particular
the documents known as J and E: see above, pp. 59 ff. Very valuable supplementary information is supplied by archaeological
discoveries, particularly by the Tell el-Amarna Letters: see
above, pp. 13 ff.

§ 1. THE EARLY LIFE OF MOSES

Much that is legendary has no doubt collected around the early
days of Moses, as around the early days of every great leader, but
it cannot too often be insisted that legendary accretions do not
disprove the historicity of the person around whom they have
gathered. The birth and preservation, the education in Royal
Egypt, the strange accident which led to his flight to Midian; how
much of these is true, how much imaginary or exaggerated, it is
impossible to state. Of the historicity of Moses, however, there
can be no real doubt.

(a) *Israel in Egypt* (Exod. 1).

We have in this chapter the setting as it were of the first act of
the great drama of Israel's deliverance. The book, after reminding
us of the small number of the original settlers (1–5), goes on to
describe their speedy growth. This multiplication of a subject
people, whilst it might be welcomed by a friendly ruler of Egypt,
was a matter for deep concern when a Pharaoh 'who knew not
Joseph' came to the throne.

There was in Egypt at this time a large slave population, a
population which might cause difficulties if outside dangers were
threatening; and such, as the monuments tell us, was the case at
this epoch. Different traditions, not necessarily contradictory,
inform us of the different methods employed by the Egyptians

to keep the Hebrews in a state of subjugation and comparative harmlessness. The earlier Judean document (J) emphasizes the forced labour which the people were compelled to render (8–12); [1] whilst the Ephraimite document (E) tells of attempts to check any further increase of population by the destruction of the male infants (15–22). The contribution of P, as seen in 13 f., is similar to that of J.

Thus we have a nation oppressed by bitter tasks, hated and feared by its masters, and subject to brutal and humiliating restrictions. It is true that in later times the abundant food provided for them (Num. 11[5]) was remembered with longing; but the value of this reminiscence must not be taken at too high a rate, since mankind commonly exaggerates present troubles and forgets those that are past, whilst it reverses the process in the case of benefits.

I. 5. In Gen. 46[8 ff.] a list of names is given making a total of seventy; in LXX of the passage (as in Num. 26) five additional names are found making seventy-five in all (as in Acts 7[14]).

7. The multiplication of terms to describe the increase of the Israelites is deliberate, and intended to emphasize their great and rapid growth.

8. *a new king*. Probably Ramses II: see Introd., p. 6.

10. *deal wisely*. A sinister suggestion: Acts 7[19] renders *subtilly* following LXX.

our enemies. Perhaps the Hittites or even nomad tribes related to Israel: see Introd., p. 6.

11. *Pharaoh*. This word is a title and not a personal name as is sometimes supposed. It means literally 'great house' to which the Turkish 'Sublime Porte' offers a ready parallel.

Pithom. The Πάτουμος of Herodotus, ii. 158. It was excavated by Naville in 1883, when inscriptions giving Ramses II as its founder were discovered.

Raamses. This site is not so well identified, it is perhaps *Tell er-Retabeh* some ten miles west of Pithom where Flinders Petrie carried on excavations. It is possible, however, that *Raamses* is not a place-name at all, and that we should read Pithom of Raamses.

14. *the field*. This suggests that agriculture as well as building was performed by the Hebrews.

21. *houses*. That is families as in 2 Sam. 7[11]; 1 Kings 2[24], &c.

---

[1] Aristotle, *Politics*, viii (v), 11, mentions forced labour as a method employed in breaking the spirit of a people.

22. Gressmann, a well-known German scholar, thinks that this command was regarded by the narrator as specially given in order to prevent the survival of Moses (see next section); in any case it can only have been enforced for a short time, otherwise the whole race would have been wiped out. Like the command to the *two* midwives in v. 15 it supposes that the Hebrews were very few in numbers, otherwise the river would have swarmed with dead bodies and been intolerable.

'They made their lives bitter in hard service, in mortar and in brick.'
A modern Egyptian brickmaker at work

(b) The Birth of Moses (Exod. 2$^{1\text{-}10}$).

Owing to the command of Pharaoh that all boys were to be drowned at birth the parents of Moses place him in an ark made of bulrushes or papyrus, and entrust him to the Nile. He is found there by the daughter of Pharaoh himself, and her interest and affection being aroused she adopts the Hebrew baby and brings him up as her son.

Such is the story of the early days of the great deliverer and law-giver of the Israelite people, a story which must have been re-peated time after time long before it came to be written down. Similar stories of the birth and miraculous preservation of national heroes are, of course, very common; the examples of Cyrus (Herodotus, i. 110 ff.) and Romulus (Livy, i. 4) may be adduced, and in earlier Semitic legend the closely parallel account of the first Semitic king of Babylon, Sargon of Akkad. This monarch was born secretly of a poor woman who placed him in a basket of reeds and floated him on the River Euphrates where he was found by a gardener and adopted as his son.

Josephus (*Antiq.* II, ix. 3 ff.) relates that the future eminence of Moses was foretold before his birth, and Gressmann suggests that this prophecy had become known to Pharaoh who thereupon ordered the destruction of the Hebrew *boys* as a precaution (cf. the massacre of the Innocents by Herod).

II. 1. *a daughter of Levi.* Better *the* daughter (as in Num. 26⁵⁹); cf. 6²⁰.

3. The word for *ark* seems to be of Egyptian origin.

bulrushes. The Egyptian practice of making vessels of papyrus is mentioned by Pliny (*Nat. Hist.*, xiii. 22) and by Lucan (*Phars.*, iv. 136).

slime. That is bitumen or asphalt. In the legend of Sargon the mouth of the basket is closed by pitch.

flags. The word is that used for the Red Sea (i. e. Sea of flags or reeds).

5. *the daughter of Pharaoh.* Ramses II had fifty-nine daughters. Legend has given to this one various names, such as Thermouthis (Josephus) and Merris (Eusebius).

10. *became her son.* Cf. Acts 7²²; Heb. 11²⁴.

Moses. The word is of Egyptian origin and founded on *mosi* = born; the name Aḥmosi for example = the moon is born. The fact that Moses had an Egyptian, and not a Hebrew, name is a guarantee for his origin in Egypt, an inventor would not have dared to give him a foreign name.

Because, &c. This explanation is not grammatically possible, and since it presupposes a knowledge of Hebrew in an Egyptian princess not likely on other grounds.

(c) *The Flight to Midian* (Exod. 2¹¹⁻²²).

This section consists of four vivid scenes from the early life of the deliverer, four scenes in which he shows his care for his oppressed fellow-countrymen and also his care for any who are so suffering. Two of them are located in Egypt, two in Midian.

Egyptian nobles hunting wildfowl in the reed banks of the Nile, the scene of Moses' discovery by Pharaoh's daughter

The scenes in Egypt record (a) that Moses found one day an Egyptian ill-treating a Hebrew and after cautiously making sure that there were no onlookers, slew the oppressor: and (b) his finding a similar thing going on next day between two Hebrews; he attempted to interfere but was met with a reply which showed him that his deed was known. Nothing remained but instant flight.

The country to which his steps were led was Midian, a somewhat ill-defined territory lying east of Canaan. Here, like Jacob when flying from his home (Gen. 29 ff.), he came to a well, and the opportunity was given him of helping the daughters of the ruling priest from the bad-mannered shepherds. The sequel to his act of kindness was an invitation to the priest's dwelling. Here Moses found a second home, and for many years he was content to live there as shepherd to the priest, in due time marrying his daughter.

A parallel to this experience of Moses has been found in the story of Sinuhe, an important personage in Egypt, who fled to the desert, made friends with a Bedawi chief, and finally married his daughter: see *Camb. Anct. Hist.* i, pp. 226 ff.

II. **12.** The caution of Moses, rather than his sensitiveness, seems here to be emphasized; another man would have rushed in without thought of the consequences.

14. Jealousy over the good fortune of Moses may have been at the back of the reply. That his fellow-countrymen should have known who he was, when presumably the Pharaoh was ignorant, is strange though not impossible.

15. The flight of Moses before persecution or danger finds a parallel in the similar action of Jacob (Gen. 27^{43}), of David (1 Sam. 19^{12}), and Elijah (1 Kings 19^3).

16. *the priest of Midian.* This seems to mean not that he was the sole priest, but the chief priest, perhaps also the secular head of the clan.

daughters. In the present day unmarried girls of good family still care for the flocks.

18. *Reuel.* In E he is called Jethro (3^1, 18^1, &c.). It is possible that he had two names, but more probable that different traditions exist. In Jud. 1^{16} (Heb.) 4^{11} he is called Hobab.

19. *An Egyptian.* A tribute to Moses' manner and dress.

22. *Gershom.* The name is explained by a pun on the Hebrew word *ger*, which means sojourn.

(d) The Call of Moses (Exod. 3$^{1-12}$).

The account in this passage is a combination of the two documents J and E. P has preserved a separate account which now appears as 6$^{2-13}$.

In the present account we are told of the way in which Moses was aroused from his life of forgetfulness by a divine visitation. The straying of his sheep, in the writer's mind no doubt providential, may have led him to the mountain of God, or merely the need for finding fresh pasture. Hither he came and, to his amazement, he saw a bush apparently on fire, and yet remaining unconsumed. On turning aside he heard a voice telling him that the place was a sanctuary and must not be trodden with sandalled feet.

In the presence of the God of his fathers Moses was afraid. But soon reassuring words were spoken and the heavenly voice informed Moses that the sufferings of his fellow-countrymen in Egypt had not gone unnoticed. God Himself had come to deliver them and to lead them into a fruitful land from which the present inhabitants would have to be expelled.

The shepherd is then told that he himself must go down to Pharaoh and act as God's representative in leading out the people from Egypt. Some critics think that the earlier narratives which tell of the wonderful preservation of Moses and of his adoption by the princess were later additions intended to glorify the great Israelite leader, and that originally he was nothing more than a shepherd. The present passage certainly gives no hint that Moses had ever been in Egypt, or that he had reason to fear the offence for which he had fled thence being remembered against him. His shrinking may have been the natural timidity so often found even in the most intrepid of God's messengers: cf. Jeremiah (1$^{6\,ff.}$).

III. 1. *Horeb.* The name used in E and D for the better-known Sinai of J and P. It is possible that originally they were two distinct places which tradition has identified.

2. *the angel of the LORD.* 'When LORD is printed in capitals it represents the divine personal name generally rendered Jehovah. This word is not the original Hebrew but is made up of a combination of the consonants of the personal name (jhwh) with the vowels of the Hebrew for Lord, which in reading was substituted for it. The exact form of the name of the God of Israel has been lost, though it was probably Jahweh. The angel was really a manifestation of God Himself.'

3. *a flame.* Cf. 19[18]; Ezek. 1[27], 8[2]: also Homer *Od.*, xix. 39 for fire as revealing the divine.

6. The continuity of revelation is secured by this assurance.

8. *am come down.* So 18[20], 19[11], &c. This anthropomorphic expression is characteristic of J.

a land flowing, &c. Common in J and also in D. It also occurs in Joshua 5[6]; Jer. 11[5], 32[22]; Ezek. 20[6, 15].

Canaanite, &c. For an account of these nations see pp. 16 and 112.

(e) *The Revelation of Jahveh* (Exod. 3[13-16], 6[2-9]).

The call of Moses to be the deliverer of his people was accompanied by a fresh revelation of God, consequent upon Moses' demand for information which he could hand on to the people to whom he was to be sent.

The two passages from Exodus which make up this section come respectively from E and P. Both are agreed that the name Jahveh (cf. note on p. 46 above) was now first revealed to mankind, although in J we have the statement that from the days of Enosh men had used His name in worship (Gen. 4[26]).

Gressmann has pointed out that in P there is a progressive revelation of the name of God to accompany the different covenants into which He enters with His chosen servants: with Noah as *God* simply (Heb. *Elohim*), with Abraham as *God Almighty* (Heb. *El Shaddai*), and then at Sinai with Israel as a whole as *Jahveh*. These three covenants have their separate signs or tokens; the rainbow, the rite of circumcision, the keeping of the sabbath.

III. 14. *I AM THAT I AM.* A better rendering, following Driver and others, would be *I WILL BE WHAT I WILL BE.* The thought seems to be that Jahveh will reveal Himself more and more as the days go by. 'The temper of noble adventure which belongs to faith is here shown to spring out of the very Name (i. e. Being) of Yahweh (= He will be): no one can limit the inexhaustibly fresh possibilities of One so named.' Harford in P.C.

16. *the elders.* Amongst primitive people of all races a usual thing was for government to be vested in the older members of the tribe: cf. the Roman 'Senatus', and the Anglo-Saxon 'Alderman'.

VI. 3. *God Almighty.* Heb. *El Shaddai.* The exact meaning of *Shaddai* has been lost. It may be connected with Ass. *shadu* = mountain (cf. Bel-shadua = Bel is my mountain) or possibly with the root meaning 'to destroy', though this does not fit in with the use of the title (see Gen. 17¹, 28³, 35¹¹, &c.). Another possibility is that the name contains a reminiscence of the Syrian god, *Addu* (= *Hadad*), who appears frequently in the Tell el-Amarna Letters.

not known. In J the patriarchs are represented as continually knowing God as Jahveh.

4. *established.* The usual Hebrew for entering into a covenant is to 'cut' it, this word is P's expression.

6. *redeem.* Heb. *ga'al* almost = *vindicate, reclaim.* There is no idea of making a payment to any one; just as when God is spoken of as selling His people (Judges 3⁸) one is not to suppose that He received anything. This metaphorical use of *redeem* should be borne in mind in connexion with theories of the Atonement.

8. *lifted up.* One who takes an oath raises his hand to heaven: cf. 17²⁶; Gen. 14²; Num. 14³⁰: also Virgil, *Aeneid* xii. 196.

9. *Moses spake.* The account is compressed, we are not told of any lapse of time between the receiving of the revelation and the declaration to Israel: this has led some critics to consider that P regarded Moses as being already in Egypt when God spoke to him (so 6²⁸).

(f) The Three Signs (Exod. 4¹⁻⁹).

When God called Moses and entrusted him with his mission a number of difficulties were raised by the latter. Two of them have already been related, his own timidity and feeling of unfitness (§ *d*), and his ignorance of the name of the God in whose service he was to release the people (§ *e*). We now come to a third difficulty; the probability that Israel will not receive him.

In order to meet this eventuality God gave to Moses three signs which he might work in order to convince the people of his authority and power. First of all he was commanded to throw down his stick, which immediately became a serpent; on taking it once more by the tail it returned to its original form. Then on placing his hand, by God's direction, in his garment, it became leprous, but was restored when again put back. A third sign was to be wrought, in case those already indicated failed to convince the people, by taking water from the Nile and pouring it forth when it would turn into blood.

The first and third signs have later parallels. Aaron's rod becomes a serpent in 7⁸⁻¹³ (P) and all the water of Egypt is changed into blood in 7¹⁴⁻²⁵. The former parallel is dealt with in the notes below, the latter in § 2*b*.

IV. **2.** *A rod.* Palestinian shepherds in the present day still carry rods. The rod in v. 17 (E) appears to be different and a gift from God; a further change is found in P who places the rod in the hands of Aaron.

3. *a serpent.* It should be noticed that the word is not the same as that used by P in $7^{9\ ff.}$, the latter has *tannin* which means a larger reptile, possibly a crocodile. Gressmann quotes a curious Egyptian legend of a magician who made a wax crocodile which came to life when placed in water and devoured a man, but on the magician's taking hold of its tail it became wax once more.

6. *thy bosom.* Cf. Ps. 74^{11}.

snow. So of Miriam (Num. 12^{11}) and Gehazi (2 Kgs. 5^{27}).

9. Notice the differences as well as the similarities between this sign and the first plague ($7^{14\ ff.}$).

(g) *Moses and Aaron* (Exod. $4^{10-16,\ 27-31}$).

The relations of Moses and Aaron are very obscure. In the Pentateuch as it has come down to us they are brothers, of whom Aaron is the elder (7^7). In the actual incidents of the history, however, Aaron is little more than a lay-figure who acts at the command of Moses. In the earliest document (J), apart from $4^{10-16,\ 29\ f.}$, Aaron is ignored as a medium for addressing the people; his great prominence is due to P.

Moses having had his earlier difficulties met now advances yet a fourth; he is not a speaker. The remedy for this defect is the co-operation of his brother Aaron the Levite. Moses accordingly returns to Egypt and God commands Aaron to go out and meet him. The brothers then approach the elders of Israel and, in a conference with the whole people, Aaron relates the message sent to Moses and the signs are performed. The people are convinced that God has at last remembered them and receive His message with reverence.

Such is the account of JE from which that of P differs slightly. According to P God spoke to Moses in the land of Egypt (6^{28}) and on his making the excuse of difficulty in speaking He appointed Aaron to be the prophet of Moses unto Pharaoh. At the same time God warned him that the message would not be accepted until signs and wonders had been wrought upon the Egyptians and they had learnt by bitter experience that Jahveh is God.

IV. **13.** The words of Moses seem to be an ungracious submission.

14. *the Levite.* The word must here be used of the profession, not of the tribe, since Moses himself was a Levite by descent. See pp. 51, 54.

l account in P (7¹) notice that Moses is
ractical effect is the same since in either
et and do the speaking.
lest reading of the Heb. is to take it
ot impossible, however, that they were

A Palestinian shepherd leaning on his rod

(*h*) *The Return to Egypt* (Exod. 4¹⁸⁻²⁶).

Imbedded in the early history of the Hebrews are certain
passages which seem to have come down from very primitive
times when the conception of God was very low. They have been
preserved, like fossils, to throw light on a bye-gone period. The
story of Jahveh's attack on Moses whilst he was returning to
Egypt is one of such 'fossils', another is the somewhat similar
story of the attack on Jacob (Gen. 32³³ ᶠᶠ·). In their earliest form,
in all probability, neither of these stories had anything to do with
Jahveh. The being who encountered Jacob was in all likelihood

the Demon of the Ford of Jabbok, the story, however, has been refined and made the bearer of spiritual truth. The present story has no spiritual meaning and, as it stands, is still unworthy of Jahveh and obscure in meaning.

On receiving God's command to return to Egypt Moses goes to Jethro and, without saying anything to him about his mission, requests leave to go to see how his brethren fare. This leave is readily granted. Moses then sets out with his wife and children, the latter carried on an ass, and the precious rod of God with which the signs were to be wrought. On the way he is attacked by Jahveh for some offence connected with circumcision. Zipporah, by circumcising their son and flinging down the foreskin at the feet either of Jahveh or of Moses, obtains his release.

IV. **18**. Moses does not explain his real reason for asking for leave of absence or say that it will be permanent. It may be that this and the following verse should come before the actual call of Moses, i. e. that he was already on the way back to Egypt when God commanded him to deliver Israel. This would avoid attributing deceit to Moses inasmuch as he did not explain himself to his father-in-law, and would also give meaning to v. 19 which in the present order of the text is pointless.

19. *that sought thy life.* Cf. Matt. 2[20].

20. *sons.* Only one has so far been mentioned. They were still quite small evidently.

22. *my firstborn.* Cf. Hos. 11[1]; Jer. 31[9] (with the present writer's note).

24. *sought to kill him.* Some writers regard this as signifying that a sudden attack of illness overtook him. The phrase would certainly bear that meaning, but the whole passage reads much more satisfactorily if an actual assault is understood by it.

25. *a flint.* Either because it was an old custom to use such an implement or perhaps because in the desert (*lodging-place* must not be taken to mean an inn) no other was available.

cast it. Hebrew *made it touch*: cf. Isa. 6[7]; Jer. 1[9].

his feet. Cf. Isa. 7[20] for the euphemism.

a bridegroom of blood. The meaning of this phrase is quite obscure; Gressmann thinks that it was addressed to the attacking deity.

§ 2. MOSES AND PHARAOH

Before Israel could be set free from its Egyptian bondage a great struggle had to take place, a struggle between Moses as the representative of Jahveh on the one side, and Pharaoh as the representative of earthly power and magnificence on the other. The pride of the ruler of Egypt and his stubbornness are finally overcome by a series of disasters known widely as the Ten Plagues.

The different sources from which the Pentateuch has been compiled (see Introd. pp. 59 ff.) all make mention of these plagues, though no single source names ten. It is probable that the actual number was in the original narrative eight only, as in J, and that the third and fourth, and fifth and sixth plagues respectively are really identical (see below). All the sources mention the first and the last plague, J mentions every plague except the third and the sixth, E has in addition numbers seven, eight, and nine, whilst P has two, three, and six,

Plague	1.	2.	3.	4.	5.	6.	7.	8.	9.	10.
J	×	×		×	×		×	×	×	×
E	×						×	×	×	×
P	×	×	×			×				×

In their account of the plagues the different sources make use of different terms (see Driver, *Exodus*, pp. 55 f.) and have other peculiarities. J has the fullest and most vivid account. He makes Moses go in to Pharaoh and announce the coming scourge, but it is Jahveh Himself without any magic ceremony who both brings the plague and causes it to cease. In this source Israel is represented as living apart from the Egyptians in the land of Goshen. E has been preserved in only a few instances, but enough of it remains to exhibit Moses as a great wonder-worker, and indeed the tendency of this source is to heighten or emphasize the miraculous. In P it is Aaron who works the wonders (except in 9^{10}) and there are no interviews with Pharaoh. In this source only are the Egyptian magicians introduced ($7^{11\,f.}$, $8^{7,\,18\,f.}$, 9^{11}).

Of the plagues as a whole it may be said that some natural basis can be found for most of them (see under each plague). 'The miracle consists in the unaccustomed severity of the visitation and the opportune moment of its occurrence.' (Camb. R.V., p. 38).

(*a*) *The First Plague: Water turned into Blood* (Exod. 7¹⁴⁻²⁵).

The prosperity of Egypt in all ages has depended on the Nile (cf. the recent outcry in Egypt over the Sudan irrigation scheme). Anything which might seem to injure the great river would at once affect the Egyptians. When Moses therefore announced to Pharaoh that its waters would be turned into blood he was touching a vital spot, and his threat, besides the inconvenience which it foreshadowed, would cause a superstitious fear. The Egyptian feeling for the Nile has been well preserved in an ancient hymn:

> Hail to thee, O Nile!
> Thou who hast revealed thyself to this land,
> Coming in peace, to give life to Egypt!
> Hidden God! who bringest what is dark to light,
> As is always thy delight.

The plague is based upon a phenomenon which is still to be observed. 'When the Nile first begins to rise,' says Sayce, 'the red marl brought down from the mountains of Abyssinia stains it to a dark colour, which glistens like blood in the light of the setting sun.'

It should be noticed that in P (v. 19) not only the Nile but all the waters of Egypt are similarly affected. It is difficult to imagine in this case where the magicians found fresh water upon which to conduct their experiment (v. 22). J regards Jahveh Himself as the agent of the miracle (v. 25); in P Moses commands Aaron to work it by means of his magic rod.

VII. 17. In 4⁹ the turning of Nile water into blood is intended to be a token to the Israelites.

18. Fish was an important article of diet in Egypt: cf. Num. 11⁵.

19. Not only the river itself but also the canals and reservoirs are affected in P as well as private stores.

20. *he lifted up.* This does not refer to Aaron, as the source is not P (note that only the waters of the river are affected). If it comes from E, Moses is referred to, if J, Jahveh Himself (cf. v. 25).

22. The magicians of Egypt were noted in the ancient world, see Erman, *Life in Ancient Egypt*, pp. 353 ff. They appear in P only.

(*b*) *The Second Plague: The Frogs* (Exod. 8¹⁻¹⁵).

Pharaoh remains unmoved by the pollution of the Nile, a further plague is therefore brought upon the Egyptians. A vast number of frogs suddenly appear, and penetrate even into the bedrooms of the people. So great was the number that when the

A village on the banks of the Nile

Water pouring through the Assuan Dam

THE GREAT RIVER OF EGYPT

plague ceased, on Pharaoh's showing signs of softening, piles of their dead bodies were collected.

Similar plagues of frogs are mentioned in Pliny and other ancient historians, and in the present day the inundation is accompanied by swarms of them. Again the miracle is simply the heightening of a natural phenomenon.

VIII. 2. Frogs appear in this passage only in O.T.

3. *ovens* were portable earthenware stoves and the *kneading-troughs*, like those of the modern Arabs, were shallow wooden bowls.

7. The action of the magicians only increased the woes of their countrymen.

9. *this glory*. Pharaoh was to be allowed to fix his own time for the ceasing of the plague. Similar expressions are found in Judges 7²; Isa. 44²³.

(c) *The Third and Fourth Plagues*: *Insects* (Exod. 8¹⁶⁻³²).

The plague of lice or gnats (vv. 16–19) is found in P only, and it seems to be another form of the plague of flies (vv. 20–32) which comes from J. In the one story the dust of the earth is turned into mosquitoes or some similar pest by Aaron's rod, in the other swarms of flies come up over the land.

In each story a novelty is introduced. P states that the magicians, who hitherto had kept pace with Aaron in the matter of producing miracles, at length find themselves unable to continue (v. 18): J, for his part, tells us that the plague was not allowed to touch the land of Goshen where the Israelites were dwelling (v. 22).

Each of the stories is probably based on natural phenomena, if the origin of the lice in the dust of the ground be not pressed. Mosquitoes rise up in vast swarms from their breeding places and so are like dustclouds. The flies of J would come from the piles of decaying frogs left over from the previous plague.

This plague makes an impression upon the Egyptian king, and a tardy permission is given for the people to go three days' journey into the wilderness in order to sacrifice. When the plague is withdrawn so also is the concession, and things are once more in their original position.

VIII. 16. *lice* may be retained or 'gnats' or 'mosquitoes' substituted, both meanings of the Hebrew original appear in ancient writers, but 'mosquitoes' is probably to be preferred: cf. σκνῖφες of LXX, and Herodotus, ii. 95.

19. *the finger of God*: cf. Luke 11²¹.

21. *flies* seem to have been common in Egypt (Isa. 7[18]). Probably some especially noxious type of fly is meant; Driver, following LXX, suggests the dog-fly.

22. *will sever.* It would be quite possible on natural grounds for certain districts to be free from flies when others near by were plagued by them.

Goshen is probably the territory round Saft el-Henna, the ancient *P-sapt.* The district which is situated some forty miles north-east of Cairo and covers an area of about seventy square miles had the name of *Kesem.*[1]

my people dwell. In 3[22] (E) the Israelites live amongst the Egyptians.

26. *the abomination.* That is to the scandal of the Egyptians who would see their sacred animals offered up in sacrifice (see Herodotus, ii. 38, 41 f. 46 for the sacred animals). For the expression cf. Gen. 43[32].

27. *three days' journey.* So 3[18], 5[3].

(d) The Fifth and Sixth Plagues: Murrain and Boils (Exod. 9[1-12]).

The fifth plague is found in J only, the sixth in P only; we may therefore conclude, in view of their resemblance, that the same visitation is originally referred to. An outbreak of boils or similar troubles would naturally follow upon a plague of flies or mosquitoes, so that here again we have a natural sequence. Further, a special kind of Nile-scab is not uncommon in Egypt at the time of the rising of the river; its symptoms, a number of small red blisters, would fit in with the eruption described in the text.

Once again a distinction is made between the Egyptians and the Israelites, the cattle of the latter escape (v. 4). As regards the magicians, they not only failed to produce boils, for which in their secret hearts the Egyptians were no doubt thankful, but were so badly afflicted themselves by the complaint that they were unable to appear in public.

IX. 3. *camels* were not used by the Egyptians themselves, these perhaps belonged to Bedawin merchantmen (cf. Gen. 37[25]).

murrain occurs here and Ps. 78[50], it was limited to cattle.

4. In some plagues in Egypt the Nile has been the cause of the outbreak, and cattle at some distance from it have escaped.

6. *all the cattle* if taken literally is inconsistent with 19 ff. That it should be taken literally may perhaps be inferred from the fact that

---

[1] Gardiner challenges this proposed identification, and at the best it is only a conjecture: see *Journal of Egypt. Arch.* (1918), pp. 218 ff.

no appeal is made for the ceasing of the plague since its work was done.

8. The method of Moses and Aaron is peculiar, a piece of acted magic.

(e) The Seventh Plague: the Hail (Exod. 9¹³⁻³⁵).

This plague exhibits Jahveh as the controller of the heaven from which the hail would descend, and it comes in after the failure of the previous plagues to move the stubborn Egyptian. One remarkable feature in it is contained in vv. 19 f., the warning by which those who feared the word of Jahveh might save their cattle. Storms of hail and thunder, though not unknown, are by no means common in the valley of the Nile.

The passage (vv. 14–16) which gives an explanation of God's methods of working is possibly an insertion. It tells Pharaoh that only God's concern for His glory had preserved him alive, otherwise a visitation sufficiently heavy to have destroyed him would have been sent.

IX. 16. *made thee to stand.* Cf. St. Paul's use in Rom. 9¹⁷ which is slightly different; there the question is of raising any one to power, here of preserving them alive.

18. *since . . . it was founded.* Cf. v. 24.

23. *sent thunder*: lit. *gave voices.* Jahveh is imagined as speaking from the midst of the dark cloud (cf. Ps. 29³ ᶠᶠ·).

24. *mingled with*: lit. *taking hold of itself within.* RV mg. renders *flashing continually amidst.* So in Ezek. 1⁴.

27. *righteous . . . wicked.* Better *in the right . . . the wrong* using the words with almost a legal force. Pharaoh 'anticipated Nietzsche in the doctrine that weakness is wickedness', P.C., p. 176.

30. Moses is not deceived by Pharaoh's confession of guilt, the result of fear alone.

31. *flax* was in great demand for the wrappings of mummies and for the clothing of the priesthood: see Herodotus, ii. 37. The storm evidently took place about January, the time when the barley would be ripe and the flax only in bud.

32. *spelt* is a variety of wheat.

(f) The Eighth Plague: the Locusts (Exod. 10¹⁻²⁰).

Once more a plague comes similar in character to earlier ones (cf. § c above), a swarm of locusts. This type of visitation is very common in Palestine, but not nearly so much so in Egypt (cf. the

Egyptian Agriculture. Mural decoration from a grave near Thebes. Above, on the left, are women pulling flax (Exod. 9[31])

hailstorm). It is a curious fact that in this account the writer
adopts a Palestinian stand-point since he tells us that the locusts
were finally brought up by an east wind: the truth being that a
south-east wind brings them to Palestine, a south-west to Egypt
(so Gressmann).

The effect of this plague, like its predecessor, was to work a
fleeting penitence in the heart of Pharaoh, but with its removal
he returned once more to his spirit of opposition.

X. **2.** *what things . . . upon.* The rendering *how I have made a toy
of* is more correct.

4. *locusts.* For a description see Driver's *Joel* (Camb. Bib.)
pp. 37 ff.

5. *they shall cover, &c.* Thomson, describing a swarm in the
Lebanon district, says 'the whole face of the mountain was black
with them'.

7. *a snare,* i. e. 'an occasion for destruction'.

11. Pharaoh, who evidently suspected that the request to go into
the wilderness for sacrifice was only an excuse for escaping from
servitude, grants permission for the men alone to go: the women and
children would then be pledges of their return. Though the presence
of women at festivals was not compulsory (Exod. 23[17], &c.), it was
evidently not unusual (cf. 1 Sam. 1[4 ff.]; Deut. 16[11]).

13. *wind.* Cf. 14[21]; Num. 11[31].

19. *strong west wind*: cf. Pliny, *Hist. Nat.*, xi. 35: gregatim sublatae
vento in maria aut stagna decidunt.

20. *the LORD hardened.* This is a mark of E who could not explain
Pharaoh's obstinate stupidity on merely natural grounds. Contrast
7[23], 9[35].

(g) *The Ninth Plague: the Great Darkness* (Exod. 10[21-29]).

The last of the plagues, before the great final act of the tragedy,
is now brought upon the stricken land; and again its origin can be
traced to a natural cause. The darkness was due to a great sand-
storm produced by the dreaded *Khamsīn*, a violent, electrical wind
(see the description in McNeile, *Exodus*, p. 46).

The darkness was so complete that for three days the operations
of ordinary life had to be suspended. At the end of that time
Pharaoh sent for Moses and offered to make a further concession,
the women and children might go, but the flocks and herds were
to remain. This concession was scornfully rejected by Moses, and
the demand made for a complete and free departure. In his turn

'A darkness that may be felt'. A sand-storm sweeping over Khartoum

the Egyptian was equally obstinate, and Moses was driven from his presence. Although our main sympathies are with the oppressed Israelites in their struggle for freedom, one cannot but have a certain amount of admiration for Pharaoh in his vain contest with irresistible forces.

X. 21. *may be felt.* The presence of sand and dust would be a literal fulfilment of this threat.

25. Not only is Pharaoh to let the flocks go, but he himself must provide sacrifices.

29. *see thy face . . . no more.* The immediate sequel to this declaration should probably be 11^4 which contains the forecast of the last of the plagues. The passage in 11^{1-3} which comes in between is derived from E and evidently inserted by an editor who did not notice the contradiction.

(h) The Institution of the Passover (Exod. 12^{1-28}).

Hebrew tradition connects the institution of the Passover with the flight from Egypt. It is probable, however, that it was originally a spring festival of much older standing, and indeed that the Passover was the very feast for which permission was desired by Moses in the interviews with Pharaoh. Though we have no certain knowledge of its existence previous to the exodus, yet 'in view of the many features which seem to point to something behind the interpretation given of them; in view of what we find in the observances of related peoples, so far as these are known to us; and in view of the development in the case of all the other great feasts, and the historical interpretation which came to be given of them—it is probable that we have here another instance in which Israel's religion takes up, transforms, and appropriates an existing institution.' (H.D.B. iii., p. 688.)

The various sources of the Pentateuch treat the Passover very differently. E ignores it, unless notices of the related Feast of Unleavened Cakes (*Maṣṣôth*) be connected with the Passover; J has two references, Exod. 12^{21-23} and 34^{25}, neither of them giving much information beyond bare details; JE (?) has a reference in Exod. 12^{25-27}. In D the Passover and the Feast of Unleavened Cakes seem to be amalgamated (Deut. 16^{1-8}). It is in P, as we should naturally expect, that we get full and detailed regulations. See further the articles in the Dictionaries, and Driver, pp. 405 ff., McNeile, pp. 62 ff.

The present passage gives the regulations for the Feast from

P (vv. 1–13) and from J (vv. 21–28), as well as P's rules for the Feast of Unleavened Cakes (vv. 14–20). Both accounts agree in the time, the animal to be sacrificed, and the sprinkling of the blood upon the door-posts: they also agree in giving the divine command to perpetuate the Passover. Extra details are added according to the knowledge and taste of each of the sources.

XII. **2.** *the first month.* P uses the Babylonian system of reckoning according to which the year begins in the spring, the old Hebrew method made it begin in the autumn. P also designates the months by numbers and not by names; Abib, the Canaanite name for the month is used by JED, later writers called it Nisan, the Babylonian name (Neh. 2¹; Esther, 3⁷).

3. *lamb.* The Hebrew word can also mean kid: cf. v. 5.

6. *at even*: lit. *between the two evenings.* The traditional explanation is that it was the time from 3 p.m., when the sun begins to decline, to its actual setting. The most natural explanation is the time, very short, between sunset and dark.

8. *unleavened bread.* Since the Heb. is plural *cakes* is a better rendering than bread. The want of leaven would be a reminder of the haste in which the cakes were prepared (Deut. 16³).

bitter herbs formed a kind of salad, and to a later time were a memorial of the bitter bondage of Egypt.

9. *sodden*, that is *boiled.* A different idea seems to be presupposed by Deut. 16¹⁷ (cf. also Judges 6¹⁹ᶠ·; 1 Sam. 2¹³).

11. *passover.* The Heb. *pasaḥ* is of uncertain meaning coming perhaps from a root meaning *to limp* (1 Kings 18²¹, ²⁶; cf. Isa. 31⁵).

12. *all the gods.* Jahveh will show His supreme power: cf. 18¹¹.

14. *this day.* There is a sudden transition to the Feast of Unleavened Cakes; *this day* is the first day of that feast not the Passover.

15. *leaven* was regarded as a corrupting force: cf. Mark 8¹⁶; Gal. 5⁹, &c.

cut off. Though the idea of divine punishment cannot be excluded, the main idea is excommunication; one so offending was to be put outside the covenant people.

19. *sojourner* (Heb. *gēr*). 'A man of another tribe or district who ... put himself under the protection of a clan or of a powerful chief.' (Robertson Smith.)

22. *hyssop* is probably some kind of wild marjoram which would easily be used as a whisk. Cf. Lev. 14⁴; Num. 19¹⁸. In *Aeneid*, vi. 230 the olive is similarly used.

(*i*) *The Tenth Plague: the Death of the Firstborn* (Exod. 12$^{29-36}$).

The last and most distressing of all the plagues was now inflicted upon the hard-hearted Egyptians. In all probability its origin was natural, and some sudden epidemic, such as do not seldom break out in Egypt in the spring, was the basis of the story. But as Dillmann points out 'the plague here, by its momentary suddenness, as also by its carrying off as its victims exclusively the first-born of the Egyptians, bears a wholly supernatural character. This particular form of the tradition (*Sage*) evidently first arose partly through the influence of the Israelites' spring-offering of the Passover, partly through that of the Israelite custom of dedicating the first-born, which together brought into the tradition the sparing of the houses and first-born of the Israelites, and transformed the Egyptians who perished in the plague into first-born' (quoted in Driver).

The pestilence began at midnight, and the horror of the Egyptians was such that they urged the Israelites to depart from them fearing still more terrible things. The people take from their late masters various objects of value to adorn the festival which they are ostensibly about to celebrate.

XII. **29.** *the first-born of Pharaoh.* Gressmann suggests that originally the only victim was to be the crown-prince: cf. 4^{22}.

the captive. Cf. 11^5 the bondmaid behind the mill.

31. *called for Moses, &c.* This is not really inconsistent with 10^{29}.

32. *bless me also*: that is offer sacrifices for me.

34. *their clothes.* The word means a large outer mantle which served as a covering by night as well as a cloak by day (cf. 22$^{26f.}$).

36. The story of the 'spoiling of the Egyptians' appears three times, here, 3^{22}, 11^3. It was evidently much appreciated by the Israelites. Perhaps the jewels and so forth were a loan for the purpose of attending the festival, if so the action of Pharaoh in pursuing the Israelites made any return of them impossible.

(*j*) *The Crossing of the Red Sea* (Exod. 14–15^{21}).

After leaving Egypt the Israelites fled by way of Rameses to Succoth. They were accompanied by a mixed multitude of fugitives and by much cattle (12$^{37f.}$). Instead of taking the direct way into Canaan by the sea-coast they turned towards the wilderness of Sinai. Later tradition explained this action as being due to divine overruling, since a passage through the land of the Philistines could only have been made by force of arms. In point of fact the Philistines did not settle in Palestine until a rather later period (see Sayce, *Early Hist. of Hebs.*, pp. 291 f.) and a much more serious obstacle would have been the fortresses by which the isthmus was guarded.

After travelling for some time the Israelites encamped by the Red Sea.[1] Here they were overtaken by the Egyptian forces sent out by Pharaoh to arrest them. All hope seemed lost as the sea

PHARAOH IN HIS CHARIOT PURSUING HIS ENEMIES

A beautiful painting found on a wooden casket in Tutankhamen's grave

penned them in on one side and their foes on the other; Jahveh's command came, however, that they were to go forward; and so they did, plunging into the shallow waters and, to their surprise, getting through in safety to the other side. Their escape had been made possible by a strong east wind which drove back the sea. The Egyptian chariots in attempting to follow got into difficulties in the yielding sand and mud (14[25]) and the wind dropping, the waters flowed back in their former strength and overwhelmed the pursuers.

This deliverance was ever afterwards remembered in Israel, and

[1] This name is derived from ἡ ἐρυθρὰ θάλασσα, LXX rendering of the original Hebrew which means ' sea of reeds '. How LXX got its rendering is quite uncertain.

the song of Triumph (15), although it comes from a time when Canaan itself has been conquered, still breathes the fire and enthusiasm which it aroused in an earlier generation. Tradition is here so strong, and apparently so well-founded, that to doubt the actual historicity of the deliverance—apart of course from its details—would seem to be entirely unjustified.

The scene of the passage is uncertain since the sites of the places mentioned in 14² are by no means firmly established. Some writers would place it near the modern Suez where the water is shallow and can be crossed at certain states of the tide. Others, building on the fact that at one time the Gulf of Suez extended northwards to the Mediterranean Sea, would place the crossing there; the difficulty of this theory is that although such an extension was a feature of Egypt in prehistoric times, it is by no means certain that it had not entirely disappeared by the date of the exodus. (For a full discussion see Driver, pp. 124 ff.)[1]

The overthrow of the Egyptians in the Red Sea represents the final triumph of Moses over Pharaoh, of Jahveh over the gods of Egypt. Henceforth the people of Israel enter upon a new stage of their history; the bondage of Egypt lies definitely behind them, cut off by the narrow sea through which they have just come; before them lies the desert and the years of suffering and discipline before the promised land is reached and conquered.

XIV. 2. *Pi-hahiroth* is an Egyptian word, the first part of which means 'house'. *Migdol* is Semitic and means tower, *Baal-zephon* is also Semitic and apparently means Lord of the 'North'. No clue to the sites has been discovered which commands general confidence.

5. *were fled.* Not merely gone on a pilgrimage.

7. *captains.* Some kind of military office is intended: Driver renders 'knights'. The Hebrew word comes from a root meaning 'three', and perhaps originally it meant the third man in a chariot: the Egyptians, however, had only two men in their chariots.

8. *high hand*: i.e. proudly, defiantly (cf. Num. 15³⁰).

11f. Cf. Num. 11⁵, ²⁰, &c. for similar complaints.

15. *criest thou.* Some words have fallen out as no cry has been mentioned.

19. *angel of God.* See p. 81 above.

---

[1] Dr. Box has drawn my attention to an interesting note in Mowinckel, *Psalmenstudien*, ii, p. 54 n., in which he states that *Suf* is used only of 'reeds' growing by *fresh* water, hence an inland lake is demanded; he thinks that the Red Sea was *Birket et Timsah.*

21. The miracle consisted in God's making use of natural phenomena and overruling them to the advantage of the Israelites and to
the confusion of their enemies. Josephus tells a similar story in the life
of Alexander the Great (*Antiq.* II. xvi. 5).

24. This expression shows that Jahveh was conceived of in a very
primitive manner: cf. the description of Neptune in *Aen.* i., 125 ff.

25. The wheels got stuck in the mud. A better rendering is perhaps
bound instead of *took off* (cf. LXX συνέδησεν).

31. *they believed.* For miracles as signs to be believed cf. 4[1 ff.]

XV. 4. *Pharaoh's chariots, &c.* We are not told that the king
himself was drowned (cf. Ps. 136[25]). The mummy of Merneptah, who
is probably this Pharaoh, was discovered in 1898.

8. *the heart of the sea.* Cf. Deut. 4[11]; 2 Sam. 18[14].

10. *They sank.* There is an Arab legend that their spirits can still
be seen moving at the bottom of the sea.

13 f. These verses seem undoubtedly to require a time when Israel
is settled in Canaan.

15. *mighty men*: lit. *rams.* In Isa. 14[9] 'chief ones'=he-goats. An
old chronicle describing a rising in Exeter calls the leaders 'bell-
wethers'.

16. *still as a stone.* Cf. Keats' *Hyperion*, 4 f.

> 'gray-hair'd Saturn, quiet as a stone,
> Still as the silence round about his lair.'

17. *The sanctuary.* This seems to refer to Jerusalem: see on
vv. 13 f., above.

20. *timbrels . . . dances.* Timbrels are the modern tambourines: see
further Jer. 31[4] with the present writer's notes and also Oesterley,
The Sacred Dance.

§ 3. ISRAEL AT SINAI

The route followed by the Israelites in their journey from the
Red Sea to Sinai, and from Sinai onwards until the border of the
promised land was reached, is very uncertain. It is quite probable
that some of the tribes made their entry northwards from Kadesh,
and it seems exceedingly likely that various traditions, belonging
to different tribes, have been combined into a single narrative
without regard to the inconsistencies which resulted from the
process. That this has happened in the case of Mount Sinai or
Horeb is most probable since some of the statements in regard to
it seem to require a situation near its traditional site in the modern

Sinai Peninsula, others seem to require it to be near Kadesh. In Num. 33¹⁻⁴⁹ an attempt has been made to construct a complete itinerary of the wanderings, but it conflicts with the evidence of other passages, and is itself late (for a discussion of this itinerary and a comparison of it with the other records see the notes on the passage in my commentary on Numbers in the Westminster Series).

In the following arrangement I have placed a number of incidents which in the Pentateuch stand before the arrival at Sinai after that event. The journey to Sinai along well-known routes would be easy and rapid, and the supplies brought from Egypt (Exod. 12³² ᶠᶠ·) would suffice for the needs of the people. It was when Sinai had been left and the wanderings really begun that difficulties would be likely to arise. Furthermore, in the case of all the events which have been put in the wandering period, instead of on the journey to Sinai, there are additional reasons for supposing them to have been misplaced. The narratives are as follows: (1) The Quails and Manna (Exod. 16); (2) Massah and Meribah (Exod. 17¹⁻⁷); (3) The fight with Amalek (Exod. 17⁸⁻¹⁶); (4) The visit of Jethro (Exod. 18). Each of these stories, with the exception of the fight with the Amalekites, finds parallels in the later narratives and is best dealt with in its later context. (See the notes on the separate sections for details.)

(a) The Bitter Waters of Marah (Exod. 15²²⁻²⁶).

After leaving the Red Sea and travelling through the wilderness of Shur (see note below) for three days, the water-supply came to an end. The Israelites then reached Marah (=*bitter*), where was abundant water, but it was so brackish that the people could not drink it. Moses cried to Jahveh, and he is thereupon shown a tree with healing properties; by its use the bitter water is made sweet.

Harford remarks concerning the shortage of water: 'This constant feature, so unflattering yet so true to the experience of a big caravan over desert ground, and so testing to the capacity of the leader, is one that illustrates the faithfulness of the tradition'. (P.C., p. 181.)

No tree with these healing properties is known to the modern Bedawin, but other peoples are said to adopt this method, especially the Tamils and Peruvians. (See the references in Dillmann.)

XV. 22. *Shur* (Heb.=*wall*). This district stretched to the east of the present Suez Canal.

three days. This would mean some forty-five miles at the ordinary rate of travel for a large caravan.

23. *Marah* is unknown, although some travellers would identify it with *'Ain Hawarah* (or *Howwarah*). Palmer describes this as 'a solitary spring of bitter-water with a stunted palm-tree growing near it, and affording a delicious shade. The quality of the water varies considerably at different times, and on the present occasion it was not only drinkable but palatable.' (*Desert of the Exodus*, p. 40.)

24. *murmured.* The first of a long series of complaints: cf. 17³; Num. 14, 17, &c.

26. *the diseases.* Cf. Deut. 28²⁷ (the boil of Egypt). A number of diseases are especially common in Egypt such as ophthalmia, dysentery, and a variety of skin diseases.

(b) The Revelation at Sinai (Exod. 19, 20¹⁸⁻²¹).

The account of the manifestation of Jahveh on Sinai comes from several different sources, and as it stands in v. 3 is a little difficult to follow. It is clear, however, that Israel believed that the first giving of the Law was accompanied by an exhibition of God's power in nature. There is the coming down of the storm-cloud upon the mountain top, the flashing of the lightning, and the sound of a trumpet out of the darkness (vv. 14–17 E). In J the phenomena described, the burning mountain and its quaking sides (v. 18), seem connected with some kind of volcanic activity.

The people are commanded to keep at a distance from the mount whilst Moses either alone (v. 20), or accompanied by Aaron, (v. 24), goes up to receive the divine message; even a straying beast which might chance to approach it was to be slain.

As a dramatic object-lesson calculated to impress upon the people the power and majesty of Jahveh the manifestation could not be bettered. But it was to Moses, the chosen instrument, that the real revelation was to be given.

XIX. 1. *the wilderness of Sinai.* On the site of Sinai, see above, p. 32.

3. *Jacob* as a synonym for Israel occurs mostly in passages of elevated style.

4. *on eagles' wings.* Another poetical touch cf. Deut. 32¹⁰ ᶠ. The whole passage, vv. 3*b*–6, is Deuteronomic in style. The *eagle* is probably the griffon-vulture, a magnificent bird which is still common in Palestine.

5. *a peculiar treasure*: lit. *a special possession.* LXX translates λαὸς περιούσιος (cf. Titus 2¹⁴; Eph. 1¹⁴).

6. *of priests.* The priest had ready access to God and knew His will; all Israelites were ideally to have this privilege (cf. Jer. 31³³ ᶠ·).

10. *sanctify them.* Cf. Num. 11¹⁸.

13. *no hand, &c.* The offender would be *taboo* or holy (cf. 29³⁷ ᶠ·) and any one touching him would become infected.

16. *a trumpet.* A different word is used in v. 13. The instrument was a supernatural one (cf. 1 Thes. 4¹⁶; 1 Cor. 15⁵²; Rev. 8² ᶠᶠ·).

22. *the priests.* In P priests are not set apart until Lev. 8 or possibly Exod. 32²⁹.

XX. 19. *Speak thou.* Cf. Deut. 5²² ᶠᶠ·

(c) The Covenant (Exod. 34).

The account of the Covenant in this chapter is probably J's original description and should follow 19²⁵. The references to the first tables are editorial additions, whilst vv. 5–9 seem to belong to the passage ending with 33²³.

After eliminating these additions or displacements we have an account of a covenant between Jahveh and Israel. Jahveh, on His side, will go before Israel and drive out their enemies; Israel, on their side, are to have no friendly dealings with the inhabitants of Canaan, and are to observe a series of ten commandments which are then given to them. Moses writes down the Commandments on the tables which he has provided.

In both J and D there is knowledge of a covenant prior to this one, a covenant made with Abraham (Gen. 15¹⁸, 7¹², &c.). In P there is an even earlier covenant, that with Noah (Gen. 6¹⁸, 9⁹⁻¹⁶), and the events at Sinai do not include the making of a covenant at all, that made with the Patriarch presumably being all suffi- cient.¹

XXXIV. 1. *Hew thee.* In E's account God Himself provides the tables and writes upon them (32¹⁶).

3. Cf. 19¹² ᶠ·

5 ff. This wonderful passage, one of the noblest in O. T., is con- tinually referred to in the Psalms as well as in the Prophets (Jer. 32¹⁸; Joel 2³¹; Nahum 1³, &c.).

¹ For a full discussion of the different covenants, see the article in H.D.B.

13. *pillars*, RV mg. *obelisks*. They were large stones set up near sacred places and perhaps originally were thought to be the home of the Deity Himself (cf. Beth-el in Gen. 28[18], with Driver's note in West. Comm.). These standing stones are often found in rows, and are perhaps similar to those used in ancient Celtic worship. In early days they were used in the worship of Jahveh (Hos. 3[4], 10[1 f.]; Isa. 19[19]), and even Moses is represented as erecting them (Exod. 24[4]). Here they are condemned.

Asherim. These were wooden poles set up in Canaanite sanctuaries (cf. Judges 6[25 ff.]). It is not clear whether they were substitutes for sacred trees or merely conventional emblems of an ancient Semitic goddess Asherah. See more fully Moore's article in Enc. Bib.

14. *a jealous God.* One who will not suffer His worship to be given to another (cf. 20[5]).

18. *unleavened bread.* Better *cakes*. This festival marked the beginning of barley-harvest. In 12[14 ff.], 13[3 ff.] an explanation connecting the origin of the festival with the exodus is recorded; its origin is, however, unknown.

19. *firstlings.* Cf. 13[13], 22[29 f.]

22. *feast of weeks* or harvest (23[16]). It celebrated the end of the wheat harvest.

feast of ingathering, sometimes called booths or tabernacles. It commemorated the gathering in of the fruit.

26. *seethe a kid, &c.* Again in 23[19]; Deut. 14[21]. The rite was probably magical, hence the prohibition. (See Frazer, *Folk-Lore in O.T.*, iii, pp. 111 ff.).

28. *the ten commandments.* These would seem to refer to those contained, with later additions, in vv. 11–26. The words are, however, probably a later gloss. The original contents of the decalogue are by no means certain, see *Decalogue* in Enc. Bib. and Kennett's suggestions in *Camb. Biblical Essays*, pp. 95 ff. The latter gives the following as the decalogue: (1) worship of Jahveh only; (2) the Feast of Unleavened Cakes to be kept; (3) firstlings belong to Jahveh; (4) the Sabbath to be kept; (5) the Feast of Weeks to be celebrated; (6) the Feast of Ingathering; (7) Leavened Bread to be avoided in sacrifices; (8) the Fat to be destroyed; (9) the Firstfruits belong to Jahveh; (10) a kid must not be seethed in its mother's milk.

(d) *The Golden Calf* (Exod. 32¹⁻³⁵).

The story of the golden calf is beset by difficulties (see the notes of McNeile, and of Driver), but as its value is independent of them we need not consider them here.

The story is an instance of the tendency of the Israelites ever to be drawn aside from spiritual ideas of Jahveh to lower forms of worship borrowed from other peoples. The calf, or young bull, here adopted as an image of Jahveh, was a common symbol for power amongst Semitic peoples, and especially for divine power. It is not necessary to derive this bull worship from Egypt— although a *living* bull was there venerated as an incarnation of Osiris—since the idea was already common amongst Semitic peoples and it is almost impossible to suppose that Aaron would have asked the people to accept an Egyptian representation of the Deity for their own God, the God who had just shown His superiority to all the gods of Egypt.

The story as it stands may well contain an attack on the bull-worship in North Israel and represent a similar point of view to that of the writer of 1 Kings, who condemned Jeroboam for introducing it (12²⁸ ᶠ·). The story was, in any event, a slight on the accepted worship of North Israel. It is possible that some of the priests of this worship traced their descent from Aaron and they may have regarded him as the first founder of the system.

XXXII. 1. *gods.* The Hebrew for God is always in the plural, here it is used exceptionally with a plural *verb*; hence the English translation.

2. *golden rings.* These are forbidden by the Koran.

4. *it.* Presumably the mass of metal where it had been melted down.

calf. Better 'young bull' since the same word could be used of an animal three years old (Gen. 15⁹). As the Israelites seem to have been without cattle in the wilderness, this worship may not actually have been adopted until after the entry into Canaan, though here it is attributed to Aaron.

These be thy gods. As only one calf is mentioned the plural may be aimed at the calves of North Israel.

7. *thy people.* Jahveh no longer regards Israel as *His* people: cf. Num. 11¹².

10. *of thee.* So in Num. 14¹².

15. The tables were small and the description suggests something similar to cuneiform tablets.

20. The image probably had a wooden case covered with gold plating.

An Egyptian parallel to the Golden Calf. The Cow-Goddess Hathor

22 ff. Aaron is depicted as a miserable person who makes the most contemptible excuses.

25–29. This short passage seems to belong to some different context. The people had not in the calf incident shown any desire to desert Jahveh.

30–34. Moses again intercedes for the people and offers his own life as a sacrifice for them: cf. Num. 11[15].

(e) *The Divine Guidance* (Exod. 23²⁰⁻²²; Num. 10³¹⁻³⁶).

At every stage of the history of Israel God's guiding hand was recognized by the prophets as having directed their movements. During the wanderings in the wilderness, a period of significance and interest to every Israelite, this guidance was especially needed. Tradition tells of its having been provided, but varies as to the form which the guidance took.

In Exod. 23²⁰ ᶠᶠ· Jahveh promises that His angel, who is none other than a manifestation of Himself (v. 21; cf. Gen. 24⁷), shall go before the people. In Num. 10³¹ Hobab is asked to be a guide, although it is not expressly stated that he consented, whilst in v. 33 of the same chapter the ark, the symbol of God's presence, went in advance to choose the resting place. Elsewhere (Exod. 13²¹) the pillar of fire and cloud is the guide by night and day. Thus, in different ways, the belief in God's guidance was expressed, and the faith of the nation called forth.

EXODUS XXIII. **20.** Guidance by means of an angel was a privilege enjoyed by the great fathers of the Hebrew peoples (Gen. 24⁷, 31¹¹, 48¹⁶).

21. *my name.* The name is almost equivalent to the person, and so the angel has the same authority as Jahveh Himself of whom he is a temporary manifestation.

NUMBERS X. **31.** In Exod. 18²⁷ Moses' father-in-law is said to have left the Israelites, but the opposite is inferred in Judges 1¹⁶: see further, *Numbers* (West. Comm.), pp. 61 f.

33. *went before them.* So in Joshua 3⁴ (P); but the distance there is only 2,000 cubits=about 1,000 yards.

three days' journey. Omit as a repetition from the first part of the verse.

35 f. These two prayers would seem to belong to a later time when the ark went out to war (1 Sam. 4³, 2 Sam. 11¹¹).

(f) *The Tent of Meeting* (Exod. 25¹⁻⁹, 29⁴³⁻⁴⁶, 33⁵⁻¹¹).

The first two passages come from the Priestly document and contain a command to construct a sanctuary from the various offerings made by the Israelites (25¹⁻⁹). Jahveh promises to sanctify the tent and to meet the Israelites there (29⁴³ᶠ·). This command, however, seems not to have been actually carried out until later (35²⁰⁻²³, 40¹⁷⁻³³).

In the third of the passages, which comes from E, the existence of the tent at an earlier period is assumed (33⁷). Since, however, this tent is pitched outside the camp (33⁷; cf. Num. 11⁶, ²⁴⁻³⁰, 12⁴) it differs from that of the Priestly tradition which was in the midst of it (Num. 2). A further difference is found in the custodian who in 33¹¹ (E) is Joshua, a non-Levite; whereas in P none but Levites may enter into it. The traditions agree in the demand for special offerings.

In J the tent seems not to be known, although the ark is mentioned (Num. 10³³, ³⁵ ᶠ·).

EXODUS XXV. 2. *sealskins*. The meaning of Heb. *taḥash* is not known. The Arabic *tuḥas* means *dolphin* and there may therefore be a connexion with some kind of marine animal (cf. R.V. mg. *porpoise-skins*). Others connect the word with the Egyptian *tḥs = leather*.

XXXIII. 6. *their ornaments*. It is a curious coincidence that in both P and JE the giving up of ornaments should be recorded. In the one case as offerings (25³ ᶠᶠ·), in the other by way of punishment.

7–11. These verses give an early account of the tent of meeting before it had been transformed by P into the better-known tabernacle. Some have supposed that the tent and the tabernacle were two distinct things; but such a supposition creates more difficulties than it removes.

(g) *The Visit of Jethro* (Exod. 18¹⁻²⁷; Num. 11²⁴⁻³⁰).

This story is of very great importance because it shows Moses acting under the instruction of a non-Israelite, Jethro of Midian. There are some scholars who think that Moses owed a good deal in the way of religious teaching, and ritual instruction also, to the priest of Midian. It is quite possible that the name of Jahveh may have been preserved among the Midianite descendants of Abraham when his other children who went into Egypt had lost it.

In Exod. 18¹⁻²⁷ this visit precedes the arrival at Sinai, but various pieces of evidence demand a later period: e. g. Deut. 1⁹ ᶠᶠ· belongs to the close of the stay at Horeb, and cf. v. 5 where the 'mount of God' is mentioned.

Another account of the appointment of elders is given in Num. 11²⁴⁻³⁰. This account is very valuable for the light which it throws on early ideas of prophecy.

EXODUS XVIII. 5. *at the mount of God*. The arrival at Sinai is not mentioned until 19¹ ᶠ·

11. *the LORD is greater, &c.* cf. 15¹¹. Jethro is hardly confessing a

new faith; he already believed in Jahveh, now he realizes the greatness of His power.

12. It is Jethro who offers the sacrifice to Jahveh, the others are guests or onlookers.

16. *the statutes of God and his Laws.* The laws of God were the decisions of Moses apparently.

NUMBERS XI. **25.** *they prophesied.* The effect of the spirit.

26. *written.* It is interesting to notice that there was a written register.

28. Moses is less concerned for his own reputation than is Joshua.

(h) *The Jealousy of Miriam* (Num. 12 [1-15]).

The position of women in Hebrew religion was relatively a high one, for although we hear of no priestesses as among the Greeks, the prophetic office was often held by them.[1] Amongst these prophetesses was Miriam, the sister of Aaron and Moses.

In the present narrative she (and perhaps Aaron) murmurs against the privileges of Moses. Jahveh suddenly steps in and vindicates the position of Moses as His special agent, at the same time punishing Miriam by making her a leper. Aaron makes an appeal to Moses to use his power with God on behalf of their sister, and as a result of the intercession of Moses she is cured of her disease.

NUMBERS XII. **1.** *Cushite woman.* According to Exod. 2[21] the wife of Moses was Zipporah, the daughter of Jethro. Since, however, a North Arabian people, the Kusi, appear in the inscriptions it is not absolutely necessary to suppose that a second wife is here referred to. If Jethro's visit, bringing Zipporah with him, comes immediately before the incident we have a good reason for the sudden outbreak of female jealousy.

6. *vision . . . dream.* A mark of E (Gen. 20[3, 6], 28[12], 31[11, 24], &c.). Jeremiah condemned dreams as a vehicle for revelation (see 23[25] with the present writer's note).

7. *mine house*: i. e. the whole people.

14. *spit in her face.* A strange action. Spitting was held to have a magic effect by the Babylonians and the Arabs.

---

[1] Women seem to have ministered in Hebrew sanctuaries in some inferior and probably degrading capacity (cf. Exod. 38 and 1 Sam. 2[23]).

§ 4. THE WANDERINGS

The failure of the Israelites immediately to seize the land which Jahveh, their God, had promised them was evidently a problem to the ancient Hebrew historians. They accounted for it on the ground of Israel's cowardice and want of faith after the spies sent out by Moses had made a report in which the difficulties of the task before them were by no means lightly estimated. The people in their terror refused to advance, and were thereupon condemned to a long wandering in the wilderness, the length of which was calculated so as to allow time for the whole of the unfaithful generation to perish.

According to our present Pentateuch the wilderness period was one of murmuring and lack of faith, a picture very different in its general impressions from that contained in prophets like Hosea (9^{10}, 11^1) and Jeremiah (2^2), although it agrees with Ezek. 20.

(a) *The Sending of the Spies* (Num. 13).

Before invading Canaan from the south the Israelites sent a number of men to spy out the land. The spies were instructed to bring back particulars of such things as the attractiveness of the country itself, the state of its defences, and the character of its inhabitants.

The expedition was absent for forty days, and its members, having explored the country round about Hebron (v. 21 which extends the survey to the far north, comes from P and is not reliable), bring back a puzzling report; the land was productive and well suited for settling in, but it was strongly fortified and its inhabitants were powerful and terrifying. Caleb alone stood firm amidst the general confusion and encouraged the people to trust in Jahveh and to fight bravely. His faithfulness gained for him exemption from the sentence of exclusion from the promised land which was afterwards inflicted on the people ($14^{22\ \text{ff.}}$).

XIII. 1. *the LORD spake.* In Deut. 1^{22} the people ask Moses to send out the spies.

16. *Joshua.* This and the previous verses come from P according to which (Exod. $6^{2\ \text{f.}}$) the name Jahveh was not known at the time of Joshua's birth and therefore his name could not have begun with *Jo-* which is a contraction of Jahveh.

17. *the South.* This refers not to a point of the compass but to the district south of Judah.

21. *Rehob.* This town lay near to Dan in the far north.

the entering in of Hamath. An expression used frequently of the ideal northern boundary of Israel. Its exact situation is disputed: see further, *Numbers* (West. Comm.), pp. 83 f.

22. *Hebron* lies some twenty miles south of Jerusalem, and its original name was Kirjath-arba (Judges 1[10]). It was for a time the capital of David's Kingdom.

the children of Anak. Anak (=neck) can hardly be a proper name, the phrase means people of long neck (i. e. giants).

Zoan was a city of great antiquity, its rebuilding in the nineteenth century B. C. may have been shortly after the foundation of Hebron.

28. *fenced and very great.* The fortified cities of the settled country must have been terrifying to the tribes from the wilderness. Excavations confirm the fact of the massive walls of Canaanite cities, those of Lachish, for example, were 28 ft. thick.

29. *Amalek.* The Amalekites were nomads who frequented the deserts south of Palestine.

Hittite. See pp. 4 ff., 16 above.

Jebusite. A small tribe living round Jerusalem, probably of Semitic race: they were afterwards conquered by David. Nothing is known of them beyond the scanty particulars contained in O. T.

Amorite . . . Canaanite. The *Amorites* are connected with the hill-country in Deut. 1[19 f.] In some passages, however, generally attributed to E and D, the term is used of the inhabitants of Canaan as a whole, without regard to the race to which they belong: J uses *Canaanite* with this meaning. Flinders Petrie thinks that the *Amorites* represent the 'pre-Israelite Semites' as distinguished from the 'neolithic troglodytes', the aboriginal people of Canaan for whom the term *Canaanite* should be reserved: see *Eastern Exploration*, p. 24[3]. In the Tell el-Amarna tablets *A-mur-ru* is the country round Beyrout in North Syria, *Ki-na-aḥ-ni*, the land south of Lebanon. According to E and D the *Canaanites* were the dwellers in the low-lands of west and south-west Palestine (Deut. 1[7], 11[30]; Jos. 5[1], &c.: contrast Num. 14[45]).

30. *Caleb.* Notice that Joshua is not mentioned.

32. *evil report.* Not necessarily a false report; cf. Gen. 37[2].

eateth up, &c. This perhaps means unable to support its population (cf. Ezek. 36[13 f.]).

33. *Nephilim.* Cf. Gen. 6[4].

(*b*) *The Battle at Hormah* (Num. 14$^{40\text{-}45}$, 21$^{1\text{-}3}$).

Two accounts of a conflict at Hormah during the wilderness period have come down to us, one a defeat, the other a victory. The account of the latter (Num. 21$^{1\text{-}3}$) fits badly into its context as it comes after a description of the Israelites moving south in

Hebron to-day

order to march round Edom, whereas Hormah is much farther north and a victory gained there would have opened up the country for an advance on the west side of Jordan. Burney, however, thinks that Palestine was invaded from two points and accepts the narrative of 21$^{1\text{-}3}$ in its present position (*Schweich Lectures*, pp. 28 ff.).

Wiener (*Essays in Pent. Crit.*, pp. 121 ff.) thinks 21$^{1\text{-}3}$ should come before 14^{45}. There would thus be an invasion into the Negeb which at first was successful, but met with subsequent disaster. It is interesting to notice, in view of his suggestion, that in 21³ the name Hormah is explained, whilst in 14⁴⁵ it is taken as well known. In Jud. 1¹⁷ the tribes of Judah and Simeon destroy a Canaanite city called Zephath and in consequence it got the name Hormah.

After the spies had made their report fear and panic so possessed the people that they showed their utter unfitness for undertaking so difficult and dangerous an enterprise as the conquest of Canaan. Their lack of faith brought its own punishment in the sentence of exclusion from the land (14³⁰ ff.). A fierce re-action then took place and an attempt was made, in spite of the refusal of Moses to countenance or support it, to force a way into Canaan from the south. Defeat and disaster followed this rash enterprise.

XIV. 42. *the LORD.* That is the ark, v. 44 and cf. 1 Sam. 4⁵ ff.

43. *Amalekite.* In Deut. 1⁴⁴, which is parallel to this, *Amorites* is read.

44. *the ark.* Not mentioned in Deut. 1⁴¹ ff.

45. *Hormah* is derived from *ḥerem*=*something placed under a ban*: see 21³; Judges 1¹⁷.

XXI. 1. *the King of Arad.* These words look like a gloss.

the way of Atharim. A.V. *of the spies* is improbable.

(c) The Rebellion of Korah, Dathan, and Abiram (Num. 16¹⁻³⁵).

The story of this incident as it stands at present is late and shows signs of having undergone much editing. So far as we can separate the various strands of the narrative three distinct rebellions have been combined, or perhaps it would be more accurate to say that two distinct rebellions have been combined, and then the whole has been modified.

(*a*) In our oldest source (JE) there is an account of a revolt under the leadership of two Reubenites, Dathan and Abiram, against the *secular* authority of Moses (note that in Deut. 11⁶ Dathan and Abiram alone are mentioned).

(*b*) In the Priestly source (P) the original story described a rebellion by Korah and the congregation against the peculiar status and privileges of the Levites (cf. 16³ 'all the congregation are holy').

(*c*) A later writer of the same school transformed the rebels into Levites who demanded the full rights of the priesthood (cf. 16¹⁰ 'seek ye the priesthood also').

The composite character of the narrative in itself has made for much confusion, and several inconsistencies have been overlooked by later editors: e. g. in v. 32 Korah and his associates are swallowed up, but in v. 35 they are burned with fire (cf. also 26[11] where 'sons of Korah' are mentioned).

A quite straightforward story is obtained by taking vv. 1, 2a, 12–15, 25–34 (after omitting a few references to Korah) as a continuous narrative. The revolt is then entirely secular, inspired probably by jealousy of Moses, and based on his failure to bring the people into the promised land. The rebels refuse to come to Moses on his summoning them and so, accompanied by the elders, he goes to their tents. The position and authority of Moses are then vindicated by an earthquake which swallows the rebels and their families.

NUMBERS XVI. **2.** *and On, the son of Peleth. On* plays no part in the story, and the name probably represents a dittography in Hebrew (for details see the present writer's note *ad. loc.*). *Peleth* is read as Pallu by LXX (cf. 26[8 f.]).

3. *all . . . holy.* This statement would deny the special status of *all* the Levites. Korah and his company were, it would seem, originally laymen, since Num. 27[3] recognizes the possibility of a Manassite having been amongst them.

6 f. The matter is to be settled by ordeal.

13. *a prince.* Cf. Exod. 2[14].

15. *I have not taken, &c.* So Samuel protested (1 Sam. 12[3]).

22. *all flesh.* Jahveh is recognized as something more than a mere tribal deity.

24. *the tabernacle of Korah, &c.* The word *tabernacle* is never used of a human dwelling; read as in 17[13] *the tabernacle of the LORD.*

30. *into the pit.* Heb. *Sheol.* The unseen regions beneath the earth. Charles distinguishes three stages in the conception of *Sheol,* of which this is the earliest corresponding to the Homeric Hades, see *The Doctrine of the Future Life* passim. For the beliefs regarding the underworld in classical literature see R. S. Conway's essay on 'The Growth of the Underworld' in his volume, *New Studies of a Great Inheritance.*

(d) Manna and Quails (Exod. 16[1-21]).

Amongst the many stories of the divine help preserved in Israel, those connected with the miraculous supply of food occupy a foremost place. It is natural that it should do so since a shortage of food in the desert is a dangerous and trying experience, and one far from uncommon.

The interest aroused by the story is shown by the fact that it is included in all three sources J, E, and P. Furthermore it appears in two separate places in the combined narrative, in the present passage before the sojourn at Sinai, in Num. 11$^{4\,ff\cdot}$ after that event. The later position seems the more natural.

That some real happening forms the basis of the account is more than probable. Manna is still found, and quails, when migrating, still fall to the ground in weariness. The sudden discovery of either or both of these unexpected supplies of provision by a hungry people would not unnaturally be attributed to the favour of their God—and shall we question the truth of their thought?

Exodus XVI. **2.** It is the common lot of leaders of large bodies of people to be blamed for any shortcomings, and leaders of caravans are in particular liable to such complaints.

3. *Egypt.* The slavery is forgotten, the luxuries alone are remembered.

4. *rain bread.* Cf. Ps. 78$^{24\,f\cdot}$; Joshua 6^{31}.

13. *the quails.* *Quails* are a kind of partridge and valued as a delicacy; their use as food is very ancient (see Herodotus, ii. 77). In the present context nothing further is said about them (but see Num. 11).

14. *round.* Better *flake.* For other descriptions of the manna see v. 31 (P) and Num. 11$^{7\,ff\cdot}$ (JE). The sweet juice of the *Ṭarfa,* which exudes from the tree and forms small white grains, is evidently meant: see further, McNeile's note on the passage.

15. *what is it?* The sound of the Hebrew resembles the word *mān* (=manna), hence the punning attempt to explain it.

21. *it melted.* We are not told how the manna preserved in the pot (v. 33) was preserved from this fate.

(e) Massah and Meribah (Exod. 17$^{1-7}$; Num. 20$^{2-13}$).

Shortage of water, like shortage of food, was a common incident in the wanderer's life in the desert. The two passages above seem to contain variant accounts of the same incident (cf. especially the explanation of the name Meribah in Exod. 17^2 and Num. 20^3). No doubt murmurings by reason of shortness of water occurred more than once in the wilderness period, but the similarity in detail is so close that it is best to conclude that we have here simply duplicate narratives.[1]

The story as told by the writer is simple and straightforward—The people demand water, Moses at the command of Jahveh takes his rod, and in the presence of the assembled people smites the rock with it, whereupon an abundant supply is forthcoming. For some reason or other, which does not appear in the narrative, Moses, in carrying out the command, offends against Jahveh and is in consequence excluded from the promised land.

NUMBERS XX. 1. *in the first month.* The year is not mentioned perhaps because the editor felt the difficulty of reconciling the present position of the story with that of Exod. 17[1-7].

3. *our brethren.* A reference to the fate of Korah and his companions (16[31 ff.], 46[ff.]).

5. *out of Egypt.* This speech suggests that the incident belongs to the early part of the wanderings.

8. *the rod.* Probably Aaron's rod which blossomed (17[10]).[2]

10. *Hear now ye rebels.* Moses forgets that the revolt is not against himself but against Jahveh. It has been suggested by Cornill that in P's account Moses and Aaron had refused to strike the rock and that these words were spoken to them by Jahveh. This would give a reason, otherwise lacking, for their punishment for want of faith (v. 12).

13. *Meribah.* Perhaps the well of Kadesh-Meribah was originally the scene of judgements (cf. En-mishpat of Gen. 14[7]).

(f) *The contest with Amalek* (Exod. 17[8-16]).

The contents of the story suggest that it belongs, not to the early part of the wanderings as its position in the narrative suggests, but to their close. Joshua, who is mentioned for the first time, comes upon the scene without any introduction; he is a grown man and of sufficient reputation as a warrior to be put in command of the Israelite forces. Moses, on the other hand, appears to be an old man (v. 12) and no longer fit to lead Israel to battle.

The story is a beautiful illustration of the power of intercession, and must always be an immense consolation to those who for one

---

[1] So Burney, *Judges*, p. 110.
[2] In early examples of Christian art our Lord, when changing the water into wine, is depicted as holding the rod of Moses in His hand (see Trench, *Miracles*[11], p. 125, note 3).

reason or another are cut off from active labour for some cause to which they have devoted themselves. Millais' picture of the three old men on the hilltop watching with anxious eyes the glittering dust of the contest below them at once comes into the mind on reading the passage.

EXODUS XVII. 8. *Amalek.* The Amalekites were a Bedawin tribe, forerunners of similar nomadic Arabs of the present day. The incoming Israelites must have seriously damaged their pasture grounds and not unnaturally they resented the presence of the newcomers.

Rephidim is possibly the upper part of the *wādy Feiran*, but the site is by no means certain.

9. *Joshua.* Contrast the picture of the warrior and chief with the representation of 24¹³, 33¹¹ where he is merely a young man and Moses' attendant.

the hill. There is a hill in the *wādy Feiran* named *Jebel el-Taḥuneh* (='windmill Hill') which would be suitable for viewing the battle.

10. *Hur.* Here and 24¹⁴ (E). Tradition makes him Miriam's husband and a brother-in-law of Moses and Aaron.

14. *Write this.* The hatred of Amalek seems to require some deeper cause than this attack (cf. Num. 14⁴⁰ ᶠᶠ·; Deut. 25¹⁷ ᶠᶠ·).

15. *Jehovah-nissi*: lit. *Jahveh is my banner*: cf. Gen. 22¹⁴; Judges 6²⁴.

16. Cf. 1 Sam. 15²⁴.

(g) *The Brazen Serpent* (Num. 21⁴⁻⁹).

After leaving mount Hor the people again break out into complaining. A plague of serpents is sent to punish them, or, if the incident has any historical origin (see below), a large number of serpents is suddenly encountered soon afterwards. Moses makes a brazen serpent and those sufferers who look to it are cured of their ill.

The incident is referred to by St. Paul in 1 Cor. 10⁹ and by our Lord Himself (John 3¹⁴).

This bronze serpent was worshipped at Jerusalem up to the time of Hezekiah (2 Kings 18⁴). Perhaps the whole story originated in a legend which grew up round the serpent in the Temple. At the same time serpents were often connected with healing in the ancient world. See farther, the Additional Note, *The Bronze Serpent* in *Numbers* (West Comm.) pp. 139 ff.

NUMBERS XXI. 6. *fiery serpents.* The *serpents* are probably called *fiery* because their bites set up an inflammation. Serpents are very common in the deserts of Palestine.

9. *made a serpent.* Cf. the mice, &c., made by the Philistines (1 Sam. 6⁴: see notes on p. 165 below).

(h) The Conquest of the East Jordan Territory (Num. 21²¹⁻³⁵).

Having marched round Edom the Israelites in their journeying found themselves at the Amorite frontier. Messengers were sent to the king asking for permission to cross his territory and assuring him of the intention of the people to avoid doing any damage or giving cause of complaint. Sihon refused to give passage to Israel, and tried to prevent their advance by force of arms, but in the battle of Jahaz he was utterly defeated. A neighbouring monarch, Og, king of Bashan, met a like fate at the the battle of Edrei.

The account of this last incident, (vv. 33–35) probably comes from Deut. 3¹⁻³. Writers of the Deuteronomic school in general are for some reason greatly interested in these victories over East Jordan peoples (cf. Deut. 1⁴, 2²⁴–3¹³, 4⁴⁷, 29⁷; Joshua 9¹⁰, 12⁴, &c.). According to Num. 32¹⁻⁴² the tribes of Reuben and Gad settled in the conquered territories because of their good pasturage.

NUMBERS XXI. **22.** For the contents of the message cf. that to Edom (20¹⁴ ᶠᶠ·).

23. *Jahaz.* Sometimes spelt Jahzah (Jer. 48²¹). Its exact site is unknown.

24. *Jabbok.* This stream is probably the modern *Nahr ez-Zerkā*.

25. *Heshbon.* The name has survived in *Ḥeshbân* which lies some eighteen miles east of Jericho.

27–30. This ancient ballad describes a defeat sustained by Moab, either at the hands of the Amorites or of Israel itself. It seems hardly suitable in the present context especially if Sihon (v. 29) be omitted with Jer. 48⁴⁶.

27. *they that speak in proverbs.* Better *the singers of ballads.*
be built. That is *re-built.*

29. *Chemosh.* The god of Moab. The relation of Chemosh to Moab was similar to that of Jahveh to Israel: see the Moabite Stone, Appendix, p. 238.

33. *Edrei.* Now *Edraat*, twenty-two miles north-west of Bosra.

(i) Balak sends for Balaam (Num. 22²⁻³⁵).

The defeat of the Amorites filled the neighbouring people of Moab with deadly fear. Balak their king, in consequence of this, sends for Balaam, a famous magician, in order that by getting a curse placed on his enemies he may be able to resist them.

Balaam at first refuses to come, but in the end he consents, with the warning that he is not a free agent, that which Jahveh puts in his mouth, whether blessing or cursing, he can alone utter.

The story comes from the early sources J and E, but whereas J represents the prophet as setting out without Jahveh's consent, E clearly states that the divine permission had been given (v. 20). The story is important as recognizing, even in quite early times, the possibility of a non-Israelite prophet being inspired by Jahveh. The kindly feeling for dumb animals which underlies vv. 22–33 is also interesting.

According to P Balaam suggested to the elders of Midian a scheme whereby the Israelites might be led to forfeit God's blessing (Num. 31[16]) and in warfare between Midian and Israel he met his death (Num. 31)[8]. It is from these latter circumstances no doubt that Balaam's character has suffered; in J and E he is entirely true to Jahveh's commands (willingly or otherwise) and refuses to be bribed (24[10-13]). Later Jewish thought held him in abhorrence (2 Pet. 2[15 f.]; Jude [11]; Rev. 2[14]).

NUMBERS XXII. 4. *Midian.* Here and v. 7. The mention of Midian may be due to a gloss suggested by 31[16].

5. *Pethor* is usually identified with *Pitru* on the *River* Euphrates. The objection to the identification is twofold, the great distance between Moab and the Euphrates, and the probability that the strange phrase *children of his people* is a corruption of *children of Ammon* which in Hebrew is almost identical.

6. *curse . . . this people.* The belief in the power of a curse is very ancient. Even in the Middle Ages popes and monarchs alike employed soothsayers and astrologers. For the belief amongst the early Teutons see Tacitus, *Ann.* xiii. 57.

22. This verse cannot be reconciled with v. 20.

23. *the ass saw.* The Arabs still believe that animals possess certain powers of clairvoyance.

28. Stories of animals speaking with a human voice are found amongst many peoples. A close parallel to this incident is the warning given to Achilles by his horse Xanthus (*Iliad*, xix. 400 ff.). The only other speaking animal in O. T. is the serpent of Gen. 3.

(*j*) *Balaam blesses Israel* (Num. 24 [1-13]).

As the story now stands four poems or oracles are included in it, these are almost certainly older than either J or E, and have been incorporated by the compilers into their various narratives.

Before proceeding to declare the will of Jahveh Balaam requests that altars may be built and sacrifices offered. He then proclaims the happiness and prosperity of Israel (23$^{7-10}$). Another attempt to obtain a curse has no better sequel from Balak's point of view (23$^{18-24}$). Yet a third time he endeavours to get his way, but with no success. Balak then dismisses Balaam with contempt, but

'He hath as it were the strength of the wild-ox' (Num. 24^8)
A relief from the Ishtar Gate of the temple of Marduk at Babylon

before leaving the prophet makes still further predictions of the future glories of Israel (24$^{15-19}$).

As a specimen of these oracles we may take the third. Like its predecessors it lays emphasis on the blessedness of Israel but it develops new lines of thought by dwelling on the fertility of Israel's territory, the greatness of its rulers, and the folly of those who oppose it.

NUMBERS XXIV. 1. *enchantments.* The Hebrew means *divination*, especially by observing natural objects such as the flight of birds: see Driver, *Deut.* (I.C.C.), p. 225.

3. *Balaam . . . saith.* Better *utterance of Balaam*; the word as a rule is used only of Jahveh.

4. *the Almighty.* Heb. *Shaddai.* The word may be connected with

Ass. *šadū* = mountain, the gods Asshur and Bel are called by the title *šadū rabū*.

6. A number of comparisons with objects in the natural world are used to describe the luxuriance of Israel. The text is perhaps corrupt or disordered since *lign-aloes* were not known to the Hebrews and *cedars* do not grow beside water.

the LORD hath planted. Cf. Isa. 40²¹, 61³.

7. *Agag.* Cf. 1 Sam. 15⁸. It seems strange that a king of Amalek should be used as the ideal of power.

8. *wild-ox.* Some kind of bison is meant, perhaps the same animal as the *bos urus* of Caesar, *de Bell. Gall.* vi. 28.

10. *smote his hands*, a sign of contempt (Job. 27²³; Lam. 2¹⁵).

(k) The Death of Moses (Num. 27¹²⁻²³; Deut. 34¹⁻⁶).

Jahveh commands Moses to view the promised land before he dies, and then at the prayer of Moses himself (Num. 27¹⁵ ᶠ·) appoints Joshua to be his successor. Between the forecast of Moses' death and its actual happening (Deut. 34¹ ᶠᶠ·) the rest of Numbers and the whole of Deuteronomy has been inserted by the editors of the Pentateuch.

It has been pointed out that there are many similarities between the account of the deaths of Moses and of Aaron (Num. 20²²⁻²⁹): both are warned beforehand, the last seen of them is on a mountain top, a successor is chosen and appointed, and no place of burial is known.

NUMBERS XXVII. **12.** *Abarim.* The name means *parts beyond*, and was evidently given by dwellers in Palestine to the range *beyond* (i.e. on the east of) Jordan. In Deut. 32⁴⁹ Nebo is specified and also in LXX of this verse.

14. *rebelled.* See on 20¹ ᶠᶠ·

15 ff. Different accounts of the choice of Joshua have been preserved. In D he is named on the return of the spies (Deut. 1³⁷ ᶠ·; cf. 3²¹, 31³), in the present passage (P) and in Deut. 31¹⁴ ᶠ·, ²³ (JE) he is named only a short time before his actual commission.

21. Joshua is practically to be a military commander whilst the real power is vested in the high-priest. We have here the priestly writer's idea of things as they ought to be.

DEUTERONOMY XXXIV. **5.** *the servant of the LORD.* See on Num. 12⁷ ᶠ·

6. *unto this day.* The writer looks back over a long interval of time.

PART II

In this part the invasion and settlement of Canaan or Palestine are recorded. As later writers looked back in this series of events they very naturally represented it according to their own views of what might have taken place—hence different traditions have arisen (see below on § 1).

The sources for the period are the books of Joshua and Judges, as well as part of 1 Samuel (see above pp. 62 ff.). Archaeological material is also available, especially for giving us information concerning the state of the country before the Hebrews entered it: see above pp. 12 ff..

The following are the sections:

(1) The Conquest of Canaan.
(2) The Rule of the Judges.
(3) The Struggle with the Philistines.

§ 1. THE CONQUEST OF CANAAN

Three different traditions of the conquest of Canaan have been handed down by the writers of O.T. According to the Priestly school (Joshua 13[15-21], 24) the whole country was conquered in the days of Joshua and divided up amongst the various tribes with exactly defined boundaries. The Deuteronomic writers, whilst not going so far as this, yet represent the conquest as comparatively speedy and as carried out by the united forces of all Israel under the command of Joshua (Joshua 1–12); two decisive campaigns, one in the south and the other in the north, being followed by the capture or surrender of practically all the Canaanite fortresses. The oldest account of all, however, seems to be that contained in Judges 1–2[5] in which the various tribes attempt the subjection each of its own territory, and meet with but qualified success; the conquest being a long and gradual process spread over several generations (cf. Exod. 23[30]; Deut. 7[22]).

(a) *Joshua* (Num. 27[15-23] P, Deut. 3[28] D, 31[14f., 23] JE).

In the earliest sources of the Pentateuch Joshua appears as the minister of Moses and as the guardian of the tent (see Exod. 24[13], 32[17], 33[11], JE); in addition he acts as captain of the hosts of Israel in the fierce struggle with the Amalekites at Rephidim (see pp. 117 f. above). The Priestly source also makes him one of the spies, stating incidentally that his name was changed by Moses from that of Hoshea (Num. 13[8, 16]).[1]

The above accounts of the appointment of Joshua in the place of Moses are parallel, and contain differences characteristic of the sources from which they come. P has a solemn service of dedication before the priest and the whole congregation, Joshua is chosen at the request of Moses; in JE Joshua is appointed by Jahveh when he and Moses are alone with God in the tent; in D Moses, at the divine command, himself appoints Joshua (Deut. 3[28]; cf. 31[7 f.]).

NUMBERS XXVII. **12.** *this mountain.* LXX 'Nebo' (cf. Deut. 32[49]).

14. See pp. 116 f. above.

19. *give him a charge.* Cf. Deut. 3[28], 31[14], 'I may . . . charge'.

21. *who shall enquire for him.* Joshua is dependent upon the priest's directions; contrast 12[8] (JE).

Urim. Except in this passage and 1 Sam 28[6] *Urim* is accompanied by *Thummim.* Together they formed some kind of sacred lot, but its exact nature is unknown: see further on 1 Sam. 14[41]. The words are probably connected with the Assyrian *ûrû* = *oracle* and *tâmu* = *to speak.*

23. *laid his hands.* Cf. Acts 6[6], 13[3].

DEUTERONOMY III. **28.** *charge Joshua.* See on Num. 27[19] above.

XXXI. **14.** Jahveh himself takes the initiative, contrast Num. 27[16 f.]

tent of meeting. See pp. 108 f. above.

15. *pillar of cloud.* See p. 108 above.

(b) *The Spies* (Joshua 2).

The book of Joshua opens with a charge to the new leader of the Israelites written in Deuteronomic language.

The older narrative begins with the despatch of two men to spy out Jericho. They get into Jericho and lodge with Rahab. The 'king', discovering their presence and suspecting the object which has brought them across Jordan, attempts to seize them. Rahab, however, hides them; and after nightfall lets them down by a rope from her window—the house was luckily on the wall of the city—and so they make good their escape. Before leaving Jericho they

---

[1] According to P the name Jahveh was not known until after the presumed date of Joshua's birth (Exod. 6[3]), therefore such a name, the first part of which involves knowledge of the divine name, could not have been given to him.

promise Rahab that her life and the lives of her kinsfolk will be spared when the city is captured by the Israelite troops. The story contains two realistic details, in v. 16 the necessity of avoiding the pursuers by flying to the hill country, and in v. 19 the fate which would befall any found in the streets on the entry of a conquering army.

II. 1. *Shittim.* See on Num. 25[1].

Jericho. Now known as *Tell es-Sultān* five miles east of Jordan and a mile and a half south of *Eriḥā* the modern city.

Rahab. The mother of Boaz (Matt. 1[5]).[1]

6. Cf. 2 Sam. 17[18 ff.]

7. *the fords.* Cf. Judges 3[28].

10 f. Editorial additions in the style of D. The sentiments come strangely from a heathen woman when generations later the Israelites themselves had not reached the belief in Jahveh as the sole deity.

15. Cf. David's escape from Saul (1 Sam. 19[12]), and St. Paul's from Damascus (Acts 9[25], 2 Cor. 11[33]).

16. *the mountain.* Jericho lay near the mouth of the *wādy el-Kelt* which led up into the mountains.

(c) *The Crossing of the Jordan* (Joshua 3[9]–4[11]).

This narrative is in a state of great confusion. As it stands two sets of memorial stones are erected, one on the bank of Jordan consisting of stones taken out of its bed, the other in the bed itself. Two accounts seem to have been unskilfully combined; for whereas in 3[17] the people are said to have crossed over, in 4[4 f., 10b], they are still on the far side.

The original story was intended to explain the standing stones at Gilgal; the reference in 4[3] and 4[8] to taking them out of the river probably arose from a misunderstanding of 4[5], for the natural thing would be to prepare the stones on the one bank and carry them over with the people to the other.

III. 10. *the Canaanite, &c.* See on pp. 16 & 112.

11. *the Lord of all the earth.* Not in Pent. but cf. Mic. 4[13]; Zech. 4[14], 6[5].

15. *overfloweth.* Cf. 1 Chron. 12[15]; Ecclus. 24[26], and see Robinson *Bib. Researches*, ii, pp. 494 ff., 504 ff.

16. The Arabic chronicler Nowairi has preserved an exact parallel

---

[1] The later Jews, being ashamed of her occupation and of the visit of the spies to her house, turned her into an innkeeper (cf. Josephus, *Antiq.* V. i. 2).

to this event. He records that in December 1267 a large landslide took place and the river was dammed up in such a way that its stream was quite cut off. (See P.E.F.Q.S. 1895, pp. 253 ff., Enc. Bib. 2399 f.)

Adam. Here only of a place.

Zarethan. Probably Ḳarn Ṣarṭabeh, a hill, nearly 300 ft. high, some sixteen miles north of Jericho; a ruined fortress occupies the summit. See 1 Kings 4^{12}, 7^{46}.

IV. **6.** Cf. Deut. 6^{20}.

9. *twelve stones.* LXX adds 'other'.

(*d*) *The Fall of Jericho* (Joshua 5^{13}–6^{27}).

The story of the capture of Jericho, as we now have it, would seem to have grown up by a gradual process; a literally minded generation first turned a vivid metaphor into sober fact, and a still later marvel-loving editor adorned the legend with suitable amplifications.

LXX comes nearest to what must have been the actual event (see 6$^{3f.}$ especially)—the troops take up their stations, the signal for attack is given, they rush forward raising their battle-cry—and 'the walls fall down'. By this last phrase we can best understand an unexpectedly slight resistance, perhaps even traitorous co-operation from within the city.[1]

Two later stories seem to have developed from this simple fact. In one the walls were marched round once on each of seven days, in the other seven circuits were made on the same day. Both these traditions find a place in the biblical narrative.

V. **14.** *captain of the host.* Really Jahveh Himself (6^2).

15. Cf. Exod. 3^5. Perhaps the interview was placed at Gilgal, a sacred spot.

VI. **1.** This verse interrupts the sequence and is rightly bracketed by R.V.

4. *seven* is a sacred or magic number.

5. *a long blast.* Cf. v. 10 where the shout comes after Joshua's command.

---

[1] It is interesting to notice that recent excavations at Jericho reveal no trace of such complete destruction as would be required by a literal interpretation of the phrase: see Handcock, *Archaeology of the Holy Land*, p. 101. The possibility of an earthquake shock cannot be ignored; there was *some* demolition of the walls in Canaanite times: see Driver, *Schweich Lectures*, p. 92.

17. *devoted.* A thing *devoted* is placed under a ban or made *taboo*; in practice this meant as a rule that it had to be destroyed: cf. Deut. 7¹ ᶠ·

'The Lord hath given you the city.' One of the panels from the gates of the Baptistery at Florence (by Ghiberti) showing, below, the passage of Jordan and, above, the Fall of Jericho

25. *unto this day* must mean in the person of her descendants.[1]

26. For the sequel to this curse see 1 Kings 16³⁴. According to Sellin, the Canaanite Jericho was an exceptionally strong fortress, but after the partial demolition of its walls it must have remained garden or arable land for a long period: see Driver, *Schweich Lectures,* p. 92.

---

[1] Perhaps the Kenites of Judges 1¹⁶.

(e) Achan's sin and its consequences (Joshua 7).

The capture of Jericho secured the Israelite position west of Jordan, it also opened up the way into the heart of the central highland from the east.

An expedition is sent against the small town of Ai, but the troops detached for the enterprise are defeated and driven back with some loss. A dangerous re-action thereupon takes place amongst the people at this first disaster, and their courage fails. Joshua, however, consults Jahveh and learns that the ban laid upon Jericho and its contents has been broken, and that the people in consequence can no longer rely upon the divine aid.

The sacred lot at length reveals the offender, Achan ben Zerah, who confesses his fault. He, and all his possessions, are immediately taken to the valley of Achor and destroyed.

VII. **1.** Notice the ancient conception of the solidarity of the nation; the sin of Achan is the sin of all Israel, and they must bear the consequences.

Achan. Better with LXX *Achar*; so 1 Chron. 2⁷, Josephus, *Antiq.* V. i. 14.

2. *Ai.* Probably about two miles south-east of Bethel, and some twelve miles from Jericho.

Bethaven. See on 1 Sam. 14²³.

5. *Shebarim*; mg. 'the quarries'. Dillmann suggests 'broken rocks'.[1] The text seems to be corrupt.

9. *thy great name.* A god who allowed his worshippers to be destroyed would lose his own honour.

15. *burnt with fire.* Perhaps after death, cf. v. 25.

all that he hath. The solidarity of the family (contrast Jer. 31²⁹ f.).

16 ff. Cf. 1 Sam. 14³⁸ ff.

21. *Babylonish mantle.* Heb. *a mantle of Shinar* (cf. Gen. 10¹⁰). A testimony to the spread of Babylonian influence.

24. *the valley of Achor* (that is *trouble*), cf. Hos. 2¹⁵; Isa. 65¹⁰ where even this gloomy and desolate place changes its nature upon Israel's repentance.

25. *troubled us . . . trouble.* A play on Achor.

26. *heap of stones.* Cf. 8²⁹; 2 Sam. 18¹⁷ (where see note).

(f) The Fall of Ai (Joshua 8¹⁻²⁹).

Joshua, realizing the serious consequences which would follow another disaster, marches against Ai with the whole military

---

[1] Cf. Crinkle Crags in the English Lake District.

strength of the people. A large force is sent in advance by night
to lie in ambush on the far side of the city, the rest attack it from
the front. The men of Ai come out to repel them and are drawn
away from their base by a feigned retreat of the Israelites. At a
given signal the liers-in-wait seize the deserted city and set it on
fire. The smoke of their burning homes reveals to the men of Ai
the disaster that has befallen them, and they take to flight, but
being caught between the Israelite armies are completely annihilated. The king of Ai is captured and hanged, and his city turned
into a ruin.

VIII. **2.** The spoil of Ai is not to be devoted.

11. *north side.* The movements of the two Israelite forces are a
little vague. Joshua was approaching from the east, perhaps the
local conditions made a detour to the north advisable.

12. This verse is surely another description of the original ambush
of vv. 4 and 9. Some think that vv. 10–13 come from another
account.

17. *or Bethel.* Omit with LXX. The words are hardly consistent
with the position of the ambush (v. 9).

18. *stretch out.* This signal would be hard to see at a distance.
Peake suggests that the pointing of the javelin at the city was a piece
of sympathetic magic (P.C. p. 252).

26. Cf. Moses in Exod. $17^{9\text{-}13}$.

(g) The Ruse of the Gibeonites (Joshua $9^{3\text{-}27}$).

The people of Gibeon, hearing of the might of Israel and dread-
ing the effect of their rapid advance upon themselves, send
ambassadors to make a treaty. By their words, and still more by
their equipment, the ambassadors represent themselves as the
envoys of a distant nation, and so Joshua makes a treaty with
them. The act of deceit is soon discovered; but because the
treaty had been made in the name of Jahveh it is kept. The
Gibeonites are, however, as a punishment degraded into servants
of the congregation and sanctuary.

This narrative comes from a variety of sources, or perhaps it
would be more correct to say, includes a number of insertions.[1]
These can readily be cut out, and the story then reads consecutively.

That the Gibeonites were ancient allies of Israel appears from

---

[1] The following are the insertions: from P, 15*b*, 17–21; from D, 9*b*–10,
24 f., 27*b*. Perhaps also 6*b*, 7, 14, and 16 belong to a different story in which
a treaty is made with Hivites.

K

2 Sam. 21; the present story looks as if it had been invented to present them in a ridiculous light.

IX. 3. *Gibeon*. In spite of philological difficulties this town is to be identified with *el-Jīb* five miles north-west of Jerusalem. It was a place of some importance both politically (10^2) and religiously (1 Kings 3^4).

7 *Hivites*. A small tribe of Central Palestine. In 2 Sam. 21^2 the Gibeonites are Amorites; there is, however, no necessary contradiction since the terms are used very loosely.

10. See Num. $21^{21\,ff.}$, and cf. Deut. 1^4, $3^{1\,ff.}$

12 f. The writer seems to think that shoes would wear out in the time that it would require for bread to become mouldy—a very short period.

17–21. This passage comes from another source. It is interesting as showing the high value which was attached to a promise made in the name of Jahveh; the Priestly writer was in this, at any rate, ethically far in advance of medieval churchmen who very readily broke the most solemn oaths if expediency demanded it.

(*h*) *The Battle of Gibeon* (Joshua 10^{1-27}).

The swift advance of the invading tribes, both by conquest and by alliance, alarms the petty kings of Canaan. A confederation of five of them is formed under the leadership of Adoni-zedek, king of Jerusalem. Their first step is to besiege Gibeon in order to punish the inhabitants for their defection. News of this new development reaches Joshua, who immediately marches to the relief of his allies, and by a sudden night attack overwhelms the besieging force. In the ardour of the pursuit the Israelites cross the whole of the central mountain range from east to west, and drive their stricken foes down the famous pass of Beth-horon into the foothills below. A great hail-storm added to the sufferings of the defeated army. In a fragment of an ancient poem from the Book of Jashar Joshua's fervent prayer that the going down of the sun might not rob the Israelites of the fruits of their victory has been preserved. The confederate kings were captured and put to death, and those of their people who survived the slaughter took refuge in the fortified cities.

X. 1. *Adoni-zedek*. Cf. the similar Melchi-zedek (Gen. 14^{18}); one means 'Lord of righteousness', the other 'king of righteousness'.[1]

---

[1] Zedek is taken by some scholars to be a deity: cf. Adoni-jah.

3. *Hebron.* See p. 112.

Jarmuth. Now *el-Yarmūk* sixteen miles south-west of Jerusalem.

Lachish. Now known as *Tell el-Ḥesy*, a site which has been excavated by Flinders Petrie, and by Bliss: see the latter's *A Mound of Many Cities*. It lies about thirty-three miles south-west of Jerusalem.

Eglon is situated a few miles north of Lachish. LXX renders 'Adullam'.

10. *Beth-horon.* The road running past the two Beth-horons has played a big part in the military history of Palestine: see 1 Sam. 13[18]; 1 Kings 9[17]; 1 Macc. 3[13 ff.], 7[39 ff.]; Josephus, *Bell. Jud.* II. xix. In the present day it was used by General Allenby in his operations against Jerusalem.

Azekah. See 1 Sam. 17[1]; Jer. 34[7].

Makkedah. This site also is uncertain. According to Sir Charles Warren the only possible place is *el-Mugār* in the vale of Sorek twenty-five miles west of Gibeon: see H.D.B. iii, p. 218.

11. *hailstones.* Cf. Isa. 30[30], and also Judges 5[20].

12. *the valley of Aijalon.* Below the pass of Beth-horon. Aijalon is now *Yālo*.

13. *stood still.* According to the following prose this meant that the day was lengthened. Nairne thinks that the poem was a prayer to stop the rising of the sun.[1] Homer represents similar interferences with the sun's course: cf. *Iliad*, ii. 413 f. (Agamemnon's appeal to Zeus), xviii. 239 f., *Odyssey* xxiii. 241 ff. (the delaying of the dawn by Athene).

the book of Jashar. Here and 2 Sam. 1[18]. A collection of songs such as were well known among the Arabs. Another such collection was the book of the Wars of Jahveh (Num. 21[14]).

15. LXX omits rightly.

26. Cf. the fate of the King of Ai (8[29]).

(i) The defeat of Jabin (Joshua 11[1-9]).

The series of conquests recorded in 10[28-40] comes from a later writer and is unhistorical; nevertheless, the defeat and death of the five confederate kings gave the Israelites an established footing in the south of the land. Another combination of Canaanites now threatens Joshua from the north, and once more he anticipates

[1] 'Morning began to dawn. Joshua looked eastwards and saw the sun rising over Gibeon while in a break of the clouds the moon still showed over the vale of Ajalon. Then, as the ancient song though not the later marvel-loving prose described it, he cried, Be silent, sun—O for another hour of storm and darkness; and his cry was heeded.' *Everyman's O.T.*, pp. 30 f.

an attack by moving against his enemies before they are aware of his approach. By the waters of Merom the kings had pitched their camp, and here the hosts of Israel fell upon them, and routed them as they had routed their compatriots at Gibeon. To Zidon in the north and Mizpeh in the east they pursued their enemies. After the battle Joshua destroyed the horses and chariots taken from the enemy.

It seems difficult to avoid the conclusion that this same battle is referred to in Judges 4 (see notes on that passage). The account here is very vague and probably, if the small results which followed it are any criterion, the magnitude of the victory has been much exaggerated.

XI. 1. *Jabin king of Hazor.* Cf. Judges 4[2, 7 ff.]. Hazor is in the territory of Naphtali (19[36] P) and near to Kedesh, perhaps it is represented by the modern *Tell Khureibeh,* two and half miles to the south of that place.[1]

4. *horses and chariots.* Cf. Judges 4[3, 15], 5[22]. To a people like the Israelites unpractised in the finer arts of warfare these would have much terror from their very strangeness.

5. *the waters of Merom.* There is no real clue to this site beyond the presumption that it was in the north: for a criticism of suggested places see S. A. Cook in Enc. Bib.

8. *Zidon.* The great Phoenician city nearly thirty miles to the north-west.

Misrephoth-maim. Also mentioned in 13[6]. An unknown place in the territory of Zidon.

the valley of Mizpeh. Somewhere in Mount Hermon, a valley of the upper Jordan. Mizpeh means *watch-tower.*

(j) *Joshua's Farewell* (Joshua 24).

From 11[10] to 23[16] we have a varied mass of late compositions forming for the most part what Dean Stanley called 'the Domesday Book of the Conquest of Palestine' (*The Jewish Church*, i. p. 221). Here and there authentic traditions may have survived in this collection of material, but as a whole it represents an idealized account of the conquest according to the later Jewish writers' conception of what was fitting and proper.

We now come to an early section describing the last acts of the

---

[1] According to Flinders Petrie *Khazura* of the Tell el-Amarna tablets is Hazor. Its site is eleven miles south-east of Tyre: see *Syria and Egypt*, pp. 54, 94, 173.

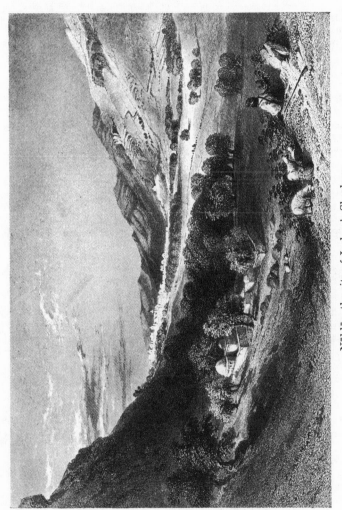

Nâblûs, the site of Joshua's Shechem

great leader. Before his death Joshua gathered all the people to the convenient centre of Shechem (cf. 1 Kings 12¹) and, after reminding them of the great acts of Jahveh in the past, exhorted them to give up their old ancestral deities and to serve Him alone. The people agree to serve Jahveh and enter into a covenant to this effect; Joshua erects a stone to be a perpetual witness of their decision.

XXIV. 1. *Shechem* is the modern *Nāblūs* an important site upon which many of the great highways converge. It lies about thirty miles north of Jerusalem between Mount Ebal and Mount Gerizim. See Gen. 34; Judges 9.

9. *Balak.* See Num. 22–24. There is no mention of actual fighting.

12. *the hornet.* Exod. 23²⁸; Deut. 7²⁰. Plagues of hornets are not unknown, but hardly on a scale sufficiently large to drive out a whole nation.

14. *the gods, &c.* The worship of other gods persisted long in Israel: cf. Isa. 65²ᶠᶠ·; Jer. 44¹⁵ᶠᶠ·; Ezek. 8¹ᶠᶠ·

26. *in the book of the law of God.* If a stone memorial were put up it would be a public appeal, an entry in a book would be an official record. The meaning of *the book of the law of God* is quite uncertain.

32. Cf. Gen. 33¹⁹.

(k) Summary of the Conquest (Judges 1–2⁵).

In the following summary the conquest does not take place until after Joshua is dead (1¹). The doings of Judah are dealt with at some length (1¹⁻²¹), as are those of 'Joseph' (1²²⁻²⁹); the rest of the tribes receive but very scanty notice (1³⁰⁻³⁶). The section closes with an account, coming perhaps from a Priestly editor, of the visit of the angel of Jahveh to Bochim, a visit whose object is to point out to the Israelites that they have themselves alone to blame for the slowness and incompleteness of the conquest.

I. 3. *Judah . . . Simeon.* Notice the personification. Both were Leah tribes (Gen. 29³³, ³⁵) and Simeon seems to have been absorbed by Judah.

my lot. For a later idea of this see Jos. 15.

5. *Adoni-bezek.* Perhaps the same as Adoni-zedek (Joshua 10³), he was apparently King of Jerusalem (v. 7).

7. *they brought.* Indefinite subject. It can hardly mean Judah (cf. v. 8).

8. *Jerusalem.* This capture of Jerusalem, unless it is really an account of the campaign of David (2 Sam. 5⁶ ᶠᶠ·), is an anachronism.

9. *the South . . . the lowland.* Heb. *Negeb . . . Shephēlah.* Technical

terms for the dry desert south of Judah and the foothills between the mountains and the maritime plain.

10. *Hebron.* See p. 112.

11. *Debir.* Now *Dāhariyeh* some twelve miles south-west of Hebron.[1]
Kirjath-sepher means 'book-town'. Sayce would make it a city of records: see *Higher Criticism and the Monuments*, p. 54. The site has recently been found at *Tell Beit Mersim*, thirteen miles south-west of Hebron.

12. *Caleb.* See p. 111 above. Like Judah he is here probably a tribe, and not an individual.

16. *the children of.* Read Hobab (Num. 10²⁹, and cf. LXXᴬ).
the city of palm trees, i.e. Jericho (Deut. 34³).

17. *Hormah* i.e. 'destruction': see Num. 21³.

18. *Gaza . . . Ashkelon . . . Ekron.* An ideal account. These Philistine cities were not captured: cf. 3³; Jos. 13³.

21. *Benjamin.* Cf. Jos. 15⁶³ where the same statement is made of Judah. A line of Canaanite strongholds, including Jerusalem, long remained and separated Judah from the other tribes.

23. *Luz.* Cf. Gen. 28¹⁹, 35⁶.

27. *Beth-shean.* Now *Beisān* south of the sea of Galilee, called by the Greeks Scythopolis. The site is being excavated by the University of Pennsylvania.

Taanach . . . Megiddo. Cf. 5¹⁹; Jos. 12²¹; 1 Kings 4¹². These places are the modern *Ta'annuk* and *Tell el-mutesellim*, the former seventeen miles west of Beisan, and the latter five miles north-west of Ta'annuk. Both towns were in the plain of Esdraelon and formed part of a chain of fortresses cutting up north Israel into two groups.[2]

Dor. On the coast south of Mount Carmel.

29. *Gezer.* Now *Tell el-Jezer* about twenty miles west of Jerusalem. It came into the possession of Israel in the time of Solomon (1 Kings 9¹⁶). The town was very ancient and recent excavations have revealed many interesting facts connected with it: see Driver, *Schweich Lectures*, pp. 46 ff.

31. *Accho.* North of Carmel, the Ptolemais of Acts 21⁷.

33. *Beth-shemesh . . . Beth-anath.* Both unknown.

34. *Dan.* Cf. 18¹ ff.

II. **1.** *Gilgal.* See Jos. 4¹⁹.
Bochim. LXX adds 'to Bethel'.

---

[1] This identification is by no means certain: see Burney, *Judges*, p. 11.
[2] For an account of the excavations at these sites, see Driver, *Schweich Lectures*, pp. 80–86, and R. A. S. Macalister, *A Century of Excavation in Palestine*.

§ 2. THE RULE OF THE JUDGES

The book of Judges, which is the chief authority for this division of the history, consists of a number of stories grouped round some remembered chief or leader. These have been set in a framework, Deuteronomic in character.

The work of the Deuteronomic school is easily recognized from such typical ideas as prosperity the reward of righteousness, and adversity as retribution for the desertion of Jahveh. Here, as elsewhere in writings of this school, the moral of the story is the most important thing about it.

For the chronology of the period see pp. 64 and 70 above.

(a) Othniel (Judges 3⁷⁻¹¹).

This short narrative comes almost entirely from the Deuteronomic editor, nothing beyond the name of the oppressor—itself of doubtful character—and of the deliverer, together with the time of the oppression, being included within the framework. There is, however, an advantage at the outset of a study of the various judges, in seeing this framework in its bare simplicity. Notice the inevitable cycle of events—sin, and unbelief, God's anger, the delivery into the hand of an oppressor, the appeal to Jahveh, the sending of a deliverer, and a period of peace before the whole process begins once again.

III. 7. *Baalim . . . Asheroth.* See pp. 49 f., 105 above.

8. *sold them.* This does not mean that Jahveh received any payment for them; an important point to remember when considering the meaning of 'ransom' since then too nothing is paid.

Cushan-rishathaim. The meaning of the later part of the name is 'double wickedness', doubtless a punning allusion to a lost original.[1] Cushan may be a reference to Ethiopia (Cush) and to the Kassite rulers of Babylon. Klostermann would connect with Husham (Gen. 36³⁴), a king of Edom (see farther in next note).

Mesopotamia. Heb. *Aram of the two rivers,* that is the land between the Tigris and the Euphrates. An expedition and subsequent oppression from Babylon at this period is by no means improbable. Others think that instead of Aram Edom was originally read (the difference in Hebrew is hardly noticeable).

[1] So Bar Cochab (son of a star), the leader of the Jewish revolt in A.D. 132–135, was called Bar Cozib (son of a lie) when his rising proved unsuccessful.

9. *Othniel.* Mentioned in 1¹³. As a Kenizzite he would live in the south of Judah and therefore a contest with Edomites rather than Arameans would be more likely.

10. *the spirit, &c.* So also 6³⁴, 11²⁹, 14⁶, ¹⁹; 1 Sam. 11⁶. 'The divine incentive to deeds of superhuman valour' (Burney).

Eastern keys. Some specimens found in excavations in Egypt
(see p. 138)

(*b*) *Ehud* (Judges 3¹²⁻³⁰).

The Israelites again forget Jahveh and Eglon, king of Moab, crosses the Jordan and seizes Jericho from which he oppresses the people. On their repentance Ehud, a left-handed Benjamite, is raised up as a deliverer. He obtains a private interview with the king, and kills him. Escaping secretly he raises the country, upon which the Moabites in panic attempt to re-cross the Jordan, but the fords having been seized against them the whole of them are slaughtered. The vigour and zest of the original story, coming down in an oral form through many generations, contrast strongly with the artificial character of the framework.

III. 12. *Eglon.* Elsewhere a place-name.

Moab. The land east of the Dead Sea.

13. *Ammon . . . Amalek.* Cf. Ps. 83⁶ ᶠ· The Ammonites were an east Jordan tribe, the Amalekites as a rule are found in the south, though as a wandering desert tribe they might join a Moabite expedition. Neither people is mentioned in the actual story.

the city of palm trees, i. e. Jericho.

15. *Ehud the son of Gera.* Cf. 2 Sam. 16⁵. Gera was probably merely the name of his clan (Gen. 46²¹).

left-handed. Cf. 20¹⁶ (also of Benjamites).

16. *a cubit*: i. e. about thirteen inches.

right thigh. The ordinary place for a hidden weapon would be the left side, Ehud's left-handedness would be an advantage in case he were searched.

17. *the present.* Better *tribute* as in 2 Sam. 8²; 1 Kings 4²¹.

18. *the people.* A train of such bearers can be seen on the Black Obelisk of Shalmaneser III.

19. *quarries* better with mg. *graven images.*

20. *summer parlour.* This would be a roof-chamber with large lattice-windows (cf. 2 Kings 1²).

23. *locked them.* By pushing the bolt, by hand.

24. *covereth his feet.* A euphemism (cf. 1 Sam. 24³).

25. *the key.* In the East a door is locked by means of a bolt, the key would be inserted from outside and pushed up to raise the bolt by means of wooden pins corresponding to holes in the bolt (see H.B.D. ii, p. 836).

26. *Seirah* is unknown.

28. *the fords.* Cf. 7²⁴, 12⁵.

(c) *Deborah and Barak* (Judges 4–5).

For the story of Deborah and Barak and the victory which they won over the Canaanites by the river Kishon we are fortunate enough to possess two distinct and separate accounts, one of them almost certainly a contemporary poem. The song of Deborah glows with fervent emotion; the call to war, the scornful notice of those tribes which did not respond, the overwhelming of the foemen, the shameful fate of the oppressor, the disappointed anticipations of his mother, are all described as if by one who actually had suffered under the oppression and rejoiced in the deliverance: 'So let all thine enemies perish, O Jahveh.'

As a work of art and as a specimen of primitive verse the poem has few rivals. In reading it we seem to hear the rattle of the Canaanite chariot wheels on the stony ground, 'The sound of many a heavily-galloping hoof', the fierce rush of the flooded Kishon, and the still fiercer rush of the mountain tribes, and the steady drive of the torrential rain falling on the quaking earth.

The prose narrative, except for the spirited description of the death of Sisera (4^{17-22}), is tame and cold by comparison with the song; it is, however, similar to the accounts of the other judges contained in the book.

There are certain discrepancies between the two narratives as they stand. The prose narrative makes the chief oppressor to be Jabin, king of Hazor (though he takes no part in the battle), in the song Sisera himself is a person of kingly state with subordinate kings under him; in the prose narrative Deborah lived on Mount Ephraim, in the song she belongs apparently to Issachar (5^{15}); there is a further difference as to those who fought for Israel; in the one account Zebulun and Naphtali supply the fighting-men (4^{10}), in the other they are summoned from all the tribes except Judah and Simeon. Possibly, too, the account of Sisera's death varies, the prose account depicts him as slain in his sleep, the song suggests that he was struck down whilst drinking: see the discussion in Burney, pp. 81 f.

Apart from these differences in detail both accounts agree in representing a Canaanite oppression being brought to an end by a battle in the plain of Megiddo, the Israelites being led by Barak with whom was Deborah. The commander of the Canaanite army, Sisera, escapes to the Kenites and is there slain by Jael.

In the prose account itself a number of contradictions occur arising probably from the writer's confusion of this battle with that against Jabin in Joshua 11^{1-9}. Kedesh-naphtali is very difficult to fit in as it lies 90 miles north of Ramah and 30 miles north of Mount Tabor, perhaps it belongs to the Jabin story.

IV. 2. *Hazor.* Near to Kedesh-naphtali (Joshua 19^{36}).

Harosheth is probably the modern *el-Haritiyyeh* on the north bank of the Kishon and some thirty-five miles from Hazor.

4. *Deborah* means *bee.* By a strange coincidence certain priestesses were called Μέλισσα by the Greeks (see Liddell and Scott).

a prophetess. Cf. Miriam (Exod. 15^{20}).

5. In Gen. 35[8] another Deborah is connected with an oak in this same locality. That the prophetess should be so far south fits in none too well with the rest of the story, perhaps she has been confused with her earlier namesake, in which case the whole verse is a gloss.

6. *Barak* means *lightning*. The name is found in Punic and Sabean: cf. Hamilcar Barcas.

Kedesh-naphtali. A few miles north of Lake Huleh, the modern *Ḳadīs*.

mount Tabor. The prominent hill at north-east end of the plain of Esdraelon, now called *Jebel eṭ-Tor*. It would be a convenient assembling point for the various Israelite detachments.

7. *the river Kishon* was a *wādy*, dry in summer but a torrent in winter. It rises near *Jenīn* and flows westward through the plain.

11. *Hobab*. See p. 80.

18. *a rug*. This is merely a guess as the Hebrew word does not appear elsewhere. Burney suggests *fly-net*.

21. *a tent-pin*. A wooden peg. In the present day women pitch the tents among the Bedawin.

V. 4. *Seir . . . Edom*. Jahveh is thought of as dwelling at Seir and coming to the help of Israel. The writer of this song, like the author of the Blessing of Moses, evidently connected Seir and Sinai (cf. Deut. 33[2]), thus placing the holy mountain in Midian (cf. note, p. 32).

6. *Shamgar the son of Anath*. See 3[31]. The two names are non-Israelite, perhaps instead of a judge he was originally a foreign tyrant.

14. *in Amalek*. Perhaps *in the vale* should be read.

After thee, Benjamin. Perhaps a battle cry (cf. Hos. 5[8]).

Machir was the principal clan of Manasseh (Joshua 17[1]).

15. *Reuben*. Cf. Gen. 49[4].

Dan . . . Asher. Burney thinks that these tribes may have been living under Phoenician protection.

19. *Taanach . . . Megiddo*. See on 1[27].

23. *Meroz*. The site is unknown.

the help of the LORD. The enemies of Israel are the enemies of Jahveh, so v. 31.

butter, i.e. curdled milk.

28 ff. These verses with terrible irony depict the anxiety of the oppressor's mother. This last scene, with its atmosphere of impending tragedy, is perfect from a literary point of view.

(d) *The Call of Gideon* (Judges 6¹¹⁻³²).

The first ten verses of chapter 6 are an introduction to the story of Gideon, for the most part consisting of frequently found ideas in stereotyped phrases, they seem to have no original connexion with the present passage.

The section itself comes from two distinct sources, each of which relates the call of Gideon and the building of an altar to Jahveh; in the manner of some ancient writers the stories are placed side by side and not combined.

The first narrative, which is vivid and forceful in style, tells how the angel of Jahveh came to Ophrah and called Gideon to be the deliverer of Israel from the oppression of the Midianites. The character of the messenger is revealed to Gideon by his treatment of the food and broth presented to him. In the second account Gideon throws down the Baal altar belonging to his father and replaces it by one to Jahveh. The men of the city seek to kill Gideon for this act of sacrilege, but his father saves his life by pointing out that if Baal is a god he can avenge himself.

VI. 11. *Ophrah.* The site is unknown, presumably it was in the neighbourhood of Shechem (9¹ ᶠ·).

the Abi-ezrite. Abiezer was a clan of Machir (Num. 26³⁰) and part of Manasseh (Joshua 17²).

in the winepress. Wheat was usually beaten out on some exposed and windy spot so that the chaff might be blown away. The winepress was usually a trough cut out of the rock where the grapes were trodden (cf. Isa. 63³).

the Midianites. Nomadic tribes distantly related to Israel: see further on Exod. 2¹⁵.

17. *a sign.* So again in vv. 33 ff.

19. Cf. Gen. 18⁶ ᶠᶠ·

20. *pour out.* Cuplike holes are found in many places in the rocks of Palestine, they formed part of the ritual apparatus of the early inhabitants: see a description in Driver, *Schweich Lectures*, pp. 51, 65, 67.[1]

21. Cf. 13¹⁹ᶠ·

24. *Jehovah-shalom*: i. e. Jahveh is peace (cf. v. 23).

25. *the Asherah.* See p. 105.

27. *ten men.* The altar was evidently an elaborate structure.

---

[1] The altar at Ophrah may have been a rock altar with these holes and the incident intended to explain it.

32. *Jerubbaal.* Jahveh was known as Baal in the early days of Israelite religion (Hos. 2[17]), and the name may originally have meant 'Let Baal (i.e. Jahveh) contend', the story here given coming later to explain the name.

(e) The Defeat of Midian (Judges 7).

The call of Gideon, like that of Saul in later times, is soon followed by the opportunity for action. The Midianites and their allies once again invade Israelite territory in considerable force and occupy the valley of Jezreel (6[33]). Gideon gathers together an army from the northern tribes, and his somewhat cowardly spirit is fortified by the signs of the fleece (6[34 ff.]).

Lest the promised victory should seem to be the result of man's power Gideon's army is reduced to three hundred men. The leader is again re-assured by overhearing a dream related by one of the Midianites and marshals his men for a night attack. They attack in three bands, each man carrying a torch and a pitcher (the story of the trumpets may belong to another source) [1] and succeed in throwing the enemy into confusion. In the subsequent pursuit the other tribes take their part and the victory is made more complete by the capture of two princes of Midian.

VII. **1.** *Harod* means *trembling.* The spring is probably '*Ain Jālūd*' two miles from Jezreel at the foot of Mount Gilboa.

the hill of Moreh. Generally identified with Little Hermon (*Jebel Neby Daḥy*). The Midianites were probably at Shunem below the hill, in which case, as Burney points out, the position of the two armies was exactly that of Saul and of the Philistines in 1 Sam. 28[4].

3. *mount Gilead,* which is east of Jordan, seems to be a mistake for Gilboa.

4 ff. The water test is obscure both as to what actually happened and its significance. The object of the test was to get a small band, and the choice may have depended on nothing else than the fewness in number of those that lapped.

8. *So . . . victuals.* Following LXX a slight emendation gives, 'And they took the pitchers of the people'. The object of the statement is to explain v. 16.

10. *if thou fear.* Cf. the request of Diomedes for a companion in similar circumstances (*Iliad*, x. 220 ff.).

14. *I dreamed.* Cf. Gen. 37[5 ff.], 40[5 ff.], 41[1 ff.], &c.

16. *trumpets.* Heb. *horns,* to be distinguished from the long metal

---

[1] See the analysis in Burney, p. 215.

trumpets of the priests: see further Driver's note in *Amos* (Camb. Bib.), p. 145, and the present writer on Num. 10^2 (West. Comm.). It is hard to suppose that each man carried a horn, a torch, and a pitcher as well.

torches within the pitchers. The torch would merely glow until waved in the air when it would burst into flame.[1]

19. *middle watch.* The night had three watches (cf. Exod. 14^{24}; 1 Sam. 11^{11}), this one probably began about 10 p.m.

20. *the sword.* Not in v. 18.

22. The places mentioned cannot certainly be identified. The object of the Midianites would be to get across Jordan as speedily as possible (cf. v. 24).

23. The tribes mentioned here (and Zebulun in addition) supplied men to Gideon's original army (6^{35}).

24. *Beth-barah.* This site is unknown, and Burney thinks the word may be due to a corruption in the text.

25. *Oreb and Zeeb.* The names mean *Raven* and *Wolf.*

(*f*) *The Pursuit beyond Jordan* (Judges 8$^{4-21}$).

This narrative seems almost a duplicate of what has gone before. In it Gideon, in order to avenge the death of his brothers (vv. 19 f.), pursues after a body of Midianites. On his way he asks for food from Succoth and Penuel, but is refused no doubt because the inhabitants feared reprisals from the Midianites. Eventually he comes upon the Midianite army encamped without fear of danger, and, surprising their camp, puts them to flight. On his return he punishes the elders of Succoth and the men of Penuel, he also slays Zebah and Zalmunna the Midianite kings. It seems hardly probable that the writer of the above account knew anything of the overwhelming defeat of the Midianites described in 7$^{15\,ff.}$, otherwise the action of Succoth and Penuel and the security of the Midianites are strange. He also ignores the large body of Israelites who were engaged in the pursuit, especially strange is the omission of all further mention of the Ephraimites.

VIII. **4**. *faint, yet pursuing.* Read with some MSS. of LXX 'faint and hungry'.

[1] Moore (Int. Crit. Comm.) refers to a passage in Lane's *Modern Egyptians*, p. 120, which illustrates this passage. It was the custom of the police in Cairo to be accompanied by a torch-bearer. 'This torch burns, soon after it is lighted, without a flame, except when it is waved through the air, when it suddenly blazes forth: it therefore answers the same purpose as our dark lantern. The burning end is sometimes concealed in a small pot or jar . . . when not required to give light.'

5. *Succoth.* Cf. Gen. 33[17]. This place and Penuel (cf. Gen. 32[30 f.]) must have been near the Jabbok, the sites have not been identified.

Zebah and Zalmunna. The words mean *sacrifice* and *shelter withheld*, and are perhaps puns upon the original names of the two leaders: cf. on 3[8].

7. Cf. Amos 1[3]; 2 Sam. 12[31].

10. The numbers are ridiculously large.

11. *Nobah.* Mentioned in Num. 32[42], the site is unknown.

Jogbehah. Burney identifies with *Agbēhāt* twenty miles east-south-east from the ford *ed-Dāmiyyeh* at which Gideon seems to have crossed the Jordan.

14. *he described.* Heb. *he wrote* as mg. There is no reason for doubting that the boy could write.

16. *taught.* Better as mg. *threshed.*

18. *Tabor.* For the mountain of this name see on 4[6]. It may be, however, that some other place is here referred to as it was some distance from Ophrah.

(g) *Abimelech's Rise* (Judges 9[1-21]).

When Gideon died he left behind him, amongst many other children, a son by a Canaanite mother. This man, Abimelech by name, combined with his father's vigour an ambitious and bloodthirsty nature. By the aid of his mother's kinsmen he slew his brothers, save Jotham who succeeded in making his escape, and so remained without a rival as despot of Shechem.

Jotham seizes an opportunity of addressing the men of Shechem and taunts them, by means of a parable, with having rejected the rule of the noble and useful trees (the legitimate sons of Gideon) in order to put themselves under a bramble! He ironically wishes that they and their king, if they really feel that they have acted justly to Gideon, may rejoice over one another; otherwise fire will be kindled amongst the thorns and will destroy the very proudest trees.

This story is interesting for the light which it throws on the relations between Canaanites and Israelites in the days before the kingship, and also because it shows the power which a determined, unscrupulous man can obtain for himself in an unsettled state of society.

IX. 1. *Abimelech.* The name seems to mean *the King* (*i. e.* God) *is father.*

Shechem. See on Joshua 24[1].

4. *Baal-berith* means *Master of the covenant,* perhaps because an agreement had been made between the men of Shechem and their Israelite neighbours over which he presided.[1]

5. *on one stone.* Perhaps slain with sacrificial rites (cf. 1 Sam. 14³³ᶠ·).

7. *the top.* Not to be taken literally, some projecting spur sufficiently near to the town for his voice to be heard.

8. *the olive.* Valuable because of its oil.

13. *cheereth God.* Wine was poured out as a libation.

15. *the bramble.* The buckthorn, a common Palestinian bush. It gave neither wood, fruit, nor shelter.

20. *the house of Millo.* A place-name, Beth-millo.

(h) The end of Abimelech (Judges 9²²⁻⁵⁹).

The gloomy forecast, or curse, of Jotham did not wait long for its fulfilment. Abimelech and his subjects soon disagreed and the men of Shechem cast off his rule. As the account now stands they were induced to do so during the excitement of a religious festival by a newcomer named Gaal. He appealed to their pride as sons of Hamor, the original lords of the city, and spoke derisively of Abimelech. The latter, warned by his governor in the city, laid an ambush and defeated the Shechemites, and Gaal and his party were driven away. Another version of the attack on Shechem (vv. 42-49) seems to be parallel to vv. 26-41 and concludes by describing the total destruction of the city.

Abimelech evidently had trouble with others of his subjects and punished them with equal ferocity. His career was suddenly brought to an end by a millstone cast upon him by a woman as he besieged Thebez.

IX. 22. *over Israel.* An exaggeration by one who looked upon the judges as rulers over the whole land.

23. *an evil spirit.* Cf. the experience of Saul (1 Sam. 16¹⁴).

25. The conduct of the Shechemites would interfere with trade.

26. *Gaal the son of Ebed.* Ebed means *slave* and may come from his enemies, we should perhaps read *obed.*

27. *cursed.* Wine loosened their tongues.

28. The text of Gaal's speech is corrupt. By a slight alteration we may read, 'Did not he . . . serve the men of Hamor, &c.'

[1] This is the first example of a temple in O. T. Macalister thinks it may originally have been Philistine: see his *Schweich Lectures,* p. 123. Sellin claims to have discovered the foundations of this temple which he describes as a square building with porticoes, three columns on each side, with a pedestal for an idol: see the report of a lecture in *The Times,* 21st Sept. 1926.

30. *he said.* Read with LXX *I would say.*

37. *the oak of Meonenim* that is *the augur's oak*, no doubt a well-known landmark.

41. *Abimelech dwelt at Arumah.* Having defeated the rebels he leaves Zebul to deal with them, and goes to Arumah, the site of which is unknown.

42. This seems to follow on v. 25.

44. Cf. the taking of Ai (Joshua 8¹⁴⁻²²).

45. *sowed it with salt.* To mark its future desolation.[1]

50. *Thebez* perhaps *Tubas* twelve miles north-east of Shechem.

54. Cf. the death of Saul (2 Sam. 1⁹).

(i) *Jephthah the Gileadite* (Judges 11).

'Jephthah . . . is the Othello of Israelitish history, a splendid barbarian, "little blessed with the soft phrase of peace," familiar with "moving accidents by flood and field", who by his valour delivers his country, and by a mysterious fate sacrifices a life dearer to him than his own.'[2]

Gilead being oppressed by the children of Ammon appoints as its chief the illegitimate son of one of its members. Being assured of his position by a solemn oath (v. 10) Jephthah opens negotiations with the king of the Ammonites. He points out that Israel in entering Canaan had respected the rights of Edom and Moab (Num. 20¹⁴, 21¹¹ ᶠᶠ·) and ought not Ammon to do the same to Israel. Just as Chemosh (!) their god gave them lands so Jahveh had given Israel lands. It should be noticed that Jephthah's argument is not really sound since the Ammonites could reply that their god was urging them into fresh conquests; moreover there is an obvious confusion between Moab, whose god was Chemosh and Ammon which worshipped Milcom.

In spite of Jephthah's diplomatic efforts, which neither party probably regarded very seriously, war breaks out and Jephthah overwhelms his foe. Unfortunately he had made a vow, before the battle, to offer up to Jahveh whatsoever should first come out to meet him on his victorious return. The victim[3] turns out to be his own daughter, but she is equal to her fate and with true heroism

---

[1] Burney quotes from the Annals of Tiglath-pileser I: 'The whole of the city (i.e. Hunusa) I laid waste, I destroyed, I turned into heaps and ruins: and salt (?) thereon I sowed.'

[2] James Strahan in P.C.

[3] Cf. Iphigenia's similar feelings in a like situation:
'And deem me blest as working good to Greece.'

feels that her life is but a small sacrifice for the nation's deliverance. She asks for two months' grace in which to mourn 'her virginity'; and then the offering is made.

Two important points should be observed in the above story—the recognition of the reality of 'other gods' (v. 24), and the apparent legality of human sacrifices in a great emergency. Both are signs that religion is still in its twilight stage.

XI. 3. *Tob.* Locality unknown,[1] mentioned also in 2 Sam. 10⁶, ⁸.

4. *the children of Ammon* lived to the east of Gilead which itself lay on the east side of Jordan.

12-28. Jephthah's speech confuses Moab and Ammon and is perhaps in a wrong context.

12. *my land.* This seems hardly suitable on Jephthah's lips, unless his sudden elevation made him speak proudly.

16. *Kadesh.* See pp. 32 f.

17. *unto . . . Moab.* These negotiations are not mentioned elsewhere.

18. *Arnon, &c.* Cf. Num. 21¹³.

19. *Sihon.* Cf. Num. 21²¹ ᶠᶠ.

29. *the spirit of the LORD.* So in 3¹⁰, 14⁶, ¹⁹, &c.

31. *whatsoever . . . it.* This should be *whosoever . . . he.* To offer a human sacrifice at a time of great anxiety was not uncommon in primitive ages, cf. 2 Kings 3²⁷.

33. *Aroer.* Probably not Aroer of v. 26 which was on the Arnon, but Aroer of Joshua 13²⁵ near Rabbah. Both *Minnith* and *Abel-cheramim=meadow of vineyards*, are unknown.

34. Cf. Miriam (Exod. 15²⁰) and the women of Israel (1 Sam. 18⁶ ᶠ·). *his only child.* Cf. Amos 8¹⁰; Jer. 4²⁶.

36. In its noble simplicity this verse shines out from the darkness of a rude and barbarous age. Both Byron in *Jephtha's Daughter* and Tennyson in *A Dream of Fair Women* have found in this unnamed Israelite maiden a subject worthy of their pens.

37. *my virginity.* She laments that she will die unmarried and childless: so, too, Antigone (Sophocles, *Ant.* 890 ff.).

39. with admirable reticence the last act of the tragedy is suggested but not described: there can be but little doubt that in the mind of the writer she was actually sacrificed.

---

[1] Thutmose III (*c.* 1500–1447 B.C.) mentions a city of Tubi amongst his conquests which may have some connexion with Tob.

(j) Micah and his Image (Judges 17).

The story contained in this and the following sections undoubtedly comes from a very early period in the history of Israel, to date it even approximately is, however, not possible.

The account begins by the abrupt mention of Micah and his confession that a certain sum of money which his mother had lost had been taken by him. With part of the silver which he then restored an image was made for Micah, to serve which he consecrated one of his sons. It chanced, however, that soon afterwards a young Levite of the tribe of Judah passed that way and Micah, learning of his qualifications, persuaded him to become his priest: to which office on the Levite's consent being obtained he consecrated him.

This passage is important for the light which it throws on the early conceptions of the Levites. The Levite here introduced was a member of the tribe of Judah, and the term Levite cannot refer to his tribe but must be used of his office (cf. Exod. 4[14]).

XVII. 1. *the hill country of Ephraim* lay some miles north of Jerusalem.

2f. These verses are in some disorder, but the sense is fairly clear. Micah was evidently afraid that the curse might come upon him.

3. *a graven image and a molten image.* The latter should be omitted as an addition. The graven image was carved from wood, the molten probably had a wooden centre overlaid with metal.

5. *of gods.* Read with R.V. mg. *of God.* Micah had a private chapel.

an ephod. See p. 52.

teraphim were evidently some kind of image having, at any rate in certain cases, a human form (1 Sam. 19[13, 16]). They were abolished by Josiah (2 Kings 23[24]).

consecrated: lit. *filled the hand of.*

6. This verse represents the opinion of a later editor who was shocked at a layman consecrating another as a priest.

10. *a father.* So called presumably from respect to his office.

12. *consecrated* better *installed.*

13. *Now know I, &c.* The Levite would know the way of obtaining blessings better than a layman, so Micah thought: magic and not religion lies behind the thought.

(*k*) *The trek of the Danites* (Judges 18).

The Danites in the early days of the conquest tried to settle to the south-west of Ephraim, but could make no headway. The tribe determined to seek a fresh home, and so spies were sent out to the north. On their way they came across Micah's Levite and obtained an oracle from him. Continuing their journey they discovered a community of Zidonians living in a desirable country, but away from powerful neighbours who could protect them, a situation well suited to the designs of the Danites.

Acting on the report of the spies, the Danites to the number of six hundred men trek northward.[1] They make a halt at Kirjath-jearim and then came to Micah's house. The images are stolen and the priest persuaded to go with the Danites. Micah, in desperation, gathers his neighbours and dependents and pursues the spoilers; he gets nothing from them, however, but insults and threats, and finally has to return home empty. The tribe goes on its way and falls upon its victims; the people are massacred, the city burnt, and a new one built which they name Dan. The image is set up and so the famous sanctuary of Dan is founded.

The story is a vivid description of a time of anarchy, when might was right, and those who could not defend themselves were at the mercy of their foes. The conception of religion which animates the Danites is very crude and has no obvious connexion with right conduct. Perhaps one of the objects of the writer of the story was to pour scorn on the great northern sanctuary which is represented as being founded with stolen images and a kidnapped priest.

XVIII. **2.** *Zorah . . . Eshtaol.* Cf. 13^{25}. *Zorah* is the modern *Ṣar'ah* fourteen miles west of Jerusalem, *Eshtaol* is perhaps *'Eshūa'* about two miles north-east of *Ṣar'ah*.

3. *knew the voice.* The meaning must be that they actually recognized him. Attempts to explain *voice* as dialect and so forth have not been successful.

5. *Ask counsel.* By means of the Ephod probably.

7. *Laish* was situated at the source of the Jordan, its site is now

---

[1] Presumably their wives and children accompanied them as their object was to make a permanent settlement. There is a vivid description of such a movement, on a much bigger scale, in the temple of Medinet Habu. Ramses III describes the approach of the invaders, who brought their wives and children in two wheeled ox-carts, and their complete defeat.

occupied by *Tell el-Ḳády*. G. A. Smith, however, prefers *Banyas* a few miles to the east.

any man. The better rendering, following some MSS. of LXX, &c., is *Syria*, this involves a very slight change in Heb. (*Aram* for *Adam*).

12. *Kiriath-jearim* means the 'city of woods' and is perhaps represented by *Qaryet el-'Enab*, some six miles north-east of *'Eshúa'* (=Eshtaol).

Mahaneh-dan, that is the camp of Dan: cf. 13[25].

15 ff. There is some confusion in the text.

30. *Moses.* Later piety read this as Manasseh inserting a small n' between the 'm' and 's' of Moses.[1]

the captivity. Either in 734 or 721 B.C.

31. *Shiloh.* See on 1 Kings 14[2].

§ 3. THE STRUGGLE WITH THE PHILISTINES

i. *The coming of the Philistines*

The Philistines first appear in Palestine in the fifth year of Ramses III (*c.* 1193 B.C.) when, according to the Egyptian records, a Libyan invasion of the Delta was assisted by a number of sea-rovers, and amongst them were the Pulasati. This people, there can be but little doubt, is to be identified with the Pelishtim (Philistines) of O.T. Their home was in Kaphtor (Amos 9[7]; Deut. 2[23]), the Egyptian *Keftiu*, and the modern Crete.[2]

The Pharaoh repulsed the invaders, and a few years later anticipated a similar movement, though this time on a much larger scale, by marching into Palestine and attacking the invaders there. Again he was successful, but in spite of defeats the Pulasati and their allies slowly pushed their way south, and before very long the whole of the coast from Mount Carmel to the borders of Egypt itself was in their hands.

It will be obvious that sooner or later these people must come into touch with the Israelite tribes, who about this time were conquering homes for themselves in the hill-country of Judah. The expansion of the Philistines southward was stopped by the Egyptian frontier, and consequently their natural outlet was eastward; whilst the Israelite tribes in the hill-country no doubt cast

---

[1] It should be remembered that in the Hebrew Bible only the consonants were printed: Moses=M-sh-h, Manasseh=M-n-sh-h.

[2] There are reasons for supposing that Kaphtor included a wider area than Crete only: see *The People and the Book*, p. 25.

envious eyes on the more desirable land which stretched below them to the sea. The story of the subsequent struggle is recorded in part of the book of Judges and in the succeeding books. The earlier stages of it form the main subject of this section.

ii. *The story of Samson*

The stories which have gathered round the figure of Samson are quite different from any others in O.T. They are different in two ways; as to their probable origin, and as to their nature. It may be said of the rest of O.T. that it comes from circles possessing some literary culture, these stories would seem to come from the heart of the people themselves. By pointing out the non-literary origin of the Samson stories it must not be supposed that an attempt to deny their literary merits is being made; such is far from being the case, for no one could read them without recognizing the vigour and naturalness which mark them, and make them works of real artistic power. They bring to us the atmosphere, rude and rustic, of the border country between the Philistines and the men of Israel. No wonder they have been preserved to us, for

Heads of Philistines. From reliefs at Medinet Habu

as Moore says: 'The scrapes into which Samson's weakness for women brought him, the way in which he turned the tables on those who thought they had got the better of him, the hard knocks he dealt the uncircumcised, and the practical jokes he played on them must have made these stories great favourites.'[1] Then as to their nature. If we leave out of account the forecast of his birth (chapter 13) and an occasional reference, there is nothing specifically religious in the entire series of tales. We have not a judge or a prophet like Samuel, but a figure almost without parallel in O. T., one indeed who reminds us of the Greek Herakles with his supreme strength and rough good humour. The narratives are also unusual in preserving for us, very thinly concealed, legend and myths such as no doubt formed a very large part of the primitive belief of the Israelite people in common with their Semitic kinsfolk. Probably many of these stories had originally nothing to do with Samson, but just as Homer wove into the *Odyssey* old tales and legends, so the Hebrews connected similar tales with Samson. The name Samson is closely connected with the Hebrew for *sun*, and it seems certain that some at least of the incidents of the hero's career are based upon the movements of the sun itself. In other words ancient solar-myths, such as are undoubtedly found amongst other races, have become attached to this Hebrew judge.[2]

(a) The birth of Samson (Judges 13²-²⁵).

The birth of Samson was foretold by the visit of an angel to his mother, who was warned that she must avoid wine and strong drink before the event took place, since her son was to be a Nazirite (see below) from the womb. The woman reported the matter to her husband, and in response to his prayer a further visit from the heavenly messenger took place. With Oriental hospitality Manoah wishes to give a meal to his visitor, and also asks after his name, with the object, so he avers, of doing him honour when his promise has come true. The angel, who has not been recognized as such by his host, refuses to receive any food, but when Manoah prepares a kid and places it on the altar he disappears in the flames. The name was also withheld from their curiosity. The terror which fell upon Manoah at the thought of having seen God was assuaged by his wife's common sense: 'If he had intended to kill us he wouldn't have taken our offering.'

[1] *Judges* (I.C.C.), p. 315.
[2] The question of solar-myths is obviously too complicated to be discussed here: those who wish for further information as to the relation of Samson to them should consult Burney's *Judges* where the matter is discussed and reference is made to further authorities.

The appearance of the messenger and his behaviour have parallels in the story of the call of Gideon (6²¹). The forecast of the birth and the manner of life to be followed by the child seem to anticipate the story of John the Baptist.

XIII. **2.** *Zorah.* See on 18².

Danites. Probably the bulk of the tribe had already left and gone north as described in ch. 18.

3. *the angel of the LORD.* See p. 81.

5. *a Nazirite* was one dedicated to the service of God. The rules which governed the life of the Nazirite and the vows which he had to undertake are described in Num. 6¹ ᶠᶠ· In some respects Samson seems to have differed from the Nazirite as there described.

6. *I asked him not.* In ancient times such questions were asked at an early stage (cf. Gen. 16⁸, 29⁴: and for an example outside O.T. Homer, *Odyssey*, iv. 60 ff., &c.).

16. *I will not eat.* Contrast Gen. 18⁸.

18. The name of God is not to be known by man as in the story of Jacob at the ford (Gen. 32²⁹).

24. *Samson.* The name is connected with *Shemesh* (*sun*). Not far from Zorah lay Beth-Shemesh where was no doubt a temple to the sun, or had been.

25. *Mahaneh-dan.* Cf. note on 18¹². It has been suggested that we should here read *Manahath-dan* and so connect the name with Manoah (cf. 1 Chron. 2⁵⁴).

(b) Samson's Marriage (Judges 14).

We hear nothing of the youth of Samson, he comes upon the scene quite suddenly in connexion with the first of the several love-affairs which form the chief interest of his life as related in the book of Judges. Nothing could be further removed from the picture which our minds might be disposed to form of one devoted to God's service.

The lady who aroused the hero's affections was unfortunately a Philistine, and on Samson's informing his parents of his choice, they were unwilling to arrange the matter. As the account now stands they eventually went down with their son and the marriage feast was begun. The confused state of the text, however, suggests that the parents were inserted by an editor—they perform no useful function in the story—in order to conceal the real nature of Samson's union or proposed union with the woman.

On the way down to Timnah, which was the home of the bride,

the hero fell in with a young lion, and by his immense strength he rent it in two. Going down again after an interval he came across the body and found that in the meantime it had been occupied by a swarm of bees. This incident formed the basis of a riddle which he put forth to the young men of the village whom he was entertaining as a preliminary to the marriage. Naturally enough, since they were quite ignorant of the circumstances of the event, they were unable to guess the answer. They then by threats got the answer from the woman, and produced it triumphantly at the very end of the stipulated time. In an access of anger Samson attacked and slew thirty young men of Ashkelon, spoiling them in order to provide the reward promised for the successful solution of the riddle. His wife's treachery disgusted him so much that he left her, probably before the marriage was consummated, and in order to console her another husband was found from amongst the wedding-guests.

XIV. 1. *Timnah* is the modern *Tibneh* about four miles south-west of Zorah.

3. *uncircumcised*. A constant reproach held up against the Philistines.

4. *it was of the LORD*. A religious touch is given to the story; but from a Christian standpoint it would have been better without it.

8. *a swarm of bees*. Cf. Virgil's method for producing bees from a carcase, *Georgics* iv. 295 ff.

14. Samson's couplet is pithy and to the point, but it gives little real information to those who had to guess the riddle.

18. *before the sun went down*. Read by a slight alteration *before he went into the (bridal) chamber*.

19. Burney regards this verse as a gloss, thinking that in the original story he left the wager unpaid since the answer had been unfairly gained. The difficulty of supposing that Samson went some twenty-three miles and returned within the day is certainly very great.

(c) Samson's Exploits against the Philistines (Judges 15–16³).

After a time Samson evidently relents and so he goes down once again to Timnah. He then discovers to his disgust the sequel to his former desertion. In revenge Samson captures three hundred foxes, and attaching a firebrand to the tails of each pair he sets on fire the corn of the Philistines. For this loss the Philistines burn up Samson's wife and her father. Samson carries the vendetta a stage farther by slaughtering other Philistines.

The next step of the Philistines was to report the matter to their vassals, the men of Judah, and to request them to give up the offender. To his fellow-countrymen Samson makes no resistance, and as a result he is handed over bound to his enemies. The spirit of the LORD, however, came mightily upon him; he broke his bonds and, snatching up the jaw-bone of an ass, he slew his captors. His effort had left him exhausted, but in response to his cry Jahveh caused a spring to burst forth.

Samson seemed unable to learn from experience, and again he put himself in the hands of his enemies; this time by going to pay a visit to Gaza whither he was drawn by the attractions of another

Samson and the lion. A Minoan ring-bezel of about 1400 B.C., showing a hero slaying two lions

Philistine woman. The gates were shut against him, but nothing daunted he carried them on his shoulders to the top of a distant mountain!

XV. 4. *three hundred foxes*. Some commentators think that jackals should be read since foxes do not go about in packs. This is to give too high a value to the details of the narrative; the writer is obviously trying to make the marvels as great as possible.[1]

[1] There can be but little doubt that the story here is connected in some distant way with the custom at the Roman *Cerealia* described by Ovid, *Fasti*, iv. 679 ff. Foxes with firebrands tied to their tails were let loose in the Circus and hunted away. Some scholars derive this ceremony from a Semitic source. Like the *Robigalia*, which was in later times connected with it, it seems to have been intended to keep away mildew from the corn; the mildew or rust being signified in the one case by the brands and red colour of the foxes, in the other by red poppies which were sacrificed to the spirit of mildew. An interesting detail is that this rust was thought to be caused by the rays of the sun; Samson is thus represented as acting

8. *Etam.* A city of this name is situated not far from Bethlehem (2 Chron. 11⁶).

9. *Lehi* means jawbone, its site is unknown. The name is probably far older than the story and may have been given to some feature of the landscape which resembled a jawbone.[1]

19. *the hollow place.* Heb. *the Mortar,* also the name of a place near Jerusalem (Zeph. 1¹¹).

En-hakkore means *the spring of the caller* (cf. v. 18), the original meaning, however, was probably *Partridge Spring* since this bird is named the caller in Heb.[2]

20. A conventional formula usually at the end of the narrative.

XVI. 1. *Gaza* was about thirty miles to the south of Zorah. It is still a place of importance.

3. The gate consisted of two posts from which the doors hung with a bar let down into the posts to secure it. Samson plucked up the whole thing and carried it some forty miles to a hill near Hebron! The story reminds one of some of the exploits of Thor and the Norse heroes.

(d) Samson and Delilah (Judges 16⁴⁻³¹).

Once more the Israelite hero falls under the influence of a woman: this time quite possibly his charmer was of his own race. Whether Delilah was a Philistine or not, however, she was willing, in return for an enormous bribe, to do the work of the Philistine lords. They commissioned her to discover the source of his more than human strength, which according to the belief of those days was presumed to have some magic basis. Three times Samson deceived her with false information, but at last being wearied by her pestering he told her that he was a Nazirite, and that his strength lay in his hair. This time the Philistines made no mistake, the giant was bound with brazen fetters, his eyes put out, and himself deposited in prison.

After a time his hair began to grow and with it his strength to return. Accordingly, when he was brought out by the Philistines to make sport for them at a great religious festival, he managed to

like the sun-god who destroys the corn of his enemies by sending amongst it the mildew. See Burney, *Judges,* pp. 393 f.; Frazer, *Spirits of the Corn,* &c., i, pp. 296 f.; also Warde Fowler, *Roman Festivals,* pp. 88 ff.

[1] Cf. the name of the cape in Laconia mentioned by Strabo, VIII. v. 1, *Ὄνου γνάθος.*

[2] It is interesting to notice that certain types of springs breaking forth from the earth were sacred to Heracles (Athenaeus, xii. 512).

Cretan (=Philistine) gladiatorial cameo. The 'Boxer' Vase from
Hagia Triada (see also p. 179)

get hold of the two pillars which supported the house where his tormentors were gathered together and exerting himself to the uttermost he brought down the building and involved all in a common destruction.

This final scene lends itself to a mythological interpretation and may represent, as Burney says, the setting of the sun: 'By pulling down the western pillars which were thought to support the vault of heaven (Job 26[11]) the sun overwhelmed himself and the world with the darkness of night.' Whether this is so or not, and quite apart from its origin, the story is immensely important as an illustration of the low ideas which were current amongst certain of the people of Israel—even of those who compiled the O.T.[1] The belief that Samson's strength lay in his hair is on a par with similar pieces of superstition in various parts of the world (see Frazer, *Folk-Lore in O.T.* ii. pp. 484 ff.); but worst of all, it is not for offences against the moral law that Samson meets with disaster, but because of an infringement of a magic ordinance, by letting his hair be cut. We can understand the vehemence of the prophets and the harsh measures to which they resorted when we see the religious conceptions of some who imagined that they were genuine followers of Jahveh.

XVI. 4. *the valley of Sorek.* The word signifies a certain kind of vine, and the valley to which it gave its name lies just below Zorah. It is now called *Wady eṣ-Ṣarār*.

5. *eleven hundred pieces of silver*=about £150.

7. *withes.* Better *cords of sinews*; *green* should be rendered *fresh*.

13. The Heb. text is defective here, but LXX supplies what is missing: *If thou weavest the seven locks of my head along with the web, and beatest them up with the pin to the beam, then shall I be weak like other men. And it came to pass while he slept that Delilah took the seven locks of his head and wove them, &c.*

21. *put out his eyes.* Cf. 2 Kings 25[7]. A common form of punishment.

23. *Dagon.* Probably a Semitic deity taken over by the Philistines when they settled in Palestine. The Jewish tradition that he was represented by a figure half man and half fish has no evidence to support it and seems to have been suggested by the resemblance of the name Dagon to the Heb. *dagh = fish.*

---

[1] Perhaps the pressure of public opinion accounts for the presence of this and similar stories in O.T., the common people insisting that such favourites should not be left out.

25. *may make us sport.* The people of Crete from whence the Philistines came were, to judge from their frescoes, very fond of gladiatorial games. H. R. Hall suggests that they introduced the custom into Palestine (cf. 2 Sam. 2^{14}).[1]

27. *men and women.* The mixing of the two sexes at a public meeting was not a Semitic custom, but similar gatherings are depicted in a fresco at Cnossus in Crete: see *Camb. Anct. Hist.* ii, p. 290.

29 f. It is a little difficult to know what exactly happened, no doubt we must allow for some exaggeration. R. A. S. Macalister suggests that the common people were on the roof and the lords under a portico: see his *Schweich Lectures*, p. 123. He also points out that before the building of Solomon's temple at Jerusalem all such buildings are associated with the Philistines (except the temple at Shechem, Judges 9^4, where see note).

(e) The Birth of Samuel (1 Sam. 1).

There now comes upon the scene the figure of one who was more worthy to play the part of a judge and leader in Israel. Like his predecessor he was dedicated to Jahveh from the womb.

The story opens with the visit of a certain Elkanah of Ramah to the house of God at Shiloh for the purpose of making the annual sacrifice. He was accompanied by his two wives, the favourite of whom, Hannah, had no children. Stung by the taunts of her rival the poor woman was praying in the tent for a child when the high-priest Eli noticed her and, attributing her conduct to drunkenness, reproved her. Hannah explained the situation and departed with the good wishes of the old man. After a time her prayers and vows received the longed-for answer—a son was born to her. In accordance with her promise Samuel, for so the child was named, was given back to God; and when old enough was taken to the temple there to remain as an attendant on Eli.

The story throws an interesting light on the social and family life of the Israelites. Quarrels such as that here depicted must have been common where polygamy was practised (cf. also Leah and Rachel), and a favourite wife an object of envy and hatred.

I. **1.** *Ramathaim-zophim.* Read *of Ramah, a Zuphite.* The site of this *Ramah* is not certainly known, it was probably the city of the same name which comes into the prophet's later life (cf. 9^4, 10^2, &c.); this seems to have lain to the north of Benjamin.

3. *Shiloh.* See on 1 Kings 14^2.

[1] See *Camb. Anct. Hist.* ii, p. 290.

5. *a double portion.* This is not the meaning of the Heb. which is obscure. LXX reads *a single portion, because she had no child, yet, &c.*

9. *Eli.* The place of *Eli* in the ecclesiastical history of Israel is a very difficult question. Before the time of Solomon his house evidently fulfilled priestly functions (1 Kings 2²⁷), but he is omitted from the lists in 1 Chron. 6¹⁻¹⁵. The name of *Eli*, although it is Semitic, does not appear to be Israelite.

11. *no razor.* Cf. Samson (Judges 13⁵).

14. Drunkenness was no uncommon feature of religious festivals (cf. Judges 9²⁷; Amos 2⁸; Isa. 28⁷).

16. *daughter of Belial.* The expression *son of Belial* is common, the phrase used here does not occur elsewhere; its general meaning is *daughter of worthlessness*, 'a bad lot' in common speech.

20. *Samuel.* The name means on the face of it *Name of God*,[1] it has no connexion beyond a slight similarity of sound with *asked*: this latter word is the meaning of Saul.

(*f*) *The Call of Samuel* (1 Sam. 3).

The story of Samuel's call is one of the best known in O.T. Its great interest lies in the fact that God chose a child to be the medium of His revelation of Himself. When all seemed dark and hopeless in Israel, a weak old man at the head of affairs, his worthless sons defrauding and oppressing the people, and no vision or direction from Jahveh, suddenly the rumour spread that once more the divine head of the nation had appeared at Shiloh.

One night as Samuel was lying down to sleep in the house of God a voice came to him. Not knowing as yet anything of Jahveh the child thought that his master needed something and ran to him. He was told to go back to bed. Three times the same thing happened, and then Eli perceived that there was something in it beyond his comprehension, that the hand of God was working out His purposes. The next time Samuel having replied as he had been bidden received a message of condemnation and punishment for Eli and his house. In the morning the old priest got from his little servant, who desired to shield his master from the evil tidings, the full account of what had been said: it was accepted with true Oriental fortitude, it was God's will let it be done.

The story throws a strong light on the opinion which was held of Samuel, and the tradition of the bad times under Eli and his

---

[1] Those who are interested in the subject may refer to Driver, *Notes on the Heb. Text of Sam.*, p. 19, for other suggestions; Driver's conclusion is that the above meaning is the obvious one on every ground.

sons; though it may have been exaggerated by a rival priesthood —the sons of Zadok—part of its value lies in the revelation which it gives of the circumstances which later made a kingship inevitable.

III. 1. *no open vision.* Cf. 28[6]. The word rendered *open* in R.V. means literally *spread abroad* and a better translation would be the mg. *frequent.*

3. *in the temple.* To the later Israelites the presence of a small temple servant, one who was an Ephraimite and not a Levite by birth, in the place where the ark was must have been something of a shock. By later regulations the ark was kept in the Holy of Holies and no one was allowed to go near it save the High Priest, and he only on one day in the year (Heb. 9[7]: cf. Exod. 30[10]).

10. *came and stood.* A very primitive conception of the deity underlies this statement, God is thought of as acting as a man would need to do.

10–18. These verses are very like 2[27 ff.]

20. *Dan to Beer-sheba.* The extreme northern and southern limits of the land, a distance of about 140 miles. The phrase was proverbial (cf. Judges 20[1]).

(*g*) *The loss of the Ark* (1 Sam. 4[1-11]).

Israel being defeated in an encounter with the Philistines somewhere near Lydda decides to renew the battle, but before doing so to send for the ark from its home at Shiloh. On the arrival of this talisman, with its guardians the two sons of Eli, Hophni and Phineas, a great shout of joy and confidence went up from the camp. The Philistines at first alarmed by the news soon recover their courage, and in the subsequent fighting the Israelites are once more defeated, this time so decisively that the army breaks up in panic and even the ark is left to the victors. The two sons of Eli—like many since their day—do what they can to atone for worthless lives by dying nobly in defence of their charge.

IV. 1. *Eben-ezer.* This place ought to be distinguished from that in 7[12] which was evidently many miles to the south. The meaning of the name is *stone of help* but the exact site of the place is lost.

Aphek, is probably the place of the same name mentioned in Joshua 12[18]. It lay somewhere near to Lydda in the plain of Sharon, and was the scene of a battle between the Syrians and Israel in later times (1 Kings 20[26]).

4. *cherubim.* Cf. Gen. 3[24]; Isa. 6[2]; Ps. 18[10].

2546·8   M

6. *Hebrews.* This name is only applied to the Israelites by foreigners. Strictly speaking it belonged to other tribes as well, to all in fact who came over the river with Abram.

8. *in the wilderness.* There is here either a different tradition or an error on the part of the writer, the Egyptians were not plagued there.

(h) *The Ark in the hands of the Philistines* (1 Sam. 5).

The victorious Philistines carry away their trophy to place it in the temple of their god.[1] The first resting place of the ark was at Ashdod where was a famous shrine of Dagon. But the power of the Israelite trophy was evidently too great for him since he was found prostrate before it on the first morning after its arrival, and on being restored to his position was a second time found lying on the ground; this time his prostration had been made so violently that great damage had been done to him. At the same time a severe plague broke out in Ashdod which was taken to be a sign of the wonder-working powers of the deity who had plagued the Egyptians. After consultation with the lords of the Philistines it was decided to see if a change of scene might not gratify the Israelite palladium, and so it was taken to Gath; but still the plague followed it; and so it happened at Ekron where the people from the first moment of its coming anticipated the very worst.

It seems probable that some kind of plague was carried from place to place by the bearers of the ark; a plague which still worked even when the ark was restored to Israel (see on 6[19]).

V. **1.** *Ashdod*, is the modern *Esdud* which lies on the coast about thirty miles west of Jerusalem. The temple there existed down to the time of the Maccabees (1 Macc. 10[84]).

2. *Dagon.* See on Judges 16[23].

3. *they of Ashdod.* The priests (v. 5) are not specifically mentioned.

4. The text of this verse is difficult; *the stump* which appears in R.V. is supplied from the versions.

5. The sacredness of thresholds is a widespread belief (see on Exod. 12[22], and cf. Zeph. 1[8 f.]).

6. *tumours.* Driver favours the rendering of mg. *plague-boils.*

8. *Gath* is possibly the modern *Tell es-Ṣafi* which lies about ten

---

[1] Just as Mesha, king of Moab, did many years later: see Moabite Stone, lines 12 f., 17 f., where various captured objects are 'dragged before Chemosh' (Appendix, p. 238).

Harvest in the East. Above, cutting; below, carrying

miles east of Ashdod and therefore nearer to Israelite territory. The village was the site of Blanchegarde the famous castle of the Crusaders.[1]

10. *Ekron* is likewise of uncertain identification though many scholars find its site at *'Akir* twelve miles north-west of Beth-shemesh and about the same distance due north of Gath. A theory has recently been advanced which would equate it with *Dhikerin* a few miles south-west of Gath: see Macalister, *Schweich Lectures*, pp. 74 f.

(i) *The return of the Ark* (1 Sam. 6–7[1]).

After seven months of plague the Philistines call together their ecclesiastical advisers and at their suggestion, since all realized at length the superior power of the ark of the God of Israel, determine to send it back, together with rich offerings. This they hope will have the effect of staying the pestilence from which their land is suffering.

The gifts which they choose are five golden models of the boil which has afflicted them, and five golden mice, for it seems that the land of the Philistines as well as their persons had also been afflicted by a plague (see farther on 6[1]). To convey the ark two cows are chosen, and, in order to test the real holiness and power of Jahveh, they are taken from their calves and set on their way by themselves. Forgetting the call of nature the animals turn away from their calves and convey the ark straight to its own land. Then the Philistines knew without any doubt that it was Jahveh who had been oppressing them.

The Israelite city which received the ark was Beth-shemesh. The men of the city were busily engaged in cutting their wheat, for it was the time of harvest, when suddenly they looked up, and to their amazement saw the treasured symbol and resting-place of their God coming back to its own land. The cattle are slain and offered up as a sacrifice, and there is great joy in all hearts. Suddenly, however, a fierce epidemic breaks out and many of the citizens die from its effects. The pious attribute this disaster to the profane curiosity which had led some to look into the sacred object, and like the men of Ashdod they persuade their neighbours to take over from them the dangerous privilege of being the guardians of such a holy thing. The men of Kiriath-jearim ac-

[1] The site now favoured is *'Arak el-menshiyeh*: see S. A. Cook, *Expos. Times*, 1926, p. 488.

cordingly come down and convey the ark to the house of Abinadab
and no ill effects follow; the plague had spent its force.

It is a remarkable fact that when David attempted to bring up
the ark to Jerusalem difficulties were also experienced and for
a time its journey was delayed (2 Sam. 6).

VI. **1**. At the end of the verse LXX adds *And their land swarmed
with mice* (cf. Exod. 7[28]).

2. *priests and diviners*. We know very little of the ecclesiastical
organization of the Philistines. Diviners were not allowed in Israel
(Deut. 18[10]: where see Driver's note in I.C.C.).

3. *guilt offering*. Though this term was later used of one of the
Jewish sacrifices, here as in 2 Kings 12[16] it means merely a compensation for any discomfort or loss which may have been sustained.

4. Some kind of sympathetic magic seems to lie behind the pre-
sentation of these objects. Peake refers to Wundt, *Elements of Folk
Psychology*, pp. 438 ff., where examples are given of sufferers carrying to a sanctuary figures of those parts of the body in which they are
afflicted. The mice probably had much to do with the spread of the
plague, though this fact would not of course be known in that age.

12. *Beth-shemesh* is the modern *'Ain Shems*, it lies fourteen miles
west of Jerusalem.

14. *a great stone*. This may have been already a sacred stone or
merely a convenient form of altar.

15. This verse represents a later point of view and is really supplementary to v. 14 since it repeats the sacrifices. The presence of
Levites was necessary for genuine sacrifices.

20. *the LORD*. It is important to notice that Jahveh and the ark
are practically identified.

21. *Kiriath-jearim*, is perhaps *Qaryet el-'Enab* which lies some ten
miles north-east of Beth-shemesh.

come down. *Qaryet el-'Enab* is much higher than *'Ain-Shems* =
Beth-shemesh.

PART III

In this part of the history the rise of the Hebrew monarchy is recorded, an event which later generations—as they tried to estimate its effect upon the religious and political life of the people—regarded with very different feelings. To some the monarchy had been a mistake and even a curse, to others it was a divine institution. These different feelings are reflected in the different accounts which have come down to us.

The sources from which our knowledge is derived are parts of the books of Samuel and Kings. The following are the sections:

(1) The Rise and Decline of Saul.
(2) The Reign of David.
(3) The Reign of Solomon.

§ 1. THE RISE AND DECLINE OF SAUL

In 1 Sam. 8 there is preserved a dramatic account of Israel's demand for a king. This story is inconsistent with 1 Sam. 9–10^{16} since it represents Samuel as opposed to the change, and even Jahveh Himself as offended. There is in this section a continuance of the double strand of narrative which was noticed above. One strand favours the monarchy; the other, and later, regards it as a misfortune; one depicts Saul as a brave and religious man; the other as rebelling against the commands of God delivered by Samuel, and as jealous and vindictive by nature.

The early, popular opinion of Israel's first monarch is preserved in the poem of 2 Sam. 1$^{17\,ff.}$

(a) The choice of Saul (1 Sam. 9–10^{16}).

Saul, a young Benjamite, goes in search of his father's asses. Failing to find them, at the suggestion of the servant who accompanied him, he paid a visit to Samuel at Ramah. The prophet recognizes in the handsome young giant the future king of Israel, and taking Saul to the sacrificial feast to which he is going, gives to him the place of honour. Saul stays the night with Samuel, and next day is secretly anointed by him. His anointing is followed by a change of heart, and on his encountering a band of prophets, as Samuel had foretold, he joins in their frantic prophesyings.

IX. **1.** *mighty man of valour*: better man of substance.

2. *Saul*: Heb. *Sha'ul=asked* (of God): cf. 1^{20}.

4. *Shalishah* (cf. 2 Kings 4^{42}) . . . *Shaalim*: unknown places.

5. *Zuph*: perhaps the name of a person, but see Driver on 1^1.

8. *fourth part of a shekel of silver*: a trifling sum, about 8*d*., though worth more in those days.

9. *Prophet* . . . *Seer.* An explanatory note which would be better after v. 11.

12. *high place*: a sanctuary: see p. 46.

14. *within the city*: better *gate* by a slight change in Hebrew: cf. v. 18.

16. *the Philistines.* The great deliverance of 7^{13} is evidently not known to the writer.

17. Cf. 16^{12}.

24. *that which was upon it*: read *the fat tail*; this is still a choice portion in the East, its taste resembles that of marrow.

25 f. *he communed . . . early*: read with mg. (=LXX) *They spread a couch for Saul . . . and he lay down.*

X. **2.** *Rachel's sepulchre.* Said to be at Ephrath (=Bethlehem according to gloss on Gen. 35^{19}, 48^7), but near to Ramah according to Jer. 31^{15}, where see my note in West. Comm.

Zelzah: unknown.

3. *oak of Tabor*: or terebinth; the site, which is unknown, must not be confused with Mount Tabor.

to God: i.e. to the sanctuary.

5. *the hill*: Heb. *Gibeah*: cf. 13^3.

the Philistines: see on 9^{16}.

7. *occasion*: see $11^{4\ \mathrm{ff.}}$

8. A gloss to connect with $13^{7b\ \mathrm{ff.}}$

10. Cf. Samson (Judges 14^6, &c.).

he prophesied: i.e. behaved like a modern dervish.

11. *Is Saul, &c.*: cf. 19^{24}.

12. *who is their father?* Prophetic inspiration is not hereditary and may come upon any one.

14. *Saul's uncle*: cf. 9^3, &c., *father*.

(*b*) *Saul's opportunity* (1 Sam. 11).

Soon after Saul's anointing the occasion arises upon which he is able to take the lead in Israel. Jabesh-gilead, being threatened by Nahash the Ammonite, sends messengers through Israel; these come to Gibeah, and Saul, who is apparently unknown to them, suddenly comes forward and takes control of the situation. He gathers an army, and attacking the unsuspecting Ammonites, puts them to flight.

XI. 1. *Then Nahash*. The last sentence of 10²⁷ should be joined on, and the whole translated, with LXX, *And it happened about a month later that Nahash, &c.*

Jabesh-gilead: see Judges 21⁸.

2. *right eyes*. The left eye was hidden by the shield, a one-eyed man would therefore be useless as a warrior.

7. Cf. Judges 19²⁹.

8. *Bezek*. Now *Khirbet Ibrik* on the west of Jordan, a convenient point from which to attack Nahash.

11. *the morning watch*. The last of the three watches into which the Hebrews divided the night (cf. Judges 7¹⁹).

12–14. An editorial insertion to reconcile the coronation of v. 15 with that already narrated, from another source, in 10¹⁷ ᶠᶠ·

15. *peace offerings*: better *thank offerings*. The flesh was eaten in part by the worshippers.

(c) *Jonathan's Exploit and its sequel* (1 Sam. 14).

Jonathan and his armourbearer attack a post of the Philistines and throw them into confusion; an earthquake increases their panic. Saul and the Israelites, taking advantage of the confusion, attack them and gain a decisive victory pursuing the fugitives as far as Aijalon. During the pursuit Saul had put a 'taboo' on all food, Jonathan in ignorance taking a little honey breaks it. The exhausted people fly upon the cattle and eat them without draining off the blood, a serious offence against what was thought to be divine law. Saul next contemplated attacking the Philistines by night, but, being unable to obtain any response from the oracle, he concludes that in some way Jahveh has been offended. An inquisition by lot reveals Jonathan as the unwitting cause, and Saul is only prevented from putting him to death by the remonstrances of the people.

XIV. 2. *Gibeah*: read Geba.

Migron: site unknown.

4. *Bozez . . . Seneh*: the meaning of the former name is unknown, the latter perhaps=*thorny*. The exact position of these two crags is uncertain (see Driver, *Notes on Heb. Text of Sam.*², p. 106, with sketch-map).

11. *hid themselves*. Cf. 13⁶. There still exists in Palestine, especially

east of the Jordan, a number of underground cities. One at *Beit Jibrin* has been described as follows: 'Small holes in the hill-side, difficult to discover, give admission to extensive labyrinths of passages and chambers.' Macalister, *Century of Excav. in Pal.*, p. 217.

14. *half a furrow*: about 12 yards.

15. *an exceeding great trembling*: Heb. *trembling of God*: cf. panic, from the god Pan.

18. *the ark*: read with LXX *ephod*.

23. *Beth-aven.* This place is about four miles north-west of Michmash, and would probably lie on the route to Aijalon (v. 31). Lucian reads Beth-horon, which some prefer.

24. The object of this 'taboo' was probably to retain the divine favour (cf. vv. 37 ff.), not to save precious time.

27. *his eyes were enlightened*: i.e. he was refreshed (cf. Ps. 13⁴, 19⁹).

29. *hath troubled.* A very strong word (cf. Joshua 7²⁵; Judges 11³⁵; 1 Kings 18¹⁷ ᶠ·).

31. The distance was more than twenty miles. *Aijalon* is the modern *Yalō* (cf. Joshua 10).

32. *with the blood.* A custom repulsive to the Hebrews (Gen. 9⁴; Lev. 17–26; Ezek. 33²⁵, &c.).

35. *the first altar*: this implies that he made others afterwards; the writer regards Saul as particular about religious ordinances.

37. Cf. 28⁶.

38 ff. Cf. Joshua 7¹⁶ ᶠᶠ·

41. *Shew the right* (Heb. *Thummim*). LXX has evidently preserved the true text: *Why hast thou not answered thy servant this day? If this iniquity be in me or in Jonathan my son Jehovah God of Israel, give Urim; but if it be in thy people Israel, give Thummim.*

43. *lo, I must die.* Hebrew gives no idea of shrinking from this fate, but a readiness to meet it.

47–51. These verses seem to be an editorial summary of Saul's reign.

(d) The Rejection of Saul (1 Sam. 15).

In response to the divine command, delivered through the mouth of Samuel, Saul gathers the people together in order to destroy Amalek and its possessions. The friendly Kenites having been got out of the way the whole tribe is annihilated, only Agag the king and the choicest cattle being spared. This last act was a breach of the instructions given to Saul, and Jahveh declares to Samuel that such disobedience makes Him repent His choice of

Saul. Samuel goes to Saul and, after reproving him, slays Agag with his own hands. The prophet and the king then part in sorrow, and so far as we know (19[23] is late and unreliable) they did not meet again.

XV. 2. *which Amalek did.* Exod. 17[8-16].

3. Amalek and all its possessions is to be 'devoted' or 'banned'.

4. *Telaim*: the same place probably as Telem in South Judah (Joshua 15[24]). The numbers seem greatly exaggerated.

5. *the city.* As the Amalekites were nomads this must not be taken to mean a fortified place: perhaps it was a tribal sanctuary.

6. *the Kenites.* See Judges 1[16].

7. *Havilah . . . Shur.* Wellhausen thinks the phrase is borrowed from Gen. 25[18]. *Havilah* is probably in north-east Arabia; for *Shur*, see Exod. 15[22].

11. *wroth*: cf. Jonah 4[1].

12. *Carmel*: now *el-Kurmul*, seven miles south of Hebron, not to be confused with Mount Carmel.

a monument: i.e. to his victory: cf. 2 Sam. 18[18].

15. *to sacrifice.* The people would eat of these sacrifices, hence they had not destroyed the cattle.

22 f. These verses form a short oracular poem in the Hebrew. The teaching is that of the pre-exilic prophets, that obedience is greater than sacrifice (cf. Amos 5[21ff.]; Hos. 6[6]; Mic. 6[6ff.], &c.).

23. *witchcraft*: Exod. 22[18]; Deut. 18[10].

teraphim: some kind of image (Gen. 31[19]; 1 Sam. 19[13]); unfavourably regarded here, Gen. 35[2ff.] (E), and 2 Kings 23[24]; but cf. Hos. 3[4].

28. *hath rent*: cf. 1 Kings 11[29ff.]

29. *Strength*: better with mg. *Glory.*

repent: cf. Num. 23[19]; Jer. 18[8].

32. *delicately*: LXX *tremblingly.*

33. Agag as part of the banned nation was slain before God's altar. The story seems to come from a time when the hatred of foreigners was intense.

(e) The Choice of Saul's successor (1 Sam. 16).

The account of the anointing of David (1–13) is probably late, but the story of his first meeting with Saul (14–23) seems earlier than the account in the following chapter. Samuel is commanded to forget his grief for Saul and to go to Bethlehem and there anoint a son of Jesse in his place. After some delay David the youngest is chosen. Saul, meanwhile, had become subject to

attacks of some obscure mental disease. On his servants recom-
mending music as a remedy David is brought to him. The king is
instantly drawn to him and attaches him to his person.

XVI. 4. *Comest thou peaceably?* To this writer Samuel is still the
judge and lawgiver.

11. With David's absence cf. that of Saul (10²²).

David and his harp. A miniature from the Ormesby Psalter.
Fourteenth century

13. *David*: his name is suddenly introduced. No one else bears it
in O. T., but it seems to have been the name of a deity east of Jordan:
see the Moabite stone, l. 12, Davdoh (App. p. 238).

14. *evil spirit*: cf. 1 Kings 22²³; some kind of demon possession is
intended.

16. Music brought inspiration to Elisha (2 Kings 3¹⁵).

19. *with the sheep*: cf. v. 11, 17¹⁵, &c.

20. *an ass . . . with bread*: Heb. is peculiar and *ass* is probably
a corruption of some number; read *five (or ten) loaves of bread*.

22. *stand before*: i. e. attend upon.

(*f*) *David and Goliath* (1 Sam. 17–18⁵).

This story may have arisen around the camp-fire, as men in later ages discussed the national hero; it cannot be reconciled with 16¹⁴⁻²³. Large parts of the present narrative are omitted from some MSS. of LXX perhaps on account of this inconsistency: viz. 17¹²⁻³¹, ⁴¹, ⁵⁰, ⁵⁵⁻⁸, 18¹⁻⁵. It may be, however, that these parts are later additions to an originally simpler story; but even then 17³³, ³⁸, ⁴⁰, ⁴² do not suit the armour-bearer of Saul. According to another tradition Goliath was slain by Elhanan (2 Sam. 21¹⁹).

The narrative as it stands may be summarized as follows. The Israelite and Philistine armies being encamped opposite one another, the former are dismayed by the challenge to single combat issued by a gigantic Philistine. David is sent to the camp with food for his brothers and hearing the challenge offers to meet Goliath. Rejecting the arms of Saul he goes forth to meet his enemy with a sling and stones and succeeds in slaying him, finally cutting off his head with his own sword. He is then brought back and formally introduced to the king. Jonathan, Saul's son, is strongly drawn to the heroic shepherd boy and they become sworn friends.

XVII. **1.** *Socoh*: probably modern *esh-Shuweikeh*, fourteen miles west of Bethlehem.

Azekah: the site is probably *Tell Zakariya*. It was an important fortress (Jer. 34⁷).

Ephes-dammim: site unknown.

2. *vale of Elah*: an important strategic position, the key to other valleys, now the *Wady es-Sunt*.

4. The giants amongst the Philistines may have been descended from the aboriginal inhabitants (cf. Macalister, *The Philistines*, pp. 60 f.). The height of Goliath was 9 ft. 6 in.

5 ff. The description of Goliath's armour shows that it was very similar to that of Hector (*Iliad*, vi. 318 ff.). Were both sets made by Phoenician smiths? Notice that the offensive weapons are of iron, the defensive of bronze.

9. The appeal to single combat was frequent in Greek and Roman history, but not so common amongst the Semites.[1]

13. The names agree with 16⁶ ᶠᶠ.

---

[1] Challenges to single combat were not, however, unknown to the Semites. The custom was kept up for centuries by the Arabs: see Sell, *Battles of 'Badr and of Uhud*, pp. 23 f., 53.

20 ff. The description of David's holiday is very vivid.

28. The feelings of the eldest brother are easy to understand.

37. The living faith of David's answer is the really valuable part of the story.

39. Inconsistent with 16[18].

43 ff. Such taunts help to point the moral.

51. The use of Goliath's own sword finds a parallel in the story of Sinuhe referred to above (p. 80), for that hero dispatches an opponent with his own battle-axe.

52. *Gai*: read *Gath* with LXX. It lay some ten miles west of Socoh whilst *Ekron* was sixteen miles to north-west.

54. *Jerusalem*: a careless anachronism; see 2 Sam. 5[6-9].

tent: this suggests the soldier, not the shepherd boy on a visit to the army.

55. Neither Abner nor Saul knows who David is.

XVIII. **2.** Cf. 16[22].

4. The change of clothes was part of the covenant: see Robertson Smith, *Religion of the Semites*[2], p. 335.

(g) *Saul's jealousy* (1 Sam. 18[6-9, 20-28], 19[1-17]).

On the return from battle the women who come out to meet the victors place David above Saul. The king's jealousy is aroused, and he makes various attempts on David's life; amongst other means employing his daughter Michal as a bait to lure David to destruction. Jonathan succeeded in temporarily patching up the quarrel, but Saul's jealousy is once more aroused and David only escapes by the resourcefulness of his wife. The passages selected are all ancient though probably not from the same source. Important MSS. of LXX omit 18[10 f., 17-19, 29 -30].

XVIII. **6.** Cf. 2 Sam. 6[5]; Jer. 30[19].

21. *the hand of the Philistines.* Cf. v. 17.

25. *dowry*: better *purchase price*, the woman was bought from her father, as amongst the Greeks (*Iliad*, xvi. 178; *Odyssey*, xxi. 160 ff.).

27. *two hundred*: read *one hundred* with LXX and 2 Sam. 3[14].

XIX. **9 f.** Cf. 18[10 f.]

11. *in the morning*: when he came out.

12. See on Joshua 2[15].

13. *teraphim*: see 15[23].

pillow . . . clothes: what exactly was done is not quite clear.

(*h*) *David and Jonathan* (1 Sam. 20$^{1-10,\ 18-39}$).

The narrative in this chapter, except certain editorial additions, is early, though it is not possible to say in what context it should appear.

Jonathan agrees to test his father's feelings towards David; the latter is to absent himself from the king's table on the new moon, and Saul's comments on his conduct will reveal his attitude. Saul inquires the reason for David's absence, and being told by Jonathan that he has been compelled to attend a family sacrifice at Bethlehem, the king in an outburst of rage casts his spear at his own son. Jonathan leaves the banquet in anger and next day manages to let David know, by a pre-arranged sign, that his life is in danger and that he ought to fly.

XX. **1.** The first part of the verse is editorial.

2. *it is not so.* No knowledge is shown of 19$^{1\,ff.}$

5. *new moon*: cf. 2 Kings 4^{23}; Amos 8^5.

11–17 seems to be inserted from another source; notice that Jonathan is here the suppliant.

19. *the stone Ezel*: read with LXX *yonder heap of stones.*

20 ff. The proposed sign is simple and not likely to betray either party.

25. *stood up*: this hardly makes sense, LXX and Lucian make it clear that Jonathan was opposite to his father.

26. *not clean*: only those who were ceremonially 'clean' could attend a sacrificial meal.

31. *shall surely die*: lit. *is a son of death,* a graphic phrase.

33. Cf. 18^{11}, 19^{10}.

40–42. This seems to be an addition. If an interview had been possible there would have been no need for the sign.

(*i*) *David's visit to Nob* (1 Sam. 21$^{1-9}$, 22$^{6-23}$).

David's flight may have been the immediate sequel to his escape from Saul's messengers (19^{12}). He arrived at Nob where he was received by Ahimelech the priest. Quieting Ahimelech's suspicions on account of his being alone, David obtained from him holy bread and the sword of Goliath. Unfortunately for the priests the chief of Saul's herdsmen, an Edomite named Doeg witnessed the whole matter. He reported the priest's conduct to Saul and was commanded by him to slay the whole body of the priests of Nob—Saul's other servants having refused to do so—

and afterwards he destroyed their city and all that belonged to them.

XXI. 1. *Nob*: about one mile north of Jerusalem and not far from Anathoth (Isa. 10³²).

Ahimelech: called Abiathar in Mark 2²⁶ where this incident is referred to; Abiathar was really his son (22²⁰).

trembling: David's condition—he had probably been in hiding for some time and was evidently short of food—alarmed the priest.

4. Warriors were regarded as engaged on a sacred task: see Robertson Smith, *Religion of the Semites²*, p. 455.

6. *shewbread*: lit. *bread of the Presence*, no doubt regarded originally as food for the deity.

7. *detained*: either because he was unclean and waiting to enter the sanctuary (so Driver: cf. Jer. 36⁵ with my note); or because he was actually in the sanctuary undergoing purificatory rites (P.C.).

chiefest of the herdmen: better *mightiest of the runners*; cf. 22¹⁷f.

9. The author of this narrative knew of David as the slayer of Goliath (cf. p. 172 above).

ephod: not here a garment (cf. 22¹⁸).

XXII. 6. *in Ramah*: read with LXX *in the high-place*; this involves a slight change in the Hebrew but is preferable to mg. *in the height*.

8. *conspired*: cf. v. 13; suspicion of conspiracies is a mark of certain types of mental disease.

14. Ahimelech was ignorant, or professed to be so, of any quarrel between Saul and his son-in-law.

15. *to inquire of God*: Ahimelech picked out the untrue part of the accusation, and denied that.

(j) David spares Saul's life (1 Sam. 26).

Two stories are told of David's clemency to Saul, the one contained in this chapter which is perhaps more primitive in form, and one in 24 located at Engedi. Both are probably based on the same incident.

Saul hears that David is in hiding in the wilderness of Ziph, and having collected a comparatively large body of men he tries to track him down. David, however, accompanied by Abishai, succeeds in entering Saul's camp. They make their way to the place where the king lies asleep and Abishai is with difficulty restrained from killing him. Taking Saul's spear and the cruse of water which was near his head they depart without injuring any one. Standing on a neighbouring hillside David taunts Abner with the carelessness of his guard. Saul recognizes David, and, realizing his own narrow escape, in response to David's pleas gives up his pursuit.

XXVI. 1. *Hachilah*: usually identified with a ridge five and a half miles east of Ziph, now called *Dahr el-Kōlā*.

2. *the wilderness of Ziph*: a plateau south-east of Hebron; it is partly covered with scrub and contains many caves.

5. *the place of the wagons*: the camp was arranged like a Boer laager.

6. *the Hittite*: see p. 16, above.

Zeruiah: David's sister according to 1 Chron. 2^{16}; the unusual mention (here and elsewhere) of the mother rather than the father is, however, suspicious.   It may be a relic of matriarchy.

8 f. Cf. $24^{4f.}$

12. *a deep sleep*: cf. Gen. 2^{21}.

19. *the LORD*: i. e. by the evil spirit which He had sent upon him.

an offering: this sacrifice was thought to be sufficient to stop the divine anger.

Go, serve other gods: Jahveh could only be worshipped in His own land (cf. 2 Kings 5^{17}).

20. *a flea*: read with LXX *my life*.

a partridge: cf. 24^{14}.

(k) David at Gath (1 Sam. 21^{10-15}, 27).

In 21^{10-15} David is described as going to Gath from Nob. This passage is almost certainly a variant account of the present flight; it is of special interest, however, because it represents David as pretending to be mad.

David in despair of keeping out of Saul's hands flies to the Philistines, and is received by Achish, king of Gath. The latter, at his request, gives him Ziklag as a dwelling-place for himself and his men. From Ziklag David makes continual raids upon the Amalekites and other tribes to the south, this policy was calculated to gain for him the favour of the men of Judah; and as he represented to Achish that he was raiding his own countrymen the king also was satisfied.

XXI. 10. *king of Gath*: Achish[1] may have been the chief of the Philistine lords, or possibly he is called *king* by mistake. In later history Gath disappears, the leading city being Ashdod.

---

[1] Achish in LXX is 'Αγχους, and, as Hitzig pointed out, the name is no doubt the same as the Trojan Anchises.

XXVII. 5. David probably found it difficult to live in close relations with the Philistines.

6. *Ziklag*: site uncertain, possibly *Zuḥēlīgeh*, twenty-two miles south-west of Gath. According to the Egyptian inscriptions the Zakkala were a tribe in alliance with the Purasati or Pulesati (=Philistines), their name may be preserved in Ziklag.

8. *the Geshurites*: not Geshur east of Jordan.

the Girzites: perhaps Gizrites, i.e. the people of Gezer (cf. 1 Kings 9¹⁶).

the Amalekites: see Exod. 17⁸ᶠᶠ·

of old: better *from Telam* (see 15⁴).

Shur: see 17⁷.

10. Truthfulness was not a Hebrew virtue (cf. Gen. 20², 27²⁴, 37³², &c.).

Jerahmeelites: a tribe incorporated into Judah.

12. *for ever*: the other Philistine lords were wiser (29¹⁻⁴).

(*l*) *The witch of En-dor* (1 Sam. 28³⁻²⁵).

This passage, the date and exact context of which are uncertain, is interesting in view of the cult of Spiritualism, and as an illustration of the superstition of the natural man.

After the death of Samuel the Philistines again invade Israel. Saul failing to get advice by means of dreams, or oracles, or through his prophets, determines to consult a witch or 'medium'. He goes in disguise to En-dor and there takes part in a 'seance'; the medium professes to bring up Samuel who holds a conversation with the king foretelling nothing but disaster. Saul is so overcome that for a time he refuses to take food, but is at last persuaded to do so.

XXVIII. 4. *Shunem*. Now *Sōlem*, three and a half miles north of Jezreel. The probable position of the Midianites in Judges 7¹.

Gilboa. Now *Jebel Fuqūʻa*, a ridge five to twelve miles south and south-east of Shunem.

6. *Urim*: see 14⁴¹.

7. *En-dor*. Now *Endūr*, three and a half miles north-east of Shunem and therefore behind the Philistine lines.

12. *the woman saw*: notice that Saul sees nothing.

13. *a god*: better *gods*, i.e. supernatural beings.

14. *a robe*: cf. 15²⁷, not a very convincing piece of evidence, however.

15. *Samuel said*: perhaps the witch took the part by ventriloquism.

16 ff. If the speech put into the mouth of Samuel was actually delivered by the witch, it was an opportunity for her to obtain revenge on the persecutor (28⁹).

19. *with me*: cf. Caesar's appearance to Brutus in *Julius Caesar*, Act IV, Sc. 3. LXX reads *with thee be fallen*.

(m) The Death of Saul (1 Sam. 31, 2 Sam. 1¹⁻¹⁶).

The two accounts of Saul's death differ only in detail; in both he is represented as so exhausted as to be unable to escape from his enemies. In one account after vainly commanding his armour-bearer to slay him he falls on his own sword (1 Sam. 31⁴), in the other a similar request to an Amalekite is carried out. The story of the Amalekite may have been invented by himself in order to gain the favour of David; if so it was a ghastly failure, and led to the narrator's own death (2 Sam. 1¹⁶). After the battle the Philistines discovered the bodies of Saul and his three sons; they cut off the head of the king and sent it round their cities, the body they fastened to the wall of Beth-shan. The blackness and horror of Saul's end is relieved by one ray of light—the gratitude of the men of Jabesh-gilead, who made a long night march and rescued the body of their benefactor from shameful exposure.

XXXI. **4.** *abuse me*: cf. Judges 16²⁵.

10. *his armour*: cf. 21⁹.

the house of the Ashtaroth: the temple of Astarte at Ashkelon mentioned in Herodotus, i. 105.

Beth-shan:[1] now *Beisān*, the Greek Scythopolis, a fortress commanding the east entrance to the valley of Jezreel.

11. Cf. 11¹ ᶠᶠ·

12. *all night*: the distance is about ten miles as the crow flies.

burnt them: cremation was not a Hebrew custom; but there may have been the desire to save the bodies from further disgrace, or even some vague religious intention (see Robertson Smith, *Religion of the Semites*², p. 373).

14. *the LORD'S anointed*: cf. 1 Sam. 24⁶, 26¹¹.

2 Sam. I. **1, 2 ff.** Described in 1 Sam. 30. Cf. 1 Sam. 4¹² ᶠᶠ·

(n) David's Lament (2 Sam. 1¹⁷⁻²⁷).

This exquisite poem, which formed part of the collection known as the Book of Jashar (see p. 131), is without doubt the work of

---

[1] Very extensive archaeological operations are being carried on at this site on behalf of the University Museum of Philadelphia.

David himself. After desiring that the tidings of Israel's defeat might not be published in the Philistine towns, he goes on to celebrate the valour of Saul and Jonathan, and calls on the women of Israel to weep for them. The poem ends with a special lament over Jonathan and an expression of the writer's own personal sorrow. Driver points out 'that no *religious* thought of any kind appears in the poem: the feeling expressed by it is purely *human*'.

I. **18.** *the bow*: R.V. supplies *the song of*; the text seems corrupt.

21. *not anointed*: shields were oiled to keep them in good condition: cf. Isa. 21^5; Virgil, *Aeneid*. vii. 626.

23. *eagles*: the griffon-vulture is the bird really meant.

§ 2. THE REIGN OF DAVID

The authorities for the reign of David are excellent, and for the most part seem to be based on contemporary sources. One continuous narrative covers the whole reign and there is thus an absence of that contradiction which makes the story of Saul so complicated. Chapters 7 and 8, however, are Deuteronomic in character, and seem to be insertions; whilst 21–24 form an appendix of which 21, 23$^{8\text{-}39}$, and 24 are of an early date.

The importance of these narratives can hardly be exaggerated since they give unique insight into the religious and social conditions of the early monarchy.

(a) David at Hebron (2 Sam. 2).

The death of Saul was followed by the setting up of two rival kingdoms in Israel. David, in response to a divine direction, seized Hebron and was made king by the men of Judah. Presumably he was still a Philistine vassal. The other kingdom had its headquarters at Mahanaim beyond Jordan, and its nominal head was Ish-bosheth, the son of Saul; the real power, however, was in the hands of Abner, the captain of the host.

Relations between the two kingdoms were not friendly, and a battle was fought at Gibeon. Fighting began by a contest between twelve men from each side:[1] this was followed by a general engagement in which the party of David was victorious. During the subsequent pursuit Asahel, the brother of Joab the captain of

[1] The scene is very suggestive of the 'Boxer Vase' found at Hagia Triada in Crete: see illustration p. 157 above and Hall, *Anct. Hist. of Near East*, p. 418.

David's army, was slain by Abner. After inflicting many losses on Benjamin, the men of Judah were recalled and the two armies marched away into the night.

II. 1. *Hebron*: see p. 112.

5. David's action was no doubt partly due to the recognition of the nobility of their conduct, partly a matter of policy (cf. 1 Sam. 30²⁶).

8. *Ish-bosheth*: his name was really Esh-baal, *bosheth* (=*abomination*) being substituted for *baal*, when the latter term was no longer applied to Jahveh: cf. 3²⁰.

Mahanaim: east of Jordan, an unknown site on the border of Gad and Manasseh.

9. *Ashurites*: perhaps Asherites.

all Israel: that is, leaving out Judah.

10*a*. An editorial note of doubtful value.

12. *Gibeon*. See on Joshua 9³.

pool. Cf. Jer. 41¹². There are still at *El-jib* 'the remains of an open reservoir or tank, into which the surplus waters flow'. Enc. Bib. col. 1719.

13. *Joab*: the famous captain of David's host.

14. The challenge comes from Abner.

16. *Helkath-hazzurim*: *field of flints*; a slight change in Hebrew gives *sides* instead of *flints*, a reference to the manner of death demanded by *wherefore*.

22. Abner does not wish to provoke a blood-feud.

23. *the hinder end*: Heb. is difficult; possibly Abner reversed his spear and struck backwards as he ran, the butt-end would hardly pierce through a man.

24. *Ammah . . . Giah*: not known.

27. Heb. means that if Abner had not made his appeal the pursuit would have gone on till morning; R.V. is not clear.

29. *the Arabah*: the Jordan valley above the Dead Sea.

Bithron: unknown.

32. *the day brake upon them*: a vivid touch (cf. Gen. 19²³).

(*b*) *The treachery and death of Abner* (2 Sam. 3⁶⁻³⁹).

Abner's growing power aroused the anger of Ish-baal who quarrelled with him. In revenge Abner determined to transfer the crown to David, and conspired with the elders of Israel to this end. He pays a visit to David's camp, in the absence of Joab, to arrange matters. After leaving he is brought back by messengers from Joab, who has meanwhile returned, and treacherously murdered

Part of the Davidic wall at Jerusalem, showing a stretch of Roman plaster of a later house built on to its south side

A breach in the outer Jebusite wall at Jerusalem

by him. David is horrified at the act of treachery, which is liable
to do him so much harm, and invokes a curse upon the house of
the murderer. A public funeral is held at Hebron, the king being
chief mourner. David, however, could not afford to lose the
services of Joab, and he went unpunished.

III. 8. *a dog's head . . . Judah*: the text is corrupt; possibly a scribe
mistook *dog* (*kelebh* in Heb.) for the tribe *Caleb*, and added an explanatory note.

14. *Michal*: see 1 Sam. 18²⁰ ᶠᶠ·, 19¹¹ ᶠᶠ.

16. *Bahurim*: between Jericho and Jerusalem (16⁵, 17¹⁸).

26. *Sirah*: perhaps *'Ain Sārah*, about 1 mile north of Hebron.

27. *midst*: read with LXX *side*.

30. May be editorial; Abishai is not mentioned in v. 27.

33 f. This short poem is probably by David himself.

(c) David becomes king of all Israel (2 Sam. 5).

Ish-bosheth having been murdered by two of his officers (4⁵⁻¹²),
the whole nation desires David as its king. He is anointed at
Hebron, but later makes an attack with his men on Jerusalem
which he captures from the Jebusites. Hiram sends messengers to
David. The Philistines, however, are alarmed at his growing
power and twice attempt an invasion by the valley of Rephaim;
they are on each occasion heavily defeated, David being guided by
the divine oracle.

V. 3. *a covenant*: the terms of this agreement are unknown.

4 f. Probably editorial.

6. *the Jebusites*: see p. 112.

Except thou take away, &c.: read *But the blind and the lame will
turn thee aside* (cf. mg.).

7. *Zion*: the south-west hill is now called Zion, but the hill to the
south-east seems to be required by other passages (see Driver).

8. The whole verse is obscure and corrupt.

get up: Heb. cannot bear this meaning; it should perhaps be
changed slightly to read *go up*.

watercourses: it has been suggested that there is a reference here
to the tunnels which connected Zion with the Virgin's Spring (Gihon
in 1 Kings 1³³), and so supplied it with water; some daring Israelites,
led perhaps by Joab (1 Chron. 11⁶), may have climbed up the shaft,
and·so got possession of the fortress.[1]

[1] There is a very vivid description of the possible course of events in
Macalister, *A Century of Excav. in Pal.*, pp. 173 ff.

There . . . house: read with mg. *The blind . . . cannot come into the house* (i. e. temple).

9. *Millo*: cf. 1 Kings 9[15, 24], 11[27], and the house of Millo near Shechem (Judges 9[6, 20]). The word seems to mean *filling* and to represent some kind of earthwork.

11. *Hiram*: this is a mistake, as the contemporary king was Abibaal; perhaps his help given to Solomon has been anticipated (see on 1 Kings 5[1]).

17. *the hold*: perhaps that of Adullam (cf. 23[13 f.]). Driver would place these attacks immediately after v. 3.

18. *Rephaim*: cf. Isa. 17[5 f.], a fertile plain near Jerusalem, modern *el-Baq'a*.

20. *Baal-perazim*: Jahveh is still called Baal: cf. 2[8] with note.

21. *took them*: in 1 Chron. 14[12] we are told that they burned them.

24. *marching*: the wind showing Jahveh's presence (cf. 22[11]; 1 Kings 19[11 f.]).

25. *Geba*: neither this place nor Gibeon (so LXX) is suitable; perhaps an unknown Geba.

Gezer: *Tell el-Jezer*, nineteen miles north-west of Jerusalem, the scene of the well-known excavations: see Driver, *Schweich Lectures*, pp. 46 ff., 88 ff.

(d) The bringing up of the Ark (2 Sam. 6).

The last previous mention of the ark was in 1 Sam. 7[2], its fate in the interval is unknown. After the capture of Jerusalem David determines to bring it to his new capital (1 Chron. places this incident immediately after 5[10]). Attended by all the picked warriors he goes down to Baale Judah to escort it from thence; on the way the oxen stumble and Uzzah, in endeavouring to save the ark, is suddenly struck down dead, which is taken as a sign of God's displeasure. David thereupon abandons his attempt to reach Jerusalem, and leaves the ark in the house of Obed-edom, a man of Gath. Finding, however, that Obed-edom is prospering, he concludes that the divine anger is stayed, and the rest of the journey is completed without further difficulty. Carried away by religious zeal David leaps and dances before the ark and arouses the scorn of Michal. Her ironic greeting of the king on his return is met by a bitter reply, and Michal is apparently put aside by David.

VI. 1. *Baale Judah*: probably another name for Kirjath-jearim (Joshua 15[9 f.]) where the ark had been left (1 Sam. 7[1]). Baale should be Baalah (Joshua 15[9 f.]) or Baal (Joshua 15[60], 18[14]).

5. *all manner . . . of fir wood*: read with 1 Chron. 13⁸ *all their might* (cf. v. 14) *and with songs.*

7. To touch the ark was regarded as an act of sacrilege. The death of Uzzah may have been due to natural causes, or this whole story may merely be an attempt to explain the place-name.

10. *the Gittite*: presumably a Philistine.

14. *a linen ephod*: rather a scanty garment (cf. v. 20).

20. *How glorious was the king*: better *How the king hath got him honour.*

22. The text is obscure and possibly corrupt.

(e) The Temple planned (2 Sam. 7¹⁻¹⁷).

This section is Deuteronomic in character and seems to have been composed after the greater part of the history.

David proposes to build a house for the ark, and is at first encouraged in his project by Nathan the prophet. A message, however, is sent to the latter, and he informs the king that the temple will not be built by himself but by his son. The throne is assured to the seed of David for ever.

VII. 3. *Nathan said, &c.*: this is an interesting case of a prophet mistaking the divine will.

7. *tribes*: read *judges* with 1 Chron. 17⁶.

11. Instead of David's building a house for Jahveh, Jahveh will make a 'house' for him.

(f) David's Sin (2 Sam. 11).

This section comes from the earlier source. It tells how David falls in love with Bath-sheba, the wife of one of his officers, a Hittite named Uriah, and commits adultery with her. The king makes an attempt to conceal his deed, but the self-denial of Uriah renders it unsuccessful. David then sends a message to Joab suggesting a plan for bringing about the death of Uriah. The latter is accordingly abandoned in a skirmish, and slain by the men of Ammon. On hearing the news the king takes Bath-sheba into his harem. The story shows the depths to which an Oriental despot can descend, and the nobility of Uriah makes the abject treachery of his master all the darker.

XI. 1. *the time when*: the Assyrian armies went out regularly year after year on vast plundering expeditions.

Rabbah: now *'Amman* on the Jabbok, twenty-three miles east of Jordan.

2. *very beautiful*: it is noteworthy that there are no parallels among the Hebrews to Medea and Helen, no legends of women who, by their beauty, caused international complications.

3. *the Hittite*: evidently a mercenary soldier.

11. *the ark*: cf. 1 Sam. 4³.

21. *Jerubbesheth*: i.e. Jerubbaal: see 2⁸.

Thebez: for the incident, see Judges 9⁵⁰ᶠᶠ.

'At the time when kings go out to battle.' An Assyrian war-chariot

(g) David's Repentance (2 Sam. 12¹⁻²⁵).

David was not allowed to enjoy the fruits of his crime in peace. The prophet Nathan quickly came to him with a message of condemnation. He did not come, however, as Elijah would have done with violent denunciations, but by arousing the king's sense of justice got him unwittingly to condemn himself. The parable of the ewe lamb is beautifully told and in itself well calculated to arouse the interest of the shepherd king. When David's sorrow has been stirred up, then comes denunciation, but mingled with it the promise of forgiveness; but because the sin has been so notorious, punishment equally striking must follow; the child of Bath-sheba will die.

The story of the child's illness and death, and of David's conduct in relation to it, is vividly told, and the action of the king and the comments of his servants are exactly true to experience. Whilst the child lived the father wept and fasted, clinging to the last remnants of hope; when the child was dead he accepted bravely the punishment laid upon him.

XII. 7. *Thou art the man*: a sudden dramatic turn to the parable: cf. Isa. 5⁷.

10–12. A later addition based on what actually happened.

(h) *Absalom's Rebellion* (2 Sam. 15).

The sin of David quickly reproduced itself in his own family (cf. the case of Jacob who was deceived by his own children just as he had deceived Isaac); and Ammon, one of his sons, was murdered by the servants of his half-brother Absalom because of an offence committed against Tamar, Absalom's sister. The offender fled to Geshur, but after three years he was allowed to return.

After his return Absalom made it his business to ingratiate himself with his father's subjects, and by his sympathy and ease of manner won their hearts. At last he felt strong enough to make an attempt on the kingdom itself and gathered his partisans together at Hebron. David hears of the conspiracy and, accompanied by his ministers and escorted by the Philistine guard, flies from Jerusalem. Zadok and the Levites bearing the ark went with the king at first but were commanded to return to the city. David and his followers go on their way mourning and are met by Hushai the Archite. The latter is sent to Jerusalem in order that he may gain Absalom's confidence and together with Zadok keep the king informed of his plans.

XV. 1. Cf. Adonijah (1 Kings 1⁵).

3. *no man deputed*: the neglect of the administration of justice was a frequent cause of discontent (cf. 1 Sam. 8³‚ ⁵).

5. Caesar won the goodwill of the Romans by pleading their causes and because of his courteous manner to every man (see Plutarch).

7. *forty*: read *four* with Syr., Lucian, &c.

12. *Giloh*: in the hill-country of Judah (Joshua 15⁵¹), perhaps *Jāla*, five miles north-west of Hebron.

17. *Bethmerhak*: read with mg. *Far House*. The whole of this pas-

sage is a little obscure, but by means of LXX it is possible to reconstruct the story: David and his servants halt at the last house in Jerusalem till all his followers have gone past; he tries to send back a recently arrived contingent of mercenaries under Ittai the Gittite, but they remain faithful.

18. *Cherethites . . . Pelethites*: both probably Philistine tribes, Pelethites is in fact a variant of Pelishtim (=Philistines). The custom of having a bodyguard of foreigners is common; cf. the Swiss guards of the French kings.

23. *towards the way of*: this does not represent Heb. (see Driver). Lucian supplies *olive*—the people pass before David by the way of *the olive tree of the wilderness*.

25. David relies on the divine favour, not on a 'talisman' such as was the ark.

27. *Art thou not a seer?*: the text is suspicious; priests are never called seers.

37. *friend*: the king's friend was probably an official title (cf. 1 Macc. 2¹, 10¹⁶, &c.).

(i) The Rival Counsellors (2 Sam. 16¹⁵–17¹⁴).

When David heard that his counsellor Ahithophel had joined the conspiracy against him he despaired (15³¹) until he met Hushai and sent him back to undermine his influence. By his flattering approach to Absalom and his skill in turning even the latter's scornful reproaches to his ends, he won the rebel's confidence. From that moment the success or failure of the conspiracy depended on the result of the struggle between the two advisers. Ahithophel saw quite rightly that violence and speed are the two great requisites for a successful rebellion. His first piece of advice, that. Absalom should publicly take possession of his father's harem, and thus make the breach between them final, was followed out. His second piece of advice, that he himself with a considerable force should pursue the fugitives, and slay the king, was rejected; Hushai pointing out that such a course might involve a slight check, since the king and his guard were experienced warriors, which would have disastrous consequences. Hushai advised Absalom not to move until his army was large enough to make victory certain. Absalom's failure to act quickly may be compared with Hannibal's refusal to follow up the victory of Cannae by dispatching a body of cavalry to seize Rome (Livy, xxii. 51).

XVI. **22.** *a tent*: the bridal tent; it survives in the canopy still used in Jewish weddings.

XVII. **3.** *the man . . . returned*: awkward and not really an accurate rendering of Heb.: read with LXX *as a bride returneth to her husband*: *thou seekest but the life of one man.*

9. David's escapes from Saul would give point to this.

11. *in thine own person*: cf. v. 1, a subtle appeal to Absalom's vanity.

(j) The Defeat and Death of Absalom (2 Sam. 18–19⁸).

David, having received news of Absalom's plans by means of his friends in Jerusalem (17¹⁵ ᶠᶠ·), determined to make a stand against the rebels at Mahanaim. The army marched out in three divisions, but the king himself, at the strong desire of the people, remained with the reserves in the city. The various divisional commanders were charged by David to spare Absalom if he fell into their hands.

The battle was fought in the forest of Ephraim, and resulted in the rout of the followers of Absalom who were pursued over a wide area. Absalom himself was caught in an oak as he fled on his mule and the matter being reported to Joab, he slew him with his own hand, in spite of being reminded of the king's charge. The body was cast into a pit and a great heap of stones placed over it.

Joab sends a messenger to David with news of the victory; he is, however, outrun by Ahimaaz who informs the king of the issue of the fight, but professes ignorance of the fate of Absalom. The official messenger follows quickly telling of the death of the rebel. David is apparently more distressed over the death of his son than uplifted by the success of his arms. Joab reproves him with rough soldierly language and David, suppressing his grief, shows himself to his victorious troops.

XVIII. **2.** The division of an army into three bodies was a favourite method (cf. Judges 7¹⁶; 1 Sam. 11¹¹). Two of the commanders were Israelites, the third *Ittai the Gittite*, a mercenary captain (15¹⁹ ᶠᶠ·).

3. Cf. 17².

6. *the forest of Ephraim.* This locality is unknown. It is a little strange that the tribe of Ephraim should give its name to a forest or jungle west of Jordan: see, however, G. A. Smith, *Hist. Geog. of the Holy Land*, p. 335 n.

8. *the forest devoured.* The wild, rocky country would be full of pitfalls for a flying army.

9. *his head caught.* Nothing is said of his hair catching, which is the traditional explanation.

14. *three darts.* Following LXX; Heb. has *rods*.

17. *heap of stones.* Cf. Joshua 7²⁶, 8²⁹. Perhaps to prevent his spirit troubling them: see Tylor, *Primitive Culture*, ii. 29.

18. The monument may have had a religious character (see P.C.), but probably it was merely intended to preserve his memory. For *the king's dale*, cf. Gen. 14¹⁷.

no son. The three sons of 14²⁷ must have died before him.

21. *the Cushite.* An Ethiopian (cf. Jer. 13²³ with the present writer's note). Joab may have insisted on a foreigner bearing news which the king would regard as bad.

23. *the Plain.* The name given to the Jordan valley where it widens out north of the Dead Sea. Ahimaaz took a longer route, but one much easier for a runner.

24–27. This scene is very like 2 Kings 9¹⁷ᶠᶠ.

28. *all is well*: better *Peace*, the usual Oriental greeting.

XIX. 3. Notice the vividness of the description.

(k) *The Revolt of Sheba* (2 Sam. 20).

The fight of David and the death of Absalom had left the nation without a head. David was apparently not willing to return to Jerusalem unless the people actually invited him (19¹³). The matter, however, was arranged through Zadok and Abiathar, the priests, though a quarrel between Judah and Israel destroyed the harmony of the proceedings (19⁴¹ᶠᶠ·). An actual rebellion broke out led by a Benjamite named Sheba; and David ordered Amasa, whom he had made commander-in-chief in Joab's place, to gather together the militia of Judah to crush it. Some delay occurred and David sent Abishai with the Philistine guards and the standing army to pursue Sheba. They met with Amasa and his troops, and Joab who was with Abishai murdered him by treachery, and took command of the whole force. Sheba, who does not seem to have had any very great following, had taken refuge in Abel of Beth-maacah; Joab surrounded the city and began an assault upon it. The citizens, following the advice of a 'wise woman', put Sheba to death and threw down his head to Joab; the army then withdrew without any further attack.

XX. 1. *Bichri.* Perhaps the same as Becher (Gen. 46²¹).

4. *Amasa.* Absalom's captain (17²⁵) whom David had taken into his service.

5. *tarried longer.* Probably he had difficulty in collecting the men of Judah after having fought against them so recently.

7. *Joab's men.* LXX reads *Joab.*

8. R.V. is a free rendering of Heb. which is unintelligible.

14. *Abel, and to.* Read *Abel of.* Now *Abil,* a village in the far north, some four miles west of Dan.

15. Regular siege operations were being carried on.

16. *a wise woman.* Half witch, half prophetess.

18–19*ᵃ*. This passage is difficult. Probably we should read with Driver (following LXX): *Let them ask in Abel and in Dan whether that had ever come to an end which the faithful of Israel had established.* Abel claimed to be loyal to national tradition.

(l) *The story of Rizpah* (2 Sam. 21¹⁻¹¹).

The stories in 21–24 form an appendix to the account of David's reign and are grouped here perhaps because of difficulty in placing them in their proper context. This, and the following, section are important as 'illustrations of the primitive theology of Israel: misfortune . . . is regarded as necessarily the punishment of sin' (P.C.).

In the time of David there was a three years' famine which the divine oracle attributed to the guilt still resting on the nation because of the massacre of the Gibeonites by Saul. David asks the Gibeonites to name what compensation they will. They ask, not for money, but for the sacrifice of seven of Saul's descendants. Seven men are accordingly handed over and duly slaughtered. Rizpah, the mother of two of the victims, watched beside the unburied bodies of the whole number to keep off wild animals. In the end David had their bones buried with those of Saul and Jonathan in Zela of Benjamin.

XXI. 1. *It is . . . house.* Read with LXX *The guilt of blood rests on Saul and on his house.*

the Gibeonites. A treaty had been made with these Amorites by Joshua (Joshua 9). No account remains of their being massacred, though it has been ingeniously suggested that Gibeon should be read for Nob in 1 Sam. 22¹⁹: see Enc. Bib. *Nob.*

4. *silver or gold.* Money compensation for those slain was frequently taken in ancient days. Cf. ποινή of the Greeks (*Iliad*, v. 266, xviii. 498 ff., &c.) and the 'wergild' of the Teutons: see Stubbs, *Constitutional Hist.* i. 179.

6. *hang.* The word is rare and its exact meaning uncertain, perhaps crucifixion.

The interior of the Dome of the Rock at Jerusalem, showing the Rock (es-Sahra), which was the threshing-floor of Araunah the Jebusite (2 Sam. 24)

8. *Michal.* Merab should be read (1 Sam. 18[19]). Perhaps the scribe thought David took the opportunity of punishing his own wife (6[20 ff.]).

10. *Rizpah.* Cf. 3[7].

until water was poured. The exposure of the bones may have been part of a 'rain-making' ceremony: see Frazer, *Adonis, Attis, Osiris,* i. 22.

14. *his son.* Add with LXX 'and of them that were hanged'.

Zela. Cf. Joshua 18[28]. The site is unknown.

m) *The Census* (2 Sam. 24).

This passage is important because it reveals the deplorably low idea of God which prevailed in Israel. Jahveh is represented as being angry with His people and, in order to have an excuse for punishing them, He makes David commit the dreadful 'sin' of numbering them. Joab objects to the whole plan and does not mind saying so, but he is overruled. When the census had been completed David's heart smote him. A message also came, by the seer Gad, offering the choice between three forms of punishment: seven years of famine, three months of disastrous warfare, or three days of plague. David chooses plague; and a terrible outbreak takes place, so great that even Jahveh's anger is mollified, and He spares Jerusalem. At the command of Gad David buys the threshing-floor of Araunah the Jebusite, where the plague had stopped, and there erects an altar.

XXIV. 1. *again.* Probably this story followed immediately on 21[14].

he moved. 'Satan' according to 1 Chron. 21[1].

5. *Aroer.* Now *'Ara'ir* on the Arnon, east of the Dead Sea.

6. *to Gilead.* Going up to the north of the east Jordan territory.

Tahtim-hodshi . . . Dan-jaan. The text is probably corrupt beyond restoration: see however Driver *ad loc.*

7. *Tyre.* On the coast, twenty-seven miles west of Dan.

Beer-sheba. They worked from north to extreme south on the west side of Jordan, and thus went through the whole land.

10. *I have sinned greatly.* Why the taking of a census was considered a sin in early Israel it is impossible to say, though a similar superstition is still very widespread amongst ignorant people: see Frazer, *Folk-Lore in O.T.* ii. 555 ff.

13. *seven.* Read *three* with 1 Chron. 21[12].

20 ff. The story of the bargaining, conducted on truly Oriental lines, may be compared with Gen. 23[10 ff.].

24. *fifty shekels of silver*. Rather less than £7. In 1 Chron. 21[25] David pays Ornan (=Araunah) 500 shekels of *gold*, but perhaps his purchase included a wider area than the floor itself.

25. *was intreated*. Cf. 21[14].

§ 3. THE REIGN OF SOLOMON

The reign of Solomon was in the eyes of the later Jews the era of the nation's greatest splendour and power. Solomon himself, even in our Lord's day, was the type of wisdom (Luke 11[31]), and of kingly glory (Matt. 6[29]). The greatest of his achievements was the building and furnishing of the magnificent sanctuary at Jerusalem. These two facts, the importance of the whole reign, and the significance of the erection of the Temple, are reflected in the space which they occupy in the narrative. Of the whole of 1 and 2 Kings one quarter is given to Solomon, and of this quarter more than half is allotted to the temple.

The narratives are apparently arranged not chronologically but according to subject matter; and they are derived—apart from chapters 1–2 which belong to the Davidic document (see pp. 66, 179 above)—from two main sources:

(*a*) a species of Chronicle of an official nature which probably included notices of the construction of the temple.

(*b*) a number of detached accounts of the leading events of the reign; not all of one time or belonging to a single document but having certain features in common. In addition to these two main sources, or collections of sources, there are a number of editorial comments or interpolations coming from writers of the Deuteronomic school.

The character of Solomon is not at all unlike that of the Emperor Frederick II, *stupor mundi* as Matthew Paris called him. There was in each the same love of ostentation, the same intellectual curiosity, the same spirit of cosmopolitanism, and also the same disregard of the highest duties of a ruler.

(*a*) *Adonijah or Solomon?* (1 Kings 1).

At the end of his reign David apparently fell into a state of almost senile decay, and two parties were formed amongst his counsellors, each of which supported one of his sons for the succession to the throne. The oldest surviving son, Adonijah, had the backing of Joab and Abiathar the priest. In support of Solomon, however, were his mother Bath-sheba, and Nathan the prophet; they claimed that David had promised the throne to Solomon.

Adonijah gave a banquet to his brethren and his friends outside Jerusalem, and carefully excluded Solomon and his supporters. Bath-sheba, inspired by Nathan, complained to the king that they were plotting to seize the throne and that Adonijah was already receiving royal honours. David acted quickly, and calling Zadok the priest and Benaiah the captain of his bodyguard, had Solomon publicly anointed king. The sound of the rejoicings in Jerusalem was carried down to the conspirators; and news was soon brought to Adonijah of what had happened; the guests immediately dispersed and Adonijah fled to a sanctuary, he was, however, forgiven by Solomon.

I. 3. *the Shunammite.* Shunem is now *Solam,* five miles north of Jezreel. The Shulammite (Song 6[13]) may be the same person.

5. *Adonijah* was born at Hebron (2 Sam. 3[4]) and must have been between thirty and forty years of age.

chariots, &c. Cf. 2 Sam. 15[1].

7. *Abiathar.* The only survivor of the house of Eli (1 Sam. 22[20 ff.]).

8. *Benaiah* was captain of the bodyguard (2 Sam. 8[18]).

Shimei . . . Rei are both unknown.

9. *the stone of Zoheleth,* that is, *the Serpent's stone,* perhaps the modern *ez-Zehweleh.*

En-rogel, that is, *the Fuller's Spring.* By some identified with *Bīr-'Eyyūb,* south of Jerusalem.

29. The same oath is used in 2 Sam. 4[9].

33. *mine own mule.* Cf. 10[25], 18[5]; 2 Sam. 13[29], 18[9]. The mule is first mentioned in David's reign as used by royalty.

Gihon is probably the Virgin's Spring, the pool of Siloam of Joshua 9[7].

38. *Cherethites . . . Pelethites.* See p. 187.

39. *the Tent.* That pitched to cover the ark (2 Sam. 6[17]).

42. *Jonathan.* Cf. 2 Sam. 15[27 ff.], 17[17 ff.]

50. This and the case of Joab (2[28]) are the only actual examples of Israelites seeking asylum at an altar.

(b) David's last Charge (1 Kings 2[1-12]).

The genuineness of this passage has been questioned, and the suggestion made that Solomon, in order to cover himself, gave out that his execution of Joab and of Shimei came from his father's advice or command. Probably, however, the charge (except vv. 3 f., 10–12), did actually come from David. It must be admitted that it makes him come far short of a Christian standard, and shows him to be still under the influence of the superstitious ideas of his own age (see on vv. 5 and 8).

The charge opens with a number of pious injunctions in the style of Deuteronomy; it then goes on to recommend the execution of Joab on account of his bloodthirsty doings, the reward of the sons of Barzillai, and the execution of Shimei, Saul's kinsman.

II. **2.** *go . . . earth.* Cf. Joshua 23[14] (D).

3. *the law of Moses.* In Kings this seems always to mean the book Deuteronomy.

4. *heart . . . soul.* We should say 'mind' and 'heart'; the Hebrews regarded the heart as the seat of the intellect, the soul as that of the affections.

5. *Joab.* His great services to David had been mixed with utter unscrupulousness in the matter of shedding blood. David, no doubt, remembered the death of Absalom (2 Sam. 18[14]), and Solomon had his own account to settle with him for his part in Adonijah's conspiracy (1[7]).

Abner . . . Amasa. See 2 Sam. 3[22 ff.], 20[8 ff.]

and shed . . . peace. Omit as a gloss.

put the blood, &c. The treacherous murders called for revenge (cf. Gen. 4[10]), and David himself was involved in it by his failure to avenge his guest.

7. *Barzillai.* See 2 Sam. 17[27 ff.], 19[33 ff.]

8. *Shimei.* See 2 Sam. 16[5 ff.], 19[16 ff.] As a kinsman of Saul he may have been dangerous.

a grievous curse. In David's time a curse was held to have great power, and so was deemed a real injury, and as such calling for punishment.

10. *city of David.* See 2 Sam. 6[12].

(c) Solomon's Vengeance (1 Kings 2[13-46]).

After David's death Solomon carried out his father's charge as opportunity offered; and in addition he made his own position more secure by removing Adonijah.

Our sympathy goes out to Adonijah, who was apparently a foolish young man who did not realize the consequences of his own actions; to have obtained Abishag as a wife would really have been a blow at Solomon's throne (cf. 2 Sam. 12[8], 16[21 ff.]), and Solomon recognized its dangerous nature. The king's forgiveness of Adonijah ($1^{51\,ff.}$) was a most unusual piece of clemency, as an Oriental monarch almost invariably signalized his accession by removing possible rivals, and his brother seems to have presumed upon it. The removal of Abiathar from the priesthood and the death of Joab were a consequence of their part in Adonijah's attempt to seize the throne. Shimei brought his fate upon himself by breaking the regulations which Solomon had made for him.[1]

II. 13. *Bath-sheba.* The queen-mother was a very important person and the real head of the harem.

18. Bath-sheba is evidently flattered by the request coming to her.

22. *the kingdom also.* See above.

26. *Abiathar.* Possibly he had incited Adonijah to make his request; in any case, his complicity in the late conspiracy made him liable to punishment.

Anathoth. Now *'Anātā*, some three miles north-east of Jerusalem, the home of Jeremiah the prophet (Jer. 1^1, $32^{6\,ff.}$).

to death. There was a growing fear of putting a priest to death: cf. 1 Sam. 22^{17}.

27. *that . . . Shiloh.* Probably a gloss based on 1 Sam. $2^{27\,ff.}$ The Zadokite priesthood wished to claim divine sanction for their position, not merely the action of the king.

28. See 1^{50}.

31. A murderer might be taken from the altar (Exod. 21^{14}).

32. *upon his own head.* In other words, no revenge for his death would follow.

35. *Zadok.* His descendants held the priesthood until the murder of Onias in 171 B.C.

36. *in Jerusalem.* Solomon wished Shimei to be under observation.

37. *Kidron.* North-east of Jerusalem, towards Shimei's house.

39. *Achish, son of Maacah, King of Gath.* Some fifty years earlier a king of this name was reigning at Gath (1 Sam. 27^2), but his father was 'Maoch'. The similarity of the two names suggests that the same ruler is meant.

Gath. See on 1 Sam. 6^{17}.

45. *shall be blessed.* The curse of Shimei (v. 8) will become harmless.

---

[1] LXX of this section is peculiar. After v. 35 it inserts ten verses collected from other parts of the book, viz.: $4^{29\,f.}$, 3^1, 5^{15}, $7^{23,\ 27,\ 38}$, $9^{24\,f.}$, 5^{16}, $9^{13,\ 17\,f.}$; a similar series follows v. 46.

(d) *Solomon's Vision* (1 Kings 3⁴⁻²⁸).

This whole section comes from the series of detached narratives referred to above (see p. 193); vv. 6b and 14 are Deuteronomic and seem to have been supplied by the editor.

After his accession Solomon made a great festival at Gibeon. The same night God came to him in a dream with the offer of some great gift. Solomon put aside all personal ambition and requested that wisdom might be given him to govern his people aright. Pleased by his act God added to wisdom riches and honour.

The story which follows is intended to illustrate the exercise of the divine gift. Two women are brought before him, each claiming to be the mother of a certain child; the king commands the child to be divided between them; the pretended mother agrees, but the true mother, in order to save the child's life, gives up her claim. She is thus revealed by her maternal affection, and receives her child.

III. 4. *Gibeon.* Now *el-Jîb*, six miles north-west of Jerusalem. Josephus reads Hebron (*Antiq.* VIII. ii. 1).

the great high place. Perhaps because near Jerusalem, according to 2 Chron. 1³ the tabernacle was there.

5. *a dream.* Cf. 9¹ᶠ· Solomon, unlike his father, seems never to have relied on the guidance of prophets, and that in spite of Nathan's efforts to secure him the throne. In some quarters dreams were regarded as a very doubtful vehicle for a divine revelation (cf. Jer. 23²⁵ with the present writer's note).

7. *a little child.* Cf. Jer. 1⁶. Probably in both cases a hyperbolical expression. Josephus says he was fourteen (*Antiq.* VIII. vii. 8) when he came to the throne; this does not agree with 11⁴², 14²¹, according to which Rehoboam was born before Solomon began his reign.

9. *heart.* See on 2⁴.

12. *wise.* Not in the western sense of 'learned'. Skinner describes Solomon's wisdom as a 'blending of insight, shrewdness, and tact which penetrates the disguises of human action'.

18. *no stranger.* None to give evidence.

26. *her bowels yearned.* Heb. *grew warm*: cf. Gen. 43³⁰.

(e) *Solomon and Hiram* (1 Kings 5).

Hiram, King of Tyre, sends messengers to congratulate Solomon on his accession. Solomon in reply tells Hiram of his determination to build a temple to Jahveh and asks for help in getting

cedars from Lebanon. In return Solomon offers to supply food
and oil to the Phoenicians. An appendix describes the levy which
Solomon made in Israel in order to provide materials for the
temple buildings.

V. 1. *Hiram.* Better as in vv. 10, 18, Hirom. The first king of this
name; his probable dates are 968–935 B.C. He was overlord of the
Phoenician confederacy which included amongst other cities Zidon,
Arvad (Aradus), and Gebal (Byblus).

sent his servants. LXX adds *to anoint Solomon*; this would mean
that Solomon was the vassal of Tyre; it cannot be taken as decisive
in view of the absence of any other evidence of this relationship.

3–5. These verses are Deuteronomic in point of view: cf. Deut.
12$^{9 f.}$, 25^{19}.

6. *cedar trees.* The cedars of Lebanon are mentioned in inscriptions
as early as 2800 B.C.

Zidonians. In early times Zidon was the most important city of
the Phoenicians, hence the use of the name here for the whole people.

7. *rejoiced greatly.* Perhaps because Tyre was dependent on corn
from Israelite territories (cf. Gen. 49^{20}; Acts 12^{20}).

9. *the place.* According to 2 Chron. 2^{16} this was Joppa (cf. Ezra 3^{7}).

11. *pure oil*: mg. *beaten oil*, as used in the lamps of the tabernacle;
for the process, see H.D.B. iii, p. 616.

13. *a levy.* David was the first Israelite king who is said to have
used forced labour (2 Sam. 20^{24}); the system was common among
Oriental monarchs.

all Israel. Cf. 9$^{20 ff.}$

14. *Adoniram.* See 4^{6}, 12^{18}.

15. *in the mountains.* Not of Lebanon, but of Judah.

17. *great stones.* The Phoenician builders were fond of using large
stones; the custom lasted till later times, and stones of more than
60 ft. in length were not unknown.

18. *the Gebalites.* Gebal is the modern seaport of *Jebail* at the foot
of Lebanon, some twenty miles north of Beirūt.

(*f*) *Solomon's Buildings*: (i) *The Temple* [1] (1 Kings 6).

The reign of Solomon was marked by great building enter-
prises, in particular by the group of royal palaces which he erected

---

[1] The popular idea that the temple was a kind of cathedral is of course
quite wrong—it was in reality smaller than most parish churches, being
only some 100 ft. long. It was just double the size of the tabernacle
(Exod. 26$^{7 ff.}$).

at Jerusalem. The chief of these was his own palace and the
so-called House of Lebanon; smaller buildings were the King's
Chapel (the Temple) and the palace of Pharaoh's daughter.
Solomon seems to have been, like a Greek *basileus* both the
religious and the secular head of the community. His buildings
also find parallels in the pre-Hellenic period, for 'it seems probable

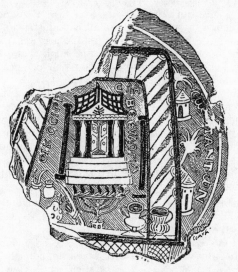

An early representation of the Temple, showing
the two detached pillars, 'Jachin' and 'Boaz' (see
p. 202). From a fragment of a glass dish of Jewish manufacture, found near Rome. About
350 A.D.

that the earliest citadels, round which the city-states grew up,
were crowned with a combined palace and temple'. See *Camb.
Anct. Hist.*, ii. 626.

To later writers the most important, however, was the temple,
which in course of time came to be the unique sanctuary of
the whole kingdom. To Solomon, no doubt, it was merely
what Beth-el was to the kings of Israel (Amos 7[13])—the Royal
Sanctuary.

The descriptions are probably very old, and from the corrupt
state of the text and the technical nature of the subject they are

often difficult to understand. Some help may be derived from Ezekiel's ideal temple (Ezek. 40-48), and to a lesser degree from Josephus's account of the Temple of Herod (*Wars*, v. 5); but perhaps the best help is to be found in the remains of Egyptian temples, since as Barnes points out, they probably influenced the form of the temple at Jerusalem. He quotes the following brief description from Breasted, *History of Egypt*, p. 61:

'Behind a forecourt open to the sky rose a colonnaded hall, beyond which was a series of small chambers containing the furniture and implements for the temple services. The central chamber in the rear was occupied by a small room, the holy of holies, in which stood a shrine hewn from one block of granite. It contained the image of the god.'

The temple of Solomon stood in a court and was approached on the east or front by a gateway or porch. It consisted of a roofed hall of stone, the inside of which was lined with cedar and variously carved and decorated. This hall was divided up into a 'nave' and a 'sanctuary', and surrounding it were a number of side-chambers or cells in three stories. The only light came from gratings which would be placed high up under the roof, according to the similar use in Egyptian temples.

VI. 1. The date of the commencement of the building operations seems to be conventional; it allows twelve generations (i.e. of forty years) from the exodus.

Ziv. The old Canaanite name for the second month, as Abib, Ethanim, and Bul were for the first, seventh, and eighth. It corresponded to April–May. A later system gave numbers to the months: see p. 97.

2. *cubit*. The length of the forearm to the tip of the fingers, about twenty inches or perhaps less. The measurement varied (cf. Ezek. 40^5, 43^{13}).

3. *the porch*. Either a porch attached to the building or possibly a gateway standing away from it after the manner of the *pylon* of an Egyptian temple.

7. This verse is probably a late addition. For the prohibition on the use of iron, see Frazer, *Taboo*, p. 230.

11–14. Lacking in LXX; they seem to come from an editor.

16. *oracle*. The word comes from Vg. *oraculum*, which is a misleading translation of Heb. *debir*, which means simply 'hinder part'.

20. *the altar*. That is, probably, the table of shewbread (7^{48}: cf. Ezek. 41^{22}).

23. *cherubim.* Mysterious figures, no doubt similar to the winged bulls and other animals found in Babylonian and Assyrian temples.

A winged bull from Nineveh, set as a guardian at the entrance to the Temple

They have a double office in O.T.; they bear Jahveh (Ps. 18¹⁰; Ezek. 1), and they act as His agents in guarding forbidden places (Gen. 3²⁴).

olive wood. Heb. 'wood of oil tree' (cf. Isa. 41¹⁹). The olive can hardly be meant, as it is too small a tree to provide wood in large pieces; perhaps some kind of pine should be understood.

38. *Bul.* See on v. 1.

(g) Solomon's Buildings: (ii) *The Palace* (1 Kings 7¹⁻¹²).

In LXX this section follows v. 51, thus bringing the descriptions of the temple and its furniture next to one another; the same arrangement is followed by Josephus. The various buildings are merely catalogued, very little description being added to the list of names.

VII. 1. *thirteen years*. According to 9¹⁰ this period runs from the completion of the temple, which itself took up seven years.

2. *the forest of Lebanon*. So called not from its situation but from the appearance of the hall with its cedar pillars. It was used as an armoury (10¹⁷) and perhaps as a court of justice (so Josephus, *Ant.* VIII. v. 2). The description contained in the following verses is very obscure.

6. *the porch of pillars*. Perhaps a hall of waiting for those who had business with the king.

7. *the porch of the Throne*. The seat of justice.

8. *for Pharaoh's daughter*. From her exalted connexions she would be the chief wife and perhaps had a separate palace, or the best portion of the palace was called after her (cf. Esther 2⁹).

12. *great court*. This surrounded all the buildings, including the temple and temple court.

(h) The Temple Furniture (1 Kings 7¹³⁻⁵¹).

This section contains an account of Hiram, a worker in metals who came from Tyre, and the works executed under his direction for the service or beautifying of the temple. These consisted of the twin pillars, Jachin and Boaz; the brazen sea supported by twelve oxen; ten portable lavers; and a number of smaller vessels.

VII. 13. *Hiram*. His name is the same as that of the king (see 5¹), though in 2 Chron. 2¹³, 4¹⁶ a longer form, Huram-abi, is used.

14. *Naphtali*. Dan according to 2 Chron. 2¹⁴ (cf. Exod. 31⁶).

brass. Better *bronze* (i.e. an alloy of copper and tin), which was well known to the ancients.

15. *the two pillars*. These pillars were not supports of the temple but stood in front of it.[1] Such pillars or obelisks were frequently found before ancient temples. Herodotus (ii. 44) describes two similar pillars at Tyre, 'one of fine gold, the other of emerald, both shining exceedingly at night'.

[1] Benzinger (*Archaeologie*, p. 251) mentions a fragment of a glass dish of the third or fourth century giving a view of the temple at Jerusalem and showing two detached pillars (cited by Skinner). See illustration on p. 199.

21. *Jachin . . . Boaz.* Perhaps 'Stablisher' and 'In it is strength'.

23. *the molten sea.* Probably copied from Phoenician or Babylonian temples and perhaps symbolizing Jahveh's power over the deep.

26. *lily.* Perhaps the lotus, a favourite Egyptian decoration.

two thousand baths. About 16,000 gallons.

Phoenician metal-work. A beautifully incised cauldron

27. *the ten bases.* Probably portable lavers similar to those discovered in Cyprus. The detailed account in the following verses is obscure.

46. *Succoth and Zarethan.* These sites are uncertain (see on Judges 8⁴ᶠ·, and cf. Joshua 3¹⁶).

48 ff. These verses seem to be a later addition.

48. *the golden altar.* The incense altar (Exod. 30¹ᶠᶠ·, 39³⁸), unknown before Ezekiel's days.

49. *the candlesticks.* Cf. Jer. 52¹⁹.

(i) The Dedication of the Temple (1 Kings 8).

The dedication began with the bringing up of the ark from Zion to the temple. The account of this event has been interpolated by a Priestly writer, some of whose additions are missing from LXX. There follows a short poetic utterance (vv. 12 f.) which may well be authentic. The whole of 8¹⁴⁻⁶¹, however, is written from the point of view of one who regarded the temple as the one lawful sanctuary in Israel; it must therefore belong to a Deuteronomic author. The account concludes with the king's blessing of his people and a catalogue of the offerings which marked the dedication.

The supplications of captives in foreign lands (46 ff.) suggest strongly the exilic period, cf. Jer. 29¹⁰ᶠᶠ·, 30¹ᶠᶠ·

VIII. 1. *Zion.* See on 2¹⁰. The name came later to mean Jerusalem as a whole.

2. *Ethanim.* See on 6¹.

3. *the priests.* These play a very subordinate part in the dedication, being merely porters.

5. Cf. 2 Sam. 6¹³.

9. *nothing.* No image; cf. Tacitus, *Hist.* v. 9, where Pompey's entry reveals only an empty sanctuary.

Horeb. See p. 81.

10. *the cloud.* See p. 108.

12 f. These verses come in (LXX where a better text has been preserved) after v. 53; they may be rendered (following Cheyne, *Origin of the Psalter,* pp. 193, 212):

The sun did Jahveh place in the heavens;
He (himself) has determined to inhabit thick darkness:
I have built a lofty palace for thee,
That thou mayest dwell there for ever.

27. There is a thought exactly parallel in a fragment of Euripides preserved by Clement of Alexandria:

'What manner of house by hands of craftsmen framed
May compass with its walls the form divine?'

65. *the entering in of Hamath.* The town is the modern *Hama* on the Orontes, 100 miles north of Damascus. The meaning of the *entering in* is uncertain; it probably signifies the northern end of the cleft between Lebanon and Hermon.[1]

the brook of Egypt. The *Wadi-el-'Arish*, not the Nile.

[1] For a discussion of different views, see Burney, *Judges,* pp. xcix f. and 63, and the note on Num. 13²¹ in my commentary in the Westminster Series.

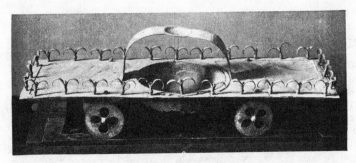

A parallel in miniature to the 'ten bases of brass.' A portable incense burner of Etruscan workmanship, found at Caere, showing Phoenician influence.

A bas-relief from the Temple of Queen Hatshepsut at Deir-el-Bahari, showing the queen of the country of Punt bringing gifts (see p. 206)

(j) The Visit of the Queen of Sheba (1 Kings 10).

The visit to Solomon of the Queen of the South, as our Lord called her (Matt. 12⁴²), was an event which appealed to the eastern mind and many legends have grown up around it. To the writer of Kings she was important as testifying to the wealth and the wisdom of Solomon; her visit, however, like that of the embassy of Merodach Baladan (Isa. 39), was probably inspired by commercial or political considerations. Appended to the story of this visit is an account of Solomon's riches and magnificence, and of the trading ventures which made them possible. The whole chapter is intensely interesting from the insight which it gives into the life of the ancient east. A remarkable parallel to this description may be found in Queen Hatshepsut's records of the cargo of her fleet, which was laden 'very heavily with marvels of the country of Punt; all goodly fragrant woods of God's land, heaps of myrrh-resin, of fresh myrrh-trees, with ebony and pure ivory, with green gold of Emu, with cinnamon-wood, with incense, eye-cosmetic, with baboons, monkeys, dogs', and so forth. (*Camb. Anct. Hist.* ii. 63.)

X. 1. *Sheba* was a nation of some antiquity (cf. Gen. 10⁷, ²⁸) in South Arabia. Its commercial importance was known to Strabo and to Pliny. A good deal of fresh light has been thrown on early Arab civilization recently by the work of Glaser and of Hommel, and important inscriptions have been deciphered.

hard questions: Heb. 'riddles' (as in Judges 14¹²).

2. *spices . . . gold . . . precious stones.* So in Ezek. 27²².

5. *his ascent.* Read with mg., following LXX, 'his burnt-offering . . . in'.

10. *a hundred and twenty talents of gold.* About £740,000 by weight. Perhaps a tribute (cf. 4²¹) in return for trading privileges.

11. *Ophir.* Opinions differ widely as to the situation of this place; some put it in East Arabia, others in South-east Africa, others, again, place it as far away as India. The first opinion, which is supported by Glaser, is most likely to be correct.

almug. The suggestion of mg., *sandal wood*, is by no means certain.

14. The sum mentioned here is more than £4,000,000 by weight, and vastly more in purchasing power.

15. *governors.* LXX renders 'satraps'; the word is Assyrian and late.

16. *target.* A large, oblong shield (cf. the Roman *scutum*).

17. *shield.* A small, circular shield (cf. the Roman *clipeus*).

The storm-god Hadad. A massive statue found in the Hittite city of
Carchemish (cf. 'when I bow myself in the house of Rimmon' (=Hadad),
2 Kings 5[18]). See p. 208

22. *navy of Tarshish.* Tarshish was Tartessus on the Guadalquivir. Ships making this long voyage had to be large in size and strongly built, and so the name seems to have come to mean any large vessel (cf. 1 Kings 22⁴⁸).

apes . . . peacocks. The names are supposed to be of Indian origin.

27. *the lowland.* See p. 134.

28. *Egypt.* Though horses were used in Egypt (see Breasted, *Hist. of Egypt*, p. 235) they do not seem to have been largely exported from it. It has been suggested that for Egypt (*Miṣraim* in Heb.) we should read *Muṣri*, a district in North Arabia mentioned in Assyrian inscriptions. H. R. Hall, however, points out that 'not long after this time the breeding of horses was actually carried on on a large scale in Egypt' (*Camb. Anct. Hist.* iii. 256, n. 1).

(k) Solomon's Adversaries (1 Kings 11¹⁴⁻⁴³).

The end of the account of Solomon's reign gives details of various troubles which arose during its course; they are grouped together here for artistic reasons in order not to interrupt the narrative of his glory and magnificence.

First we have the adventurous life of an Edomite prince named Hadad, who having been driven out of his native land found safety and fortune in Egypt. After the death of David and of Joab he returned.

Another adversary was Rezon, a vassal of the king of Zobah, who established himself in Damascus.

Thirdly there is the account of a young Israelite, Jeroboam, who was told by Ahijah the Shilonite that he would become king over ten of the tribes of Israel. In consequence he fled to Egypt where he remained until the death of Solomon brought him home again.

XI. 14. *Hadad* is the name of the storm-god known also as Rimmon, hence it is common in Palestine.

15. See 2 Sam. 8¹³ (mg.).

17. *a little child.* This seems hardly consistent with the next verse where he is evidently a grown man. Possibly two different accounts have been fused together.

18. *Midian.* See p. 80.

Paran. The desert *et-Tīh* south of Judah.

22. LXX continues, 'And Hadad went back to his country. This is the mischief that Hadad did, and he abhorred Israel, and reigned over Edom.'

23. *Rezon.* So in 2 Kings 16⁵ᶠ·

Zobah. See 2 Sam. 8³ ᶠᶠ·, 10¹⁻¹⁴.

24. *Damascus.* The great adversary of Israel. The city itself was one of the oldest and most beautiful in the world.

26. *Zeredah* occurs here only and its site is unknown.

Zeruah seems to come from the root meaning 'leprous', and was perhaps given to Jeroboam's mother by later Judaic writers to express their loathing.

27. *Millo.* See p. 183.

29. *Ahijah the Shilonite.* A prophet from Shiloh (see on 14²). Solomon's neglect of the prophets (cf. p. 197) may have caused Ahijah to encourage Jeroboam.

30. *rent it.* A vigorous piece of symbolism.

32–40. These verses are a later addition in the style of D.

40. *Shishak.* The first of the Pharaohs to be named in O.T. His real name was *Sha-sha-n-k*, and he was the first king of the XXIInd dynasty, ruling from *c.* 947 to *c.* 925 B.C.

41–43. An editorial addition.

PART IV

This part carries the history of the Hebrew peoples from the disastrous schism, which robbed them of all possibility of empire, to the death of Elisha, the inspirer of the northern kingdom's resistance to Syria. The sources are not very full (see above, p. 66) and are found mainly in the two books of Kings. The following are the sections:

(1) The Schism.
(2) The Ministry of Elijah.
(3) The Ministry of Elisha.

§ 1. THE SCHISM

The people of North and South Israel had never really been one. As far back as the time reflected in the song of Deborah Judah was evidently not regarded as part of Israel at all, at least there is no mention of the tribe. Later, after the death of Saul, David seems to have represented the southern tribe in its desire to gain supremacy, and even in David's own reign friction between the two sections of the people was not unknown. On the death of Solomon, who had obviously favoured his own tribe at the expense of the rest, the dissatisfaction of Israel broke out. Rehoboam was quite incapable of dealing with the situation, and a schism was the inevitable sequel.

(a) *The Breach between Judah and Israel* (1 Kings 12$^{1-24}$).

Critics are not agreed as to the source from which the following account comes. From a literary point of view it has resemblances to the memoirs of David's court which underlie 2 Sam. 9–1 Kings 2 (see p. 179 above); politically, however, the writer seems to be in sympathy, not with Judah and Rehoboam, but with Israel and the revolting tribes. Skinner thinks that 'on the whole . . . we have an extract from the chronicles of the Kings of Israel.'

Rehoboam, Solomon's son, goes to Shechem to be made king. A deputation of Israelites headed by Jeroboam, the returned rebel, demands as a condition of their continued loyalty a lightening of the burden laid on the people. The king asks for three days to consider this request. The interval is spent in consulting, first the older courtiers who advise him to make the required promise, and secondly, his own friends and contemporaries, who recommend a harsh reply. Rehoboam follows the advice of the latter with the result that ten tribes secede. Adoram, the head of the levy, in endeavouring to make the Israelites return to their allegiance is stoned to death, and the king himself makes a speedy escape to Jerusalem. The revolted tribes elect Jeroboam to be king of Israel.

A later writer adds a note to the effect that an attempt which Rehoboam was contemplating, to restore the unity of the people by force, was stopped by a message from Shemaiah, the man of God.

XII. 1. *Shechem.* See on Joshua 24^1. Notice that the election takes place at the Ephraimite capital.

4. *our yoke grievous.* The glories of Solomon's reign and his magnificent buildings had cost the common people dearly in the way of taxes and forced labour.

7. *good words.* The old men seem to advise a soft answer, but not necessarily a changed policy.

10. *finger . . . loins.* Evidently a common expression.

11. *scorpions.* Perhaps some particularly painful kind of scourge; the expression may, however, be proverbial.

15. *Ahijah.* Cf. 11$^{29\,ff.}$

16. Cf. 2 Sam. 20^1.

18. *Adoram.* Hardly a wise choice, unless the people were in a state to be bullied into submission.

20. This verse may be a gloss as it does not fit in with v. 3.

22. *Shemaiah.* An unknown prophet. According to LXX it was he not Ahijah who rent his mantle.

(b) *The Religious Breach* (1 Kings 12^{25}–13^{10}).

The point of view of the writer or writers of this section is late. It judges Jeroboam's acts by the standard of the Deuteronomic reform of Josiah's reign which centred all worship at Jerusalem and allowed no other sanctuaries.

After his election Jeroboam proceeded to establish his kingdom, and in order to make the breach with Judah quite permanent he inaugurated a separate system of worship having centres in the two ancient sanctuaries of Beth-el and Dan. An unknown prophet out of Judah denounces Jeroboam whilst ministering at the altar in Beth-el and foretells the destruction of the altar by Josiah; his oracle is accompanied by a double sign. Jeroboam is greatly impressed and offers refreshment and reward to the prophet, but these are indignantly declined.

The story of the visit of the prophet is evidently late and the detailed forecast of the act of Josiah has no parallel in Hebrew prophecy.[1] The whole tone of the narrative is unworthy. Wellhausen sees in it a garbled version of the visit of Amos to Beth-el in the reign of the second Jeroboam.

XII. 25. *built Shechem*. As the scene of the revolt against Rehoboam Shechem was a good choice for a capital. It also had natural advantages. *Built* means re-built or fortified.

Penuel. For some reason or other Jeroboam was compelled to transfer the seat of his government to this East Jordan town: cf. Ish-bosheth (2 Sam. 2[8]), and David (2 Sam. 17[22]).

28. *two calves of gold*. See p. 106 above.

29. *Beth-el . . . Dan*. These two sanctuaries, both of great reputation and antiquity, were situated, the one in the extreme south, the other in the extreme north of Jeroboam's dominions.

31. *all the people*. That is he did not restrict the priesthood to the tribe of Levi. The rendering of A.V. *the lowest of the people* is wrong and misleading.

XIII. 2. See 2 Kings 23[15-20].

8. *half thine house*. Cf. Balaam (Num. 24[13]).

10. *another way*. Cf. the wise men (Matt. 2[12]).

(c) *The Old Prophet* (1 Kings 13[11-32]).

The story of the visit of the prophet from Judah and his detailed forecast of events which were to happen some 350 years after his own day makes a strange and improbable narrative; its sequel is even more amazing and improbable, furthermore it exhibits a crude and unworthy idea of God.

The story goes that when the man of God was returning to Judah, having refused the king's hospitality in accordance with the command of Jahveh, he was met by an old prophet of Bethel. This latter, by a pretended revelation from Jahveh, persuaded the man of God to eat and drink. In consequence on resuming his journey he was slain by a lion. The conduct of the old prophet is both revolting and incomprehensible; having by his deceit lured a man into dishonour and death he expresses a pious desire to be buried beside him (v. 31).

The story is late as v. 32 shows, since Samaria (which was not

---

[1] The naming of Cyrus in Isa. 44[26] can hardly be adduced since the late date of the second part of Isaiah is generally admitted.

built in Jeroboam's time) is referred to. No doubt its composer wished to insist on the duty of absolute obedience to the divine commands and the danger of breaking them.

XIII. 11. *an old prophet.* The title *man of god* was evidently superior.

18. *an angel.* This is a sign of late date since angels as bearers of messages to the prophets are not found in pre-exile literature.

21. The declaration of this unpleasant oracle is like the task of Balaam.

24. The miraculous element in the story is here very prominent.

30. *Alas, my brother!* Cf. Jer. 22^{18}.

32. *Samaria.* The use of this name for the province is very late.

(*d*) *The death of Abijah* (1 Kings 14$^{1-18}$).

Abijah the son of Jeroboam falls ill. The king thereupon sends his wife in disguise to Ahijah, the prophet who had foretold his greatness, to inquire as to the chances of recovery. Ahijah was now an old man, and blind, but the ruse of Jeroboam did not deceive him, and the sorrowing mother was told that at the very moment her feet touched the threshold of the house the child would die. The story for the most part is ancient, but a Deuteronomic editor has added denunciations of Jeroboam and all his house (vv. 7–11, 13–16).

The tradition followed by LXX is different. According to it Abijah was still a young man, and Jeroboam was not yet king, when the incident occurred. The wife of Jeroboam is named Auoth. The passage is placed after 12^{24} of the Hebrew, and not here, to agree with the different version of its date.

XIV. 2. *Shiloh* was at one time the religious centre of Israel, the sanctuary which guarded the ark (1 Sam. 3^{3}). Later its importance declined, though now for a moment the presence of Ahijah gave it influence, and some terrible disaster finally overtook it (Jer. 7^{12}).

3. The giving of presents to a seer was a usual procedure (cf. 1 Sam. 9$^{7 f.}$; 2 Kings 5^{15}, 8^{8}).

cracknels. Some kind of small cake. LXX quaintly adds 'for his children'.

9. *all . . . before thee.* A common phrase (cf. 16$^{25, 30}$) but hardly suited to Jeroboam, the first King of Israel.

(e) The reign of Rehoboam (1 Kings 14²¹⁻³¹).

The reign of Rehoboam was notable for two things, the revival of Canaanite practices, and the invasion of Shishak (Sheshonk). The latter event was due to the rise to power in Egypt of a new

A relief on the temple wall at Karnak commemorating
Shishak's victory over Rehoboam

dynasty (the XXIInd), founded by Sheshonk who had been a leader of Libyan mercenaries. This invasion seems to have affected Israel as well as Judah, since Ephraimite cities are included in the tribute lists in the temple of Amon at Karnak. For the writer of Kings the chief disaster was the loss of the temple shields.

XIV. **21**. This verse gives the usual formula by which a new king's reign is summed up.

his mother's name, &c. Mentioned because of the peculiar dignity and importance of the queen-mother.

23. *pillars . . . Asherim.* See p. 105.

24. *sodomites.* Heb. *holy persons.* Prostitutes of either sex attached to the temple (cf. Deut. 23¹⁷ᶠ·).

27. *the guard.* Lit. as mg. *the runners.*

30. *there was war.* No records exist describing this, probably no regular expeditions but frontier skirmishes and border raids are referred to.

(f) *The reign of Asa* (i Kings 15⁹⁻²⁴).

Rehoboam was succeeded on the throne of Judah by Abijam. His reign was short and unimportant, and his policy merely a continuation of that of his father. His death made way for Asa whose long reign of forty-one years was a time of religious progress. Abandoning the evil habits of his immediate predecessors he attempted to purify the religion of the country and to banish foreign and base elements from it. His domestic policy seems to have been successful. In foreign affairs, however, he adopted the suicidal plan of bribing a foreign king to attack Israel which was then threatening Judah.

XV. **10**. *his mother's name.* A mistake for grandmother probably (cf. v. 2).

12. *sodomites.* See on 14²⁴.

13. *the brook Kidron.* Cf. 2³⁷.

17. *Ramah,* probably the modern *Er-Ram* some five miles north of Jerusalem. A hostile stronghold at such short distance was a grave threat.

18. *King of Syria . . . at Damascus.* There were several Syrian or Aramaean kingdoms. From this time forward they begin to play an important and threatening part in the affairs of Israel.

20. The towns mentioned show that a wide district in the north was ravaged by the Syrians. *Chinneroth* is the Sea of Galilee.

21. *Tirzah* lay probably near to Shechem though its exact site is unknown.

22. *Geba . . . Mizpah.* Asa strengthened his frontier by dismantling the threatening Ramah and building two fortresses of his own.

(g) The reign of Omri (1 Kings 16²¹⁻²⁸).

Whilst the throne of Judah had been occupied in peaceful succession by members of the house of David, and, indeed, was to continue to be so occupied till the end of the kingdom, that of Israel had a far different record. To Jeroboam succeeded his son Nadab; after a brief reign he was murdered by Baasha who thereupon seized the throne. Baasha had a long reign of 24 years and then left the crown to Elah, his son. Again a short reign was followed by murder and usurpation. The murderer, Zimri, however, had but a few days of rule when he was attacked by Omri the captain of the host. Zimri, when he could no longer defend Tirzah, set the king's palace on fire and perished in the flames.

Having disposed of Zimri the successful soldier found that he had to face another claimant to the throne, Tibni the son of Ginath who evidently had a considerable following. No details are given of the struggle which followed, but in it Tibni was overcome and met his death. Politically the reign of Omri was very important as can be seen from foreign records. To the Assyrians Israel was the land of the house of Omri even in the days when his dynasty had ceased to reign, and in the well-known Moabite stone we learn of his victories over that people. The small space given to his reign in Kings is due to the fact that the compiler's interests were religious, not political. One event, however, of high importance both for the religious and the political future of Israel is recorded, the choice and building of a new capital.

XVI. **23.** *thirty and first year.* According to vv. 15 f. Omri began to reign in the twenty-seventh year. Civil war must have lasted some four years.

24. *Samaria.* The Hebrew name is *Shōmerôn.* Our form comes from the Greek through LXX and N. T. The site is now called Es-Sebastiyyeh, a village some six miles north-west of Nāblūs. Samaria was evidently a place of great natural strength, but the excavations of the Harvard Expedition seem to show that it was not an ancient site.

(h) The accession of Ahab (1 Kings 16²⁹⁻³⁴).

Omri was succeeded by his son Ahab, perhaps the most notorious of all Israelite kings. From the religious point of view his reign was important by reason of his marriage with the Tyrian princess Jezebel (Josephus makes her out to have been the aunt of Dido

of Carthage!). Through this alliance foreign cults, as in the case
of Solomon, came into Israel, and indeed there was a real danger
of the national religion being lost in the worship of the Phoenician
Baal.

The deliberate way in which the re-building of Jericho is recorded as having taken place in the reign of Ahab (v. 34) is evidently
intended to emphasize the irreligious attitude of the age.

The site of Es-Sebastiyyeh, showing partially excavated Roman pillars

Ahab appears in Assyrian records as one of the allied kings who
fought at the Battle of Karkar in 853 B.C. (see Introduction,
p. 26).

XVI. **31.** *Jezebel.* The meaning is uncertain. Ahab in marrying
her materially strengthened his kingdom, but introduced religious
disunion.

Ethbaal is called Ithobalus by Menander (quoted by Josephus,
Antiq. VIII. xiii. 1), and reigned 887–876 B.C.

32. *house of Baal.* So Solomon, in accordance with the custom of
the time, built temples for the gods of his foreign wives (11⁷ᶠ·).

34. *build Jericho.* The town had not lain desolate from the days of Joshua, since it is mentioned in Judges 3[13] and 2 Sam. 10[5]. The tragic deaths of Hiel's two sons recalled the curse of Joshua (Joshua 6[26]).[1]

§ 2. THE MINISTRY OF ELIJAH

Into the account of the reign of Ahab there has been inserted a number of stories dealing with the life and activities of the great prophet, Elijah the Tishbite. These stories come down from a very early age and, if vividness and reality is a true test of contemporary authorship, they belong to a time but little subsequent to that of the mysterious figure around whom they have been gathered.

The importance of Elijah lies in the work which he did in opposing the introduction of a foreign religion into Israel. The conflict between Jahveh and the Tyrian Baal can be divided into two stages, corresponding fairly closely with the ministries of Elijah and Elisha respectively. In the time of Elijah there was some friendliness between prophet and king, in spite of fierce denunciations (cf. W. E. Barnes, 1 *Kings* in Camb. Bib. pp. 141 f.); in the time of Elisha, bitter hostility until Baal was crushed.

(a) The Great Drought (1 Kings 17[1-16]).

Elijah appears in the pages of Kings with startling abruptness. He stalks out of the desert into the royal presence with his message of the disastrous drought,[2] and then as quickly disappears again. By the brook Cherith his own life is preserved through the ministry of ravens commissioned by Jahveh Himself; then when the waters of the brook dry up, he goes north to Zarephath in the territory of Zidon. There a widow woman sustains him by means of a cruse of oil and a barrel of meal which are supernaturally maintained.

There is in this story, as in most of the rest, a miraculous element. Here it is of a pleasing and delightful character. The ministering ravens and the never-failing cruse fit in well with the

---

[1] Some scholars see in the statements in this verse a reference to the custom of foundation sacrifices by which human victims are buried alive under foundations to bring good fortune. Traces of such sacrifices have been found at Gezer and elsewhere in Palestine: see Driver, *Schweich Lectures*, p. 72.

[2] 'In primitive thought the destructive drought of Elijah's age would be taken as a sign of divine displeasure, especially with a bad king.' S. A. Cook in *Camb. Anct. Hist.* iii, p. 369.

kindly offices of the widow and seem to give an air of dependence
to the stern prophet.

XVII. 1. *of the sojourners*. Read with LXX *of Tishbeh*.

before whom I stand. Cf. Jer. 35^{19}.

3. *the brook Cherith*. This *wadi* must have been in the east of
Jordan (i. e. *before* Jordan) and cannot, therefore, be the *Wadi el-Kelt*
near Jericho as many have supposed.

4. *the ravens*. Hebrew can be read as *Arabs*, but LXX renders
τοῖς κόραξιν and the traditional pointing ought to be retained.

9. *Zarephath* is the Sarepta of Luke 4^{26}. It is situated ten miles
south of Zidon and at no great distance from Tyre, the seat of the
worship against which Elijah was to contend.

12. *As the LORD*. Here as usually *Jahveh*. The prophet is recognized as an Israelite and the name of his God is known.

13. *first*. The test to the woman's faith was a hard one.

(b) Elijah on Mount Carmel (1 Kings 18$^{20-46}$).

The hiding of Elijah and his subsequent flight no doubt saved
his life, otherwise he would have shared the fate of the prophets
murdered by Jezebel (v. 13). After three years of drought Elijah
appeared with his usual suddenness to Obadiah, the royal steward,
and announced that he was ready to meet the king.

When Ahab appears he challenges him to gather all the prophets
of Baal on Mount Carmel; the challenge is taken up and a great
ordeal is arranged. The people are asked to make their choice.
Two altars are built and the God who answers by fire is to be
accepted. The priests of Baal, in spite of their frantic efforts,
obtain no answer to their petitions; but the simple prayer of
Elijah receives a startling and dramatic reply. Elijah uses the
moment of victory to command a general massacre of the priests
and prophets of Baal.

Elijah and his servant return to Carmel and wait for the coming
storm which will announce the end of the drought. Then, in the
fullness of the strength given him by Jahveh, the prophet runs
before the royal chariot to Jezreel, a distance of some seventeen
miles.

The contest between the priests of Baal and Elijah on Mount
Carmel is one of the most dramatic prose narratives in all
literature, and shows that not in lyrics alone the Hebrews
could reach the highest standards of art. But high above the
dramatic interest and literary skill stands the faith of the amazing

man who single-handed could dare to challenge a whole nation, and could bring it back once more to serve its God.

Josephus preserves an interesting account from Menander of a year's drought which occurred in Phoenicia about this time. It was brought to an end by the prayers of Ethbaal, Ahab's father-in-law.

XVIII. **20.** *Mount Carmel* is a lofty ridge touching the sea at its western end. The traditional scene of the contest is *el-Muḥrakā* (=*the place of burning*), a height of nearly 1,600 ft. There are reasons for thinking that Mount Carmel was held sacred by the Phoenicians (Robertson Smith, *Religion of the Semites*[2], 156), as well as by Israel (cf. v. 30), and right through history its sanctity has been maintained.[1]

21. *How long halt ye? Halt* here means *limp*.

24. *by fire*. Fire, as an agent of divine revelation, played a great part in the life of Elijah: cf. 19[12]; 2 Kings 1[10], 2[11].

27. *he is a god*. Elijah, to judge by his irony, had risen to the belief in Jahveh as the sole God of the universe.

30. *thrown down*. Presumably by the Baal-worshippers.

31. The building of a new altar, as distinct from the repair of the old one, seems unnecessary and may be an interpolation (cf. LXX).

33. *water*. Some scholars, including Frazer (*Folk-Lore in O.T.*, iii. 67), regard this as a piece of sympathetic magic to bring down rain.

38. *the fire of the LORD*. i.e. lightning: cf. Gen. 19[24]; Num. 11[1, 3]; 2 Kings 1[12], &c.

40. *the brook Kishon* runs below Carmel. The traditional place of the massacre is *Tell el-ʿasīs* (=*the priests' mound*).

42. 'The King went up to feast, the prophet to pray'. Barnes in Camb. Bib. *ad. loc.*

45. *Jezreel* is now *Zerʿin*, some seventeen miles from *el-Muḥrakā*. It was a place of great strategic importance and gave its name to the valley.

46. *ran before Ahab*. Perhaps as one of his attendants (cf. 1 Sam. 8[11]).

[1] 'Iamblichus [*Vit. Pyth.* iii (15)], in the last days of heathenism, still speaks of Mount Carmel as "sacred above all mountains and forbidden of access to the vulgar", and here Vespasian worshipped at the solitary altar, embowered in inviolable thickets, to which ancient tradition forbade the adjuncts of temple and image. . . . The sanctity of Carmel is even now not extinct, and the scene at the Festival of Elijah described by Seetzen, ii. 96 sq., is exactly like an old Canaanite feast.' Robertson Smith, *op. cit.*, p. 256.

(c) *Elijah's flight* (I Kings 19).

Elijah's triumph on Mount Carmel and the slaughter of the prophets of Baal did not finally decide the struggle against foreign influences. Jezebel was too determined and courageous to allow even so severe a check to thwart her plans; and the people, after their sudden enthusiastic outburst, seem to have relapsed into a sullen acceptance of the royal wishes (cf. v. 14). Elijah fled to Beer-sheba in despair for his life, and then made the long journey to Horeb. At the sacred mountain he appears to have sounded the very depths of depression; no trace of hope revealed itself, he alone, so it seemed, was left to be faithful to Jahveh.

His despair was turned to hope by a divine message. In picturesque terms the writer describes the great wind rending the mountains, then an earthquake, then a fire, and last a great silence. In this account more exalted ideas of God than those held by past teachers are struggling for expression; notice especially the realization that physical phenomena of a violent and impressive kind are not adequate symbols of Jahveh's presence.

The vision is followed by a commission. Hazael is to be anointed as king of Syria, Jehu as king of Israel, and as his own successor Elisha the son of Shaphat. These three men are to be divine instruments of slaughter, and when their work is done there will still remain a remnant true to Jahveh.

Elijah leaves the mount and goes on his way to find Elisha. The latter is ready to receive the call and, turning his back on home and possessions, he follows Elijah.

XIX. **2.** *sent a messenger.* Jezebel did not dare to kill Elijah at the moment; she wished to frighten him away.

Beer-sheba is now *Bir es-Seba'* and lies at the southern end of Judah.

4. *a juniper tree.* Better with mg. *broom.*

8. *forty days.* A round number. The direct journey would not have required so long a time.

Horeb. In Pent. this name is used by E and D for the Sinai of J and P. There seems to have been a feeling in Israel that Jahveh's dwelling was still at Horeb (see Judges $5^{4 \, f.}$; Hab. 3^3; Ps. 68^8).

12. *a still small voice*: lit. *a sound of gentle stillness.* A silence which might be heard followed the storm (cf. Exod. 10^{21}: 'a darkness which might be felt').

18. *will I leave.* A.V. *have I left* is incorrect. The remnant consists, not of those at present faithful, but of those who will survive the slaughter.

19. *his mantle.* Cf. 2 Kings 2¹³ ᶠ.

(d) Naboth and his vineyard (1 Kings 21).

The order of the events in Ahab's reign is uncertain. It will be better, therefore, to leave the Syrian wars (chapters 20 and 22) to be taken together (as is done in LXX) and to pass on to the well-known story of Naboth.

The story is closely connected in point of view with chapters 17–19, but differences in style and in the situation presupposed make it unlikely that it comes from the same source or if it does that it is in its right position here.

The incident related in the story must, in its earlier stages at least, have had many parallels in Israel and Judah. The wish of the great man to lay field to field must repeatedly have clashed with the deep-rooted desire of his less fortunate neighbour to cling to the small inheritance handed down, perhaps through many generations, from his fathers.

This story is remarkable for the childish rage of the king and for the cold-blooded determination of his wife (cf. Lady Macbeth). The murder of Naboth, although his death was ostensibly a punishment for a definite crime, must have done much to alienate the sympathy of Israel from the house of Omri and to prepare the way for the successful attempt of Jehu to supplant them.

XXI. 1. *King of Samaria.* The title is strange: see on 13³².

3. Cf. Lev. 25²³ ᶠᶠ.; Num. 36⁶ ᶠ.

9. *Proclaim a fast.* This was to be done one supposes because of the horrible nature of the supposed crime.

on high mg. *at the head of.* The meaning of this is obscure, it may correspond to our 'placing in the dock'.

10. *two men.* The necessary number of witnesses in a capital charge (Deut. 17⁶; cf. Matt. 26⁶⁰).

sons of Belial. People of bad character.

14. *Naboth is stoned.* They do not mention his sons who were also put to death (2 Kings 9²⁶).

19. *even thine.* Not literally fulfilled (cf. 2 Kings 9²⁶).

21 ff. The address of Elijah follows conventional Deuteronomic lines.

(e) *Wars with Syria* (1 Kings 20).

Relations between Syria and Israel seem to have varied from time to time. Normally they were not on friendly terms, and treaties between them were little more than truces to give time to prepare for renewing the struggle. When Shalmaneser III of Assyria invaded Palestine they were both found in arms against him, but such alliances between local enemies against a foe from a distance are not uncommon and signify but little; it is even possible that, in this instance, Ahab fought as a Syrian vassal.

This chapter and 22 differ in outlook from the greater part of Kings and, indeed, of O. T. as a whole since they betray a real interest in political events. The writer, because his standard is less rigid and less theological, regards Ahab in a much more favourable light than other narrators who deal with his reign.

In the present chapter three separate incidents are described. In the first (vv. 1–22) Ben-hadad, after making humiliating demands upon Ahab, prepares to attack Samaria. By the advice of a prophet Ahab chooses out two hundred and thirty-two young men who lead a sudden sally and put the Syrians to flight. The next incident (vv. 23–34) records a victory gained by a small force of Israelites over a large Syrian army at Aphek. The defeat was so severe that Ben-hadad himself was forced to surrender. Ahab treated him mercifully and restored to him his liberty after a treaty had been made by which Israel was allowed special trading facilities in Damascus. But Ahab's clemency did not meet with the approval of the sterner minds among the nation and the king received from one of the prophets a severe condemnation for releasing one who was not only the enemy of Israel but of Jahveh also (vv. 35–43).

XX. 1. *Ben-hadad.* This name is possibly a mistaken rendering of *Bir'idri* found in the inscription of Shalmaneser. LXX reads *Son of Hadar*, which is nearer to the original since in it the final *r* has not yet been changed to *d*. *Bir* has been read as *Bar*, which means *son* in Aramaic, and so changed into the equivalent Heb. *Ben*.

thirty and two kings. An inscription found in North Syria in 1903 mentions a confederation of kings led by Bar-hadad, King of Aram. See *Camb. Anct. Hist.*, iii. 375.

12. *he was drinking.* So in v. 16. The Syrians seem to have suffered from bad leadership and want of discipline: cf. Shakespeare's description of the French before Agincourt in *Henry V*, Act III, Sc. vii.

14. *young men . . . provinces.* These would be servants of the provincial governors. The choice was perhaps an arbitrary one as in the case of Gideon's men (Judges 7$^{4ff.}$).

23. *a god of the hills.* Jahveh is constantly associated with mountains. e.g. Ex. 24^{10}, Dt. 33^2, Ezek. 6^2, Ps. 121^1.

26. *Aphek* may be the place mentioned in 1 Sam. 29^1 (see on 1 Sam. 4^1). Its exact situation is not known, but it must have been in the north on the Syrian border.

29–30. The numbers in these two verses are absurdly exaggerated.

31. 'This tribute to the humanity of the Hebrew kings, which is probably a reflection of the national character, is extremely interesting.' (Skinner.)

34. This incidental notice tells us, a fact not otherwise known, that Omri had to make concessions to the Syrians.

streets. Better perhaps *bazaars*.

36. *a lion.* Cf. 13^{24}. Lions seem to have been common.

38. *headband, &c.* A.V. by a slight change in Heb. reads *ashes upon his face. Headband* should probably, following the meaning of the cognate word in Ass., be rendered *bandage*.

40. The method employed is that of Nathan in dealing with David's sin; the king unwittingly condemns himself.

42. The offence is that of Saul in allowing Agag to live.

(f) The death of Ahab (1 Kings 22$^{1-38}$).

The treaty made between Ben-hadad and Ahab after the battle of Aphek does not seem to have been faithfully carried out by the Syrians, for the Israelite city of Ramoth-gilead remained in their possession even after the lapse of three years.

Ahab determines to attempt to enforce his rights and musters not only his own forces, but those of Jehoshaphat of Judah, who seems to have been his vassal. The official prophets promise success to the king, but Micaiah, son of Imlah, predicts, in dark and threatening language, the scattering of Israel and the death of Ahab himself.

Micaiah's words did not put a stop to the expedition, but Ahab was sufficiently impressed by them (so it may be inferred) to disguise himself and to enter the battle as a simple captain (hardly perhaps as a common soldier as Skinner suggests since he had a chariot). The Syrian king, with peculiar malignity, had commanded his captains to seek out and attack Ahab; and at first they surrounded the only person in royal robes, Jehoshaphat of

Judah. They soon found out their mistake, possibly because of the battle-cry of Jehoshaphat. Ahab, however, did not escape the judgement of God (so the writer believed), and a chance arrow pierced his harness and inflicted a mortal wound. The king was unable, or unwilling, to withdraw his chariot from the battle, and slowly bled to death. The knowledge of his fall produced a panic in the Israelite ranks and they fled to their homes, their flight, presumably, being shared by Jehoshaphat and his Judeans.

The body of Ahab was brought to Samaria and there buried. A later writer, having in mind Elijah's prophecy (21¹⁹), states that the blood from the chariot was licked up by the dogs of Samaria. He forgot that the literal fulfilment required the death of Ahab on the spot where Naboth had been stoned, and further that Ahab's repentance saved him from the consequences of his crime (21²⁹).

This chapter is very important for the study of the Hebrew conception of prophecy. Not only do we get the first instance of a division in the ranks of the prophets of Jahveh, but Micaiah, whilst admitting the genuineness of the inspiration of his opponents, regards them as deceived by Jahveh Himself.

XXII. 1. *three years*. This period is to be dated from the victory of Aphek (20³⁴).

3. *Ramoth-gilead*. The site of this place is often taken to be *es-Salt*, eighteen miles north of the Dead Sea, but a situation still further north seems to be demanded by 4¹³.

6. The prophets here called together are devoted to the service of Jahveh. From their standpoint His fortunes were involved in the conflict and so victory was promised.

8. *Micaiah*. It is strange that there is no mention of Elijah. His fitful and sudden appearances, however, would make it impossible for him to be regarded as a regular prophet who could be constantly consulted.

17. *no shepherd*. Cf. Num. 27¹⁷; Matt. 9³⁶.

19. *host of heaven*. Not the stars, but Jahveh's attendants.

25. Cf. Jer. 28⁹.

35. One wonders what thoughts went through the mind of Ahab during this long day.

(g) *Fire from Heaven* (2 Kings 1²⁻¹⁸).

Ahab was succeeded on the throne by his son Ahaziah. After reigning nearly two years Ahaziah met with an accident and, for reasons which are not given, instead of inquiring of Jahveh as to the result he sent to Baal-zebub of Ekron. Elijah indignantly stopped the messengers and turned them back, whereupon the king ordered his arrest. Two companies of soldiers who attempted to carry out the order were destroyed by lightning at the command of Elijah, and a third escaped only by the humble bearing of its terrified captain. Elijah then went to the bedside of Ahaziah and told the king that he must die.

A comparison of this passage with Luke 9[54 ff.] reveals the immense gulf between the cruder Hebrew conceptions of religion and the teaching of our Lord. The passage seems hardly to agree with the picture of Elijah given in 1 Kings 17–19, but Skinner, in calling it 'the only painful episode in all the histories of Elijah', seems to have forgotten the slaughter of the prophets of Baal in 1 Kings 18[40].

I. 2. *the lattice* was the network covering the window opening.

Baal-zebub means the *Lord of flies* and is probably connected in some obscure way with Beelzebub, the prince of the devils (Matt.10[25]).

Ekron. See p. 164.

3. *the angel of the* LORD. Not here Jahveh Himself but His messenger.

8. *an hairy man.* This probably means only that he was clothed in a garment of hair.

girdle. Cf. Mark 1[6].

13. 'The behaviour of this third captain illustrates the respect due to a prophet, which it is obviously the writer's design to inculcate.' (Skinner.)

(h) The passing of Elijah (2 Kings 2[1-18]).

The story in this section may be regarded from one of two points of view, as either the end of the life and ministry of Elijah, or the beginning of those of Elisha. From a literary point of view the second standpoint is probably correct, but for the sake of balance and completeness the narrative is here included in the story of Elijah.

That the story is more closely connected with the cycle of legends concerning Elisha than with that concerning Elijah is suggested by two facts. In the Elijah cycle Elisha has already been set apart as the successor of his master and invested with his mantle (1 Kings 19[19]), and in that cycle there is no trace of any connexion between Elijah and the schools of the prophets such as is here suggested.

The narrative describes Elijah's progress from Gilgal to Beth-el, thence to Jericho, and thence across the Jordan which is divided by the magical powers of Elijah. At each stage of the journey the older prophet tries to persuade the younger to leave him, but always in vain. As they walk on Elisha begs that a portion of the spirit of his master may rest upon him. He receives the reply that if he sees Elijah when he is taken from him, it shall be so. A whirlwind suddenly snatches Elijah away in a chariot of fire, but Elisha sees him and the mantle of the departing prophet falling from him he picks it up. Full of prophetic enthusiasm Elisha performs in his turn the miracle of dividing the waters of the Jordan, and going on impresses the prophets who meet him with his right to fill the place of Elijah.

II. 1. *Gilgal* cannot be the place named in Joshua 4[19] since it lies on the side of Jericho away from the Jordan. The name means *stone-circle*, many examples of which no doubt existed in Israel.

4. *Jericho.* See p. 125.

9. *a double portion.* That is, as the margin points out, the inheritance of an eldest son (Deut. 21[17]). Elisha wishes to be recognized as the heir and successor of Elijah.

12. *the chariots of Israel, &c.* (also in 13[14]). The prophet could do more for his country than armaments and warriors.

14. Elisha's faith in Jahveh as the *God of Elijah* after this successful appeal becomes more personal.

§ 3. THE MINISTRY OF ELISHA

The closing section of the period is concerned with the work of Elisha, the servant and successor of Elijah. His varied activities were not unlike those of his master, in fact at times it seems as if stories told of one prophet have been applied to the other (see below, p. 229), although his character and methods were very different. His work in nerving the Israelites in their great struggle with Syria is only hinted at, but his dying thoughts were with his countrymen and the monarch himself saw in Elisha one who was to the nation as valuable as its chariots and horsemen.

(a) War against Moab (2 Kings 3[4-27]).

On the death of Ahab, Mesha, king of Moab, seized the opportunity of refusing to continue an annual tribute. Jehoram of Israel raised an army, and, like his father Ahab, called upon

Jehoshaphat of Judah to furnish troops. The king of Edom also joined them, probably as the vassal of Jehoshaphat. The allies are soon in great distress because of a shortage of water and Elisha is called upon to relieve them.

In order to obtain a divine oracle Elisha required the inspiration of music. He then commanded that trenches should be dug in the valley, and promised that into them water would come without any sign of wind or rain. He promised further that the Moabites would be defeated, at the same time ordering that their land, when conquered, should be ravaged even to the cutting down of the fruit trees, a most unusual piece of severity (see on v. 19).

Elisha's promises were quickly verified by the event, for the Moabites, seeing the early morning sun shining on the water, mistook it for blood. This suggested to them the idea that their enemies had turned their swords against one another. When, however, they rushed out to spoil what they thought to be an undefended camp, they soon discovered their mistake and were overwhelmed by the Israelites. Moab now lay at the mercy of Israel and the barbarous commands of Elisha were carried out. Mesha was driven back into his last stronghold and in vain attempted a sortie with a body of picked troops. In despair he offered up his firstborn son to Chemosh whereupon the Israelites, for some cause unknown, retreated beyond the frontier.

Two very important points should be noticed in the passage: (a) the use of music as a source of inspiration by a prophet of Jahveh (cf. the modern dervish), and (b) the belief in the effectiveness of human sacrifice.

III. 4. *a sheepmaster.* The same word (Heb. *nōḳēd*) is used of the prophet Amos (1[1]), and the Arabs still call a certain breed of sheep *naḳad*.[1]

7. Jehoshaphat was vassal to Jehoram as he had been to Ahab (1 Kings 22[4]).

9. *king of Edom.* Perhaps a Judean governor, since Edom had at this time no king of its own (1 Kings 22[47]; 2 Kings 8[20]).

11. Jehoshaphat had asked the same question of Ahab (1 Kings 22[7]).

---

[1] They are described by M. A. Canney in P.C., p. 547, as 'having short legs and ugly faces but valued highly for their choice wool (cf. for their stunted growth the Arabian proverb "viler than a *naḳad*"; and see Chenery, *Assemblies of Al Harîri*, i. 452 f.)'.

which poured water, &c. Elisha is here known only as the minister of Elijah.

15. *a minstrel.* For the use of music in connexion with prophecy, cf. 1 Sam. 10⁵, and see Robertson Smith, *Prophets*, ii. 392.

16. *this valley.* Probably the *Wadi el-Ahṣā=valley of sandy water pits.* 'The peculiarity of the region is that the water from the mountains of Edom sinks beneath the surface, and is retained underground by the rocky bottom; so that a supply can almost always be obtained by digging pits in the sand.' (Skinner.)

25. The barbarous methods here employed are forbidden by Deut. 20¹⁹ᶠ.

Kir-hareseth is the modern Kerak where ancient fortifications still exist.

27. *great wrath against Israel.* Chemosh was evidently believed to have been moved by the sacrifice.

(b) The Shunammite and her Son (2 Kings 4⁸⁻³⁷).

Many traditions concerning the prophets were no doubt preserved in ancient Israel being repeated by word of mouth. Sometimes no doubt the name of the prophet who was the hero of the story would vary, and some such confusion seems to have taken place between the very similar names of Elijah and Elisha. Our story here has much resemblance to that related of Elijah in 1 Kings 17¹⁷ ᶠᶠ·, just as the multiplication of the widow's oil in vv. 1–7 may have been based on 1 Kings 17⁸ ᶠᶠ·

A wealthy lady of Shunem was in the habit of entertaining Elisha whenever he passed through Shunem. After a time she persuaded her husband to provide for him a small chamber furnished with the simple necessities of life. In return a child is born to her. Unfortunately the boy when grown older gets sunstroke which speedily proves fatal. The lady still trusts the man of God and journeys to Mount Carmel to seek his help. Elisha at first sends Gehazi, his minister, to lay his staff on the child's face, but no result follows. He thereupon goes in person and succeeds in restoring the dead to life.

IV. 8. *Shunem,* the modern *Solam,* is some five miles from Jezreel and about twenty miles from Carmel. It was the camping-place of the Philistines before the battle on Mount Gilboa (1 Sam. 28⁴).

10. *chamber on the wall.* Better as mg. *with walls.* It was not a merely temporary dwelling-place. The list of furniture is interesting.

23. *neither new moon nor sabbath.* It was apparently the custom to visit a prophet at these festivals.

27. The sacredness of the prophet's person is here emphasized as in 1⁹ *ff.*

29. *salute him not.* So in Luke 10⁴.

(c) *The Healing of Naaman* (2 Kings 5¹⁻¹⁹).

The exact period from which this well-known story comes is not certain. It was evidently a time of peace between the king of Israel and the king of Syria with the former in the position of vassal to the latter (vv. 6 ff.), both being unnamed.

Naaman, a great Syrian leader, was a leper, and, finding no cure in his own country, he seizes upon the hope, first aroused by the words of a Hebrew slave belonging to his wife, that Elisha may be able to restore him. Bearing letters from his master he comes to Samaria to the dismay of the Israelite monarch who is bidden to cure him. Elisha, however, reassures him; but, when Naaman comes to see him, he treats him in a way which the Syrian considers to be undignified, merely telling him to go and wash seven times in Jordan. It required the pleadings of his servants to make him do as he was advised. He went to Jordan and recovered.

He came back to Elisha offering rich rewards which the prophet refused, and then made a further request, that enough of the soil of Israel might be given him upon which to worship Jahveh. He begs that Jahveh will pardon him if his official duties compel him to bow down in the house of Rimmon.

V. **1.** *the LORD.* It is remarkable that Jahveh is held responsible for the victories of Naaman. It suggests the recognition of His all-sovereign power.

3. The household of Naaman seem to have been on good terms with their lord (cf. v. 13).

6. *thou mayest recover,* i.e. thou shalt. The words are a command.

12. *Abanah and Pharpar.* These names are now lost, but two great rivers, the *Nahr Baradā* and the *Nahr el-A'waj*, still water Damascus.

15. *no God.* Cf. v. 1.

17. Naaman, although he believes Jahveh to be unique, still thinks of Him as capable only of being worshipped on the soil of Israel.

18. *Rimmon* is *Rammān*, an Assyrian thunder-god better known as Hadad.

19. *Go in peace*: i.e. farewell. The phrase is conventional and expresses no judgement on Naaman's proposed conduct.

(d) *Elisha and the Syrians* (2 Kings 6⁸⁻²³).

This section provides a story full of varied interest: the supernatural knowledge of Elisha, the unseen host which protected him, and the chivalrous kindness which led him to counsel the king to spare a captured foe.

The king of Syria, suspecting that his secret plans were being revealed to Israel, since they were so repeatedly anticipated, accused his officers of treachery. In return he is informed that Elisha becomes acquainted, in some mysterious way, with all that

'Are not Abana and Pharpar, the rivers of Damascus, better than all the waters of Israel?' A mixed flock of sheep and goats watering at a stream of the *Nahr Baradā*

is going on. The king thereupon sends a force to Dothan where the prophet is then living (the writer of the story very naïvely ignores the fact that Elisha's supernatural knowledge would reveal to him the planning of this expedition as of its predecessors) to seize his person.

The prophet's servant, going out in the early morning, sees the Syrian host, but his alarm is allayed by being allowed a vision of the supernatural army guarding his master. At Elisha's prayer the Syrians become blind, in which state he leads them into the middle of Samaria where they are surrounded. The king of

Israel at Elisha's request sends them away unhurt. In return for this act of kindness the Syrian marauding bands no longer molest Israel.

VI. **8.** *shall be my camp.* A slight change in the text gives the much better reading *let us set an ambush.*

13. *Dothan* still survives in the modern *Tell Dōthān*, a green mound some twenty miles from Samaria to the north.

17. Cf. 2^{11}.

21. *My father.* The king regards the prophet with awe and veneration.

23. *came no more.* The wars between Syria and Israel seem to have been conducted in a chivalrous spirit: cf. Ahab's clemency (1 Kings $20^{32\,ff.}$).

(e) *The Rise of Jehu* (2 Kings 9^{1-26}).

Elisha held the same views of Baal worship as his master, but for a time he seems to have remained quiet. The house of Omri still reigned, Jezebel still lived, and any attempt to uproot the foreign cult would probably have been unsuccessful. Victory against Syria had apparently crowned the Israelite arms, for Ramoth-gilead had been recovered (cf. 1 Kings 21^3), though the Syrians were again threatening it (v. 14). About this time King Jehoram was wounded and had to leave the army to recover; Elisha seized his opportunity and sent down one of his followers to anoint as king a popular officer, Jehu, the son of Nimshi. The young prophet dashed into a council of officers and called Jehu out. When they were alone he anointed him, and then rushed away as mysteriously as he had come. Jehu's fellow officers began to question him about his strange visitor, but, on learning what had happened, proclaimed him as king with wild enthusiasm. Having stopped any messenger from going to Jezreel to carry the news Jehu in his chariot dashes off.

With great literary skill the scene is suddenly changed to Jezreel where the king lies sick and the watchman in his tower stands gazing across the plain. Suddenly he gives warning of an approaching body of men, and two messengers in succession gallop out to make inquiries, but fail to return. As the cavalcade draws nearer the driving of Jehu is recognized, and the king, with Ahaziah of Judah, goes out to meet him. A short interview ends in the murder of Jehoram by Jehu's own hand, and his body being thrown into the fateful field of Naboth.

IX. 1. *Ramoth-gilead.* See on 1 Kings 22³.

3. So Saul and David were anointed in secret.

7–10*a*. These verses are in the style of D and interrupt the story.

11. *this mad fellow.* The dividing-line between prophecy and insanity is narrow to the Eastern mind, both being regarded as forms of possession.

Jezebel at the window. A Phoenician carving of
a goddess looking out of a window

20. *furiously.* As one possessed, the same root as that used for *mad* in the above note. LXX, which is followed by Josephus, takes the word in the sense of 'in a meditation'.

22. *whoredoms.* That is idolatry (cf. Hos. 1², &c.).

26. The account here differs in detail from that in 1 Kings 21¹⁹, a good illustration of the way in which the biblical writers paid no heed to verbal consistency.

(*f*) *The death of Jezebel* (2 Kings 9³⁰⁻³⁷).

So long as Jezebel lived, the life of the new king would not be safe from attempts at revolt or assassination, nor would the danger of the revival of Baal-worship have been removed. When Jehu drove into Jezreel, the aged queen determined to meet her fate bravely and unhesitatingly. She greeted the new king as another Zimri, the murderer of his lord. At Jehu's command some eunuchs, who were probably among her own attendants, cast her headlong from the window; and with superb scorn he drives over her mangled body. After feasting in the palace Jehu remembers the honour due to royal blood and orders the body of Jezebel to be buried. But it was too late, the dogs had already done their ghastly work, and nothing was left but a few bones. In all their horror the words of Elijah had been fulfilled.

IX. 30. *painted her eyes*: lit. *set her eyes in antimony*. The object was to increase the beauty of the eyes: see further Jer. 4³⁰ with the present writer's note.

36. Cf. 1 Kings 21²³.

37. *as dung*. So in Jer. 7², 9²², &c.

(g) The Massacre of the Baal worshippers (2 Kings 10¹⁵⁻²⁷).

The murder of Jehoram and of Jezebel, not to mention that of Ahaziah of Judah, had been followed by the massacre of the whole house of Ahab. But even then Jehu's thirst for blood remained unsatisfied, nothing less than the extermination of all the worshippers of Baal in the land would slake it.

In his drastic policy Jehu had the co-operation of Jehonadab, the son of Rechab (it should be noted that Elisha nowhere appears), the founder of the sect of the Rechabites. According to Jer. 35 these people were ascetics, who refused to have any share in the corrupt civilization of the land with its heathen influences, preferring to retain as far as possible the simplicity of nomad life (see further the notes in my commentary on *Jeremiah*, pp. 263 ff.).

Jehu's method of destroying the followers of Baal was to proclaim a great feast at which every worshipper was to be present. On the appointed day vestments were provided for the congregation, and Jehu himself offered sacrifice, but at the end of the offering, the royal guards entered the temple and not a soul escaped them. The temple of Baal itself was afterwards desecrated.

X. 18. It is difficult to suppose that the people were deceived by Jehu's professions; force and terror no doubt compelled many of them to be present.

22. *vestments*. The wearing of sacred vestments supplied to the worshippers was not uncommon among the Arabs and kindred peoples: see Robertson Smith, *Religion of the Semites*², 451 f.

25. *the city of the house of Baal*. The text seems corrupt; perhaps some kind of inner sanctuary is meant.

(*h*) *The Usurpation and Death of Athaliah* (2 Kings 11¹⁻²⁰).

One member at least of the house of Ahab did not meet death in the massacres organized by Jehu,[1] Athaliah the widow of King Joram of Judah. On the murder of Ahaziah she seized the vacant throne and, in order to make it secure, slaughtered the surviving members of the royal family. But it happened that Jehosheba, a sister of Ahaziah, saved Jehoash, his infant son, and kept him hidden in the temple where her husband Jehoiada was chief priest. After six years of patient waiting Jehoiada showed the boy to the captains of the royal guard and had him proclaimed as king. Athaliah, attracted by the noise of the shouting, hurried to the temple; but only to meet her death, for Jehoiada ordered her to be seized and taken outside the sacred edifice and there slain. That the revolution had a religious character, as well as a political, may be seen from v. 18 where the temple of Baal is stated to have been plundered by the people and its priest put to death.

XI. **2.** *Jehosheba.* She was the wife of Jehoiada, according to 2 Chron. 22¹¹, perhaps only a doubtful authority.

4. *the Carites* were probably foreign mercenaries. The kings of Judah from the beginning of the separate kingdom seem to have had foreign bodyguards (cf. the Cherethites and Pelethites of David); we do not hear of them in the northern kingdom.

shewed them the king's son. We do not know how the captains were convinced of his being really a legitimate claimant to the throne.

12. The details here described are important and interesting. *the testimony* should perhaps be *the bracelets* (cf. 2 Sam. 1¹⁰), unless the king at the time of his coronation held in his hand a copy of the Law.

13–18a. These verses, according to a theory first advanced by Stade, belong to a different source. In them the people are the leaders in the enterprise and a religious motive is predominant.

18. *Mattan* should probably be *Mattan-Baal* = *the gift of Baal.*

(*i*) *The Death and Burial of Elisha* (2 Kings 13¹⁴⁻²¹).

Elisha is not so prominent a figure in the political narratives in Kings as we should have expected, but incidental allusions make it certain that he exercised great influence, and this last

---

[1] It is curious, as S. A. Cook points out, that Jehu did not take the opportunity of becoming king of Judah as well as of Israel (*Camb. Anct. Hist.* iii. 368).

scene is, as Skinner says, 'a pathetic tribute at once to his loyalty to the dynasty he had been the means of raising to the throne and to the great part he had played in his country's struggle for freedom.'

Joash, the king of Israel, comes down to see Elisha as the prophet lies dying and breaks down at the thought of the removal from the kingdom of its great inspiration. The old man has power enough left to encourage the king in his struggle against Syria and to assure him of victories yet to come.

After Elisha was buried men believed that supernatural power still possessed his bones, and on one occasion at least a dead body was restored to life by touching them. The story reads like a passage from Bede's *Ecclesiastical History*.

XIII. **14.** *my father*. The same address is used by the unnamed king in 6[21].

the chariots of Israel. Cf. 2[12].

17. *Aphek*. See p. 161.

eastward. Towards Damascus presumably, though north-east was a more exact direction.

20. *invaded*. The Heb. suggests continual action, *were in the habit of invading*.

APPENDIX

INSCRIPTIONS ILLUSTRATING OLD TESTAMENT EVENTS

1. *The Assyrian Eponym List.*

Part only of this List is given. The original stretches from 893 to 666 B.C. The List contains the names of the officers who gave their names to successive years as amongst the Greeks and Romans: see p. 70.

889 Tukulti-Ninura, the king.
888 Tak-lak-ana-bil-ia.
887 Abu-Malik.
886 Ilu-milki.
885 Iari.
884 Ashur-shezibani.
883 Ashur-nasir-pal, the king.
882 Ashur-iddin.
881 Imuttiaku.
880 Sha-(ilu)ma-dam-ka.

2. *The Tell el-Amarna Letters.*

These have been described in the Introd., pp. 13 ff, and extracts from them given.

3. *The Stele of Merneptah, c.* 1220 B.C.

This inscription was placed on the back of a stele of black syenite originally inscribed by Amenhotep III: see Ball, *Light from the Ancient East*, p. 129. The following extract is based on the translation in *Camb. Anct. Hist.* ii. 169.

Wasted is Tehenu,
The Hittite land is pacified,
Plundered is 'the Canaan', with every evil,
Carried off is Askalon,
Seized upon is Gezer,
Yenoam is made as a thing not existing.
Israel is desolated, her seed is not,
Palestine has become a (defenceless) widow for Egypt.
All lands are united, they are pacified;
Every one that is turbulent is bound by king Merneptah.

4. *The Moabite Stone.*

This stone, which was discovered in the ruins of Dibon in 1868, is written in Phoenician characters and it is important as being the nearest approach to an ancient Hebrew inscription which we possess. A squeeze from it is now in the Louvre at Paris. It contains an account by Mesha', king of Moab (2 Kings 3⁵), of his relations with Israel, and its language might almost have come from the book of Kings itself. The following is Driver's translation:

1. I am Mesha' son of Chemosh [Kan?], king of Moab, the Da-
2. -ibonite. My father reigned over Moab for 30 years, and I reign-
3. -ed after my father. And I made this high place for Chemosh in QRḤH, a (high place of sal-)
4. -vation, because he had saved me from all the assailants (?), and because he had let me see my pleasure on all them that hated me.[1] Omr-
5. -i king of Israel afflicted Moab for many days, because Chemosh was angry[2] with his la-
6. -nd. And his son succeeded him; and he also said, I will afflict Moab. In my days said he th(us);
7. but I saw my pleasure on him, and on his house, and Israel perished with an everlasting destruction. And Omri took possession of the (la-)
8. -nd of Mehedeba,[3] and it (i.e. Israel) dwelt therein, during his days, and half his son's days, 40 years; but (resto-)
9. -red it Chemosh in my days. And I built Ba'al-me'on,[4] and I made in it a reservoir (?); and I built
10. Qiryathen.[5] And the men of Gad had dwelt in the land of 'Ataroth from of old; and built for himself the king of I-
11. -srael 'Ataroth.[6] And I fought against the city, and took it. And I slew all the people (from)
12. the city, a gazingstock[7] unto Chemosh, and unto Moab. And I brought back thence the altar-hearth of Davdoh, and I drag-
13. -ged it[8] before Chemosh in Qeriyyoth. And I settled therein the men of SHRN, and the men of
14. MHRTH. And Chemosh said unto me, Go,[9] take Nebo against Israel. And I

[1] Cf. Ps. 118⁷. [2] Cf. 2 Kings 17¹⁸. [3] Medeba (Num. 21³⁰). [4] Joshua 13¹⁷.
[5] Kiriathaim (Num. 32³⁷). [6] Num. 32³⁴. [7] Cf. Nahum 3⁶; Ezra 28¹⁷. [8] Cf. 2 Sam. 17¹³. [9] Cf. Joshua 8¹.

Captives from Ḳarḳar

15. went by night, and fought against it from the break of dawn until noon. And I too-

16. -k it, and slew the whole of it, 7,000 men and male sojourners, and women and (female sojour-)

17. -ers, and female slaves: [1] for I devoted it to 'Ashtor-Chemosh. And I took thence the ves-

18. -sels of YAHWEH, and I dragged them before Chemosh. And the king of Israel had built

19. Yahas,[2] and abode in it, while he fought against me. But Chemosh drave him out from before me; and

20. I took of Moab 200 men, even all the chiefs; and I brought them up against Yahas, and took it

21. to add it unto Daibon. I built QRḤH, the wall of the Woods, and the wall of

22. the Mound. And I built its gates, and I built its towers. And

23. I built the king's house,[3] and I made two reser[voirs (?) for wa]ter in the midst of

24. the city. And there was no cistern in the midst of the city, in QRḤH. And I said to the people, Make

25. you every man a cistern in his house. And I cut out the cutting for QRḤH with the help of prisoner-

26. (-s of) Israel. I built 'Aro'er, and I made the highway by the Arnon.

(The rest of the Inscription is much damaged.)

5. *The Karkar Inscription of Shalmaneser III.* 853 B.C.

This inscription was made on a monolith erected near Diarbekr on the upper Tigris. It is now in the British Museum.

87.   I approached two cities of

88. Irkhulini of Hamath. Adennu, Parga, Argana, his royal city, I captured. I brought out his spoil, possessions, and

89. the riches of his palaces, and delivered his palaces to the fire. I left Argana; I approached Karkar;

90. Karkar, his royal city, I overthrew, plundered, and burned with fire. 1200 chariots, 1200 horsemen (or steeds?), 20,000 men of Adad-idri (=Ben-Hadad)

91. of Damascus; 700 chariots and 700 horsemen, and 10,000 men of Irkhulini of Hamath; 2,000 chariots, 10,000 men of Ahabbu (=Ahab)

---

[1] Cf. Judges 5[30].   [2] Jahaz (Num. 21[23]).   [3] Cf. 1 Kings 16[18].

92. Sir-i-lai (=the Israel-
    ite); 500 men of the
    Guans (=Kue or
    Cilicia); 1000 men
    of Muṣri (?=Egyp-
    tians); 10 chariots,
    10,000 men of Ir-
    ḳanata (?=Arkites)
93. 200 men of Matinu-bali
    of Arvad; 200 men
    of the Usanatians;
    30 chariots, 10,000
    men of
94. Adunu-bali the Shiani-
    an; 1000 camels from
    Gindibu the Ara-
    bian . . . 1000 men of
95. Baasha the son of Re-
    hob of Ammon;
    these 12 kings he
    took to his assis-
    tance, they marched
    to make
96. war and battle upon
    me. With the mighty
    power (or forces)
    which Ashur the lord
    had given me, with
    the mighty arms
    which Nergal, who
    goes before me
97. had given me, I fought
    with them; from
    Ḳarḳar to Gilzau
    I defeated them;
    14,000 of their war-
    riors
98. I overthrew with wea-
    pons, like Adad I
    poured a deluge
    upon them, I piled
    up their corpses, &c.

The Black Obelisk of Shalmaneser III
(see page 242)

6. The Black Obelisk of Shalmaneser III.

This famous inscription was found in the central palace of Nimrūd; it is now in the British Museum.

1. In the 18th year of my reign I crossed, for the sixteenth time
2. the Euphrates. Ha-za' ilu (=Hazael) of Damascus
3, 4. trusted to the great number of his troops
5. and assembled his troops in multitudes.
6. Saniru (=Senir, i. e. Hermon, Deut. 3⁹), a peak at the entrance to Lebanon, he made into
8. his fortress. I fought with him
9. and defeated him. 16,000
10. of his warriors with weapons
11. I destroyed 1121 of his chariots,
12. 470 of his horsemen (? horses), also his camp,
13. I took from him. He fled to save
14. his life. I followed him and
15. in Damascus, his royal city, I shut him up.
16. I cut down his plantations and marched to the mountains of
17. Ha-u-ra-ni (=the Hauran). Cities innumerable I destroyed, wasted
18. and burned, their spoils I carried away
19. without number.
21. I marched to the mountain of Bali-rasi,
22. a mount at the head of the sea,
23. and set up there my royal image. At that time
24. the tribute of the Tyrians
25. Sidonians and of Ia-u-a (=Jehu)
26. of the land of Hu-um-ri (=Omri) I received.

Above the relief representing the Israelite tribute the following inscription appears.

Tribute of Ia-u-a mar Hu-um-ri (=Jehu of the land of Omri): silver, gold, a golden bowl (?), a golden basin (?), golden cups (?), golden pails, bars of lead, sceptres (?) for the hand of the king, and balsam woods I received from him.

INDEX

A

Aaron, 31, 51, 83–122.
Abarim, 122.
Abdi-Khiba, 15, 16.
Abiathar, 42, 54, 175, 189, 196.
Abijah, 213.
Abimelech, 64, 144–6.
Abiram, 114, 115.
Abishai, 175, 189.
Abner, 41, 175, 179, 180.
Abraham, 32, 82, 104, 109, 162.
Absalom, 42, 186–9.
Accho, 135.
Achan, 35, 128.
Achish, 41, 176, 196.
Achor, 128.
Adad-nirari I, 21.
Adad-nirari II, 24.
Adad-nirari III, 27.
Adam, 126.
Addu : see Hadad.
Adoni-bezek, 134.
Adonijah, 186, 193–6.
Adoni-zedek, 130.
Ahab, 26, 44, 216–25.
Agag, 122, 169–70.
Ahaziah, 225, 226
Ahijah, 208, 209, 211.
Ahimaaz, 188, 189.
Ahimelech, 174, 175.
Ahitophel, 187.
Ahmose I, 68.
Ai, 35, 128, 129, 146.
Aijalon, 131, 168, 169.
Alexander the Great, 101.
Alfred, King, 34.
Allenby, General, 131.
Amalek, 40, 102, 112, 114, 117, 118, 123, 138, 169, 170, 176, 177, 178.
Amanus, Mount, 22.
Amasa, 189.
Amenhotep II, 68.
Amenhotep III, 2, 5, 237.
Amenhotep IV, 2, 4, 7, 13, 30.
Ammon, 38, 39, 138, 146, 147, 184.
Amon, 4, 10, 214.
Amorites, 16, 22, 33, 35, 36, 112, 114.
Amos, 52, 212, 228.
Anathoth, 196.

Antigone, 147.
Aperu, 30.
Aphek, 161, 223, 224, 236.
Arabs, 53, 101, 110, 120, 131, 172, 206, 234.
Arameans, 3, 22, 42, 223–5, 230–2.
Araunah, 191–3.
Aristotle, 76.
Arnon, 147.
Aroer, 147, 192.
Arvad, 22, 198.
Asa, 12, 44, 215.
Asahel, 179.
Ashdod, 162, 164, 176.
Asher, 16, 140.
Ashkelon, 135, 154.
Ashur-nasir-pal II, 24.
Asshur, 122.
Assyria, 1, 21–7, 43.
Athaliah, 44, 235.
Aton, 4, 7.
Azekah, 172.

B

Baal, 44, 49, 55, 141, 142, 216–21, 232–5.
Babylon, 1, 21–7, 121.
Bahurim, 182.
Balaam, 33, 34, 119–21, 212.
Balak, 33, 119–21, 134, 138–40.
Ball, C. J., 237.
Bar-cochab, 136.
Barnes, W. E., 200, 218, 220.
Bashan, 33, 119.
Bath-sheba, 184, 186, 194, 196.
Bedawin, 2, 28, 29, 30, 32, 37, 40, 80, 91, 102, 140.
Bede, 236.
Beer-sheba, 16, 161, 192, 221.
Bel, 82, 122.
Benaiah, 194.
Ben-hadad, 223, 224.
Benzinger, 202.
Beth-aven, 128, 169.
Beth-el, 51, 54, 105, 199, 211, 212, 227.
Beth-horon, 36, 131, 169.
Bethlehem, 167, 170, 171, 172, 174.
Beth-shan, 21, 135, 178.

Beth-shean : *see* Beth-shan.
Beth-shemash, 135, 153, 164, 165.
Boghaz-Keui, 13.
Box, G. H., 100.
Breasted, J. H., 2, 8, 200, 208.
Bubastis, 6, 10.
Budde, 32.
Burney, C. F., 113, 117, 135, 139-44, 146, 152, 154, 156, 158.
Byblus (Gebal), 10, 26, 198.
Byron, 147.

C

Caesar, Julius, 122, 178, 186.
Caleb, 33, 111, 135.
Canaan, 10, 16, 28, 33, 35-7, 45, 49-50, 111, 112, 123-32, 138, 214.
Canney, M. A., 228.
Carchemish, 23, 207.
Carmel, 170.
Carmel, Mount, 17, 55, 135, 219-21, 229.
Carpenter, J. E., 58, 62.
Chaldeans, 24.
Chapman, A. T., 62
Charles, R. H., 115.
Chemosh, 119, 146, 162, 228, 229.
Chenery, 228.
Cherith, 218, 219.
Cheyne, T. K., 204.
Conway, R. S., 115.
Cook, S. A., 46, 49, 50, 51, 70, 132, 164, 218, 235.
Creighton, Bishop, 58.
Crete, 150, 157, 159, 179.
Crusaders, 164.
Cushan-rishathaim, 136.
Cyrus, 78, 212.

D

Dagon, 66, 158, 162.
Damascus, 11, 18, 21, 26, 27, 125, 204, 208, 209, 215, 223, 236.
Dan, 16, 51, 112, 140, 149, 150, 153, 161, 202, 211, 212.
Dathan, 114, 115.
David, 11, 27, 41, 51, 53, 65, 80, 125, 165, 170-93, 208, 212, 233.
Dead Sea, 19, 189, 225.
Debir, 135.
Deborah, 38, 53, 64, 138-40.
Delilah, 156.

Dickens, Charles, 67.
Dillmann, 98, 102, 128.
Doeg, 174, 175.
Dor, 135.
Dothan, 232.
Driver, S. R., 13, 32, 62, 87, 91, 94, 96, 97, 100, 106, 126, 127, 135, 141, 143, 160, 162, 165, 168, 175, 179, 182, 183, 187.

E

Eben-ezer, 38, 161.
Edom, 16, 32, 33, 113, 119, 140, 228.
Edrei, 119.
Eglon, 131.
Eglon, King, 136, 137.
Egypt, 1-12, 18, 27, 42, 68, 75-101, 116, 150, 208.
Egypt, Brook of, 204.
Ehud, 64, 137, 138.
Elamites, 21, 22.
Elath, 21.
Eleazar, 51.
Elhanan, 172.
Eli, 51, 159-61.
Elijah, 44, 55, 66, 80, 185, 218-27.
Elisha, 44, 55, 66, 171, 221, 226-36.
Elkanah, 159.
El Shaddai, 82, 122.
En-dor, 177.
Ephraim, 36, 148, 149, 188.
Erman, 88.
Esau, 37.
Esdraelon, 17, 140.
Esh-baal, 41, 50, 179, 180, 182, 212.
Ethbaal, 217.
Etruscans, 8, 205.
Euphrates, 24, 26, 78, 120, 136.
Euripides, 146, 204.
Eusebius, 78.
Ezion-geber, 11.
Ezekiel, 111, 200, 203.

F

Fowler, Warde, 156.
Frazer, J. G., 105, 156, 158, 192, 200, 220.
Frederick II, 193.

G

Gaal, 145.
Gad, 33, 119.

Gad the prophet, 192.
Gardiner, A. H., 91.
Garibaldi, 40.
Gath, 162, 164, 176, 183, 196.
Gaza, 11, 135, 155.
Gehazi, 84, 229.
Gershom, 80.
Geshur, 186.
Gezer, 11, 13, 135, 177, 183, 218.
Ghiberti, 127.
Gibeah, 38, 40, 64, 167, 168.
Gibeon, 35, 36, 51, 129, 130, 179, 180, 190, 197.
Gideon, 53, 64, 141-4, 224.
Gihon, 182, 194.
Gilboa, Mount, 41, 142, 177, 229.
Gilead, 146, 147, 192.
Gilgal, 35, 36, 51, 125, 126, 135, 227.
Girgashites, 16.
Glaser, 206.
Goliath, 41, 172, 174.
Goshen, 90, 91.
Greece, the Greeks, 36, 173, 190, 237.
Gressmann, 77, 78, 82, 84, 86, 94, 98.

H

Ḥabiru, 15, 16.
Hadad, 49, 83, 207, 208, 230.
Hadad (Edomite), 208.
Hagia Triada, 157, 179.
Hall, H. R., 11, 12, 68, 159, 179, 208.
Hamath, 112, 204.
Hamor, 145, 146.
Handcock, P., 126.
Hannah, 159.
Hannibal, 187.
Harford, J. Battersby, 82, 102.
Harford-Battersby, G., 58.
Hatshepsut, 68, 205, 206.
Hattushil, 6.
Havilah, 170.
Hazael, 26, 221.
Hazor, 132, 139.
Hebron, 41, 111, 112, 113, 131, 135, 179, 186.
Henry VIII, 42.
Herakles, 152, 156.
Hermon, Mount, 17, 18, 26, 132, 204.
Herod, 78, 200.
Herodotus, 58, 78, 90, 92, 178, 202.

Heshbon, 119.
Hezekiah, 66.
Hiram, King, 182, 183, 197, 198.
Hiram, 202.
Hittites, 1, 4, 6, 9, 16, 21, 23, 30, 76, 112, 176, 185.
Hivites, 16, 129, 130.
Hobab : see Jethro.
Homer, 46, 82, 120, 131, 142, 152, 172, 173, 190.
Hommel, 206.
Hophni, 161.
Hor, Mount, 118.
Horeb, 32, 61, 101, 204, 221.
Hormah, 113, 135.
Hosea, 50, 111.
Hrihor, 10, 12.
Hur, 118.
Hushai, 186, 187.
Hyksos, 1, 28, 68.

I

Ikhnaton : see Amenhotep IV.
India, 45.
Iphigenia, 146.
Isaiah, 54.
Ish-bosheth : see Esh-baal.
Islam, 38.
Italy, 14, 40.
Ithamar, 51.

J

Jabbok, 86, 119.
Jabesh-gilead, 38, 167, 168, 178.
Jabin, 131, 132, 139.
Jack, J. W., 70.
Jacob, 37, 80, 85, 103, 153, 186.
Jael, 53.
Jahaz, 33, 119.
Jashar, Book of, 130, 131, 178.
Jebusites, 16, 53, 112, 181, 182.
Jehoiada, 235.
Jehonadab, 234.
Jehoram, 227, 228, 232, 234.
Jehoshaphat, 224, 225, 228.
Jehu, 26, 43, 44, 69, 221, 232-5.
Jephthah, 52, 64, 146, 147.
Jeremiah, 81, 110, 111.
Jericho, 21, 32, 35, 124-8, 137, 138, 217, 227.
Jeroboam, 11, 42, 43, 54, 66, 106, 209-13.

Jerusalem, 12, 18, 43, 53, 54, 101, 130, 131, 134, 165, 173, 181, &c.
Jethro, 32, 80, 108, 109, 110, 140.
Jezebel, 44, 216, 219, 221, 232–4.
Jezreel, 18, 142, 219, 229, 232, 233.
Joab, 41, 42, 179–82, 184, 188–96.
John the Baptist, 153.
Jonathan, 40, 168, 169, 172–4, 179, 190, 194.
Joseph, 8, 68.
Josephus, 51, 59, 68, 78, 101, 125, 128, 131, 197, 200, 202, 216, 217, 220.
Joshua, 34, 35, 60, 62, 109, 111–34, 190, 218.
Josiah, 66, 148, 211, 212.
Jotham, 144.
Judah, 12, 17, 37, 41–64, 66, 114, 134, 135, 139, 148, 180, 189, 210.

K

Kadesh, 32, 33, 101, 102, 147.
Kadesh (Orontes), 4.
Kalakh : see Nimrūd.
Kaphtor, 150.
Ḳarḳar, 12, 26, 43, 70, 217, 239, 240.
Karnak, 12, 214.
Kassites, 21, 136.
Keats, 101.
Kadesh-naphtali, 132, 139, 140.
Keftiu, 150.
Kenites, 127, 169, 170.
Kennett, R. H., 105.
Kent, C. F., 16, 18.
Kidron, 196, 215.
Kir-hareseth, 229.
Kirjath-jearim, 150, 165, 183.
Kirjath-sepher, 135.
Kishon, 17, 138, 220.
Klostermann, 136.
Korah, 114, 115, 117, 138–40.

L

Lachish, 13, 112, 131.
Laish (Dan), 51, 149.
Lane, E. W., 143.
Lebanon, Mount, 16, 17, 94, 112, 198, 204.
Levites, 51, 54, 84, 109, 114, 115, 148, 149, 161, 212.
Libyans, 1, 8, 9, 214.
Livy, 78, 187.

Lucan, 78.
Luxor, 5.
Lydda, 161.

M

Macalister, R. A. S., 13, 50, 135, 145, 159, 164, 169, 172, 182.
Macbeth, Lady, 222.
Machir, 140, 141.
Mahanaim, 41, 179, 188.
Manoah, 152, 153.
Marah, 101, 102.
Marduk, 121.
Mareshah, 12.
Massah, 116, 117.
McNeile, A. H., 94, 96, 106, 116.
Medes, 24, 26.
Megiddo, 13, 135, 140.
Meribah, 116, 117.
Merneptah, 6, 8, 16, 30, 70, 101, 237.
Merom, 36, 132.
Meroz, 140.
Mesha, 162, 227, 228, 238.
Micah, 148, 149.
Micaiah, 224, 225.
Michal, 173, 182, 183, 192.
Midian, 31, 46, 78, 79, 109, 120, 141–4, 208.
Migdol, 100.
Milcom, 146.
Millais, 118.
Millo, 183, 209.
Millo, House of, 145.
Miriam, 84, 110, 118, 147.
Mizpah, 51.
Moab, 33, 34, 119–21, 137, 138, 146, 227, 228.
Moabite Stone, 119, 162, 171, 216, 238–40.
Moore, G. F., 105, 143, 151, 152.
Moses, 28, 30, 34, 45–8, 59, 60, 75–122, 129, 150.
Mowinckel, 100.
Muṣri, 12.
Mutallu, 4, 6.
Mutkina, 22.

N

Naaman, 230.
Nāblūs, 133, 134, 216.
Naboth, 44, 222, 225.
Nahash, 38, 167, 168.

Nairne, A., 28, 32, 40, 58, 131.
Naphtali, 132, 139, 202.
Nathan, 184, 185, 194.
Naville, 76.
Nebo, Mount, 122.
Nebuchadrezzar I, 22.
Nefertiti, 7.
Nesubenebded, 10.
Nietzsche, 92.
Nile, 1, 30, 79, 83-9.
Nimrūd, 24, 25, 242.
Nineveh, 201.
Noah, 82, 104.
Nob, 51, 174, 175, 190.
Nowairi, 125.

O

Obadiah, 219.
Obed-edom, 183.
Oesterley, W. O. E., 101.
Og, 33, 119.
Omri, 43, 57, 216.
Ophir, 206.
Ophrah, 141, 144.
Osiris, 106.
Osorkon I, 12.
Othello, 146.
Othniel, 36, 64, 136, 137.
Ovid, 155.

P

Palestine, 12-21, 36, 45, 92, 93, 118,
  150, 168.
Palmer, E. H., 103.
Paran, 208.
Paul, St., 92, 118, 125.
Peake, A. S., 129, 165.
Pelusium, 6.
Penuel, 143, 144, 212.
Per-Ramses, 6.
Perizzites, 16.
Persia, 24, 56.
Pethor, 22, 120.
Petrie, Flinders, 76, 112, 131, 132.
Philistines, 9, 11, 17, 38, 40, 98, 99,
  145, 150-79, 182.
Philo, 59.
Phinehas, 161.
Phoenicians, 17, 18, 198, 203 ; see
  also Tyre, Zidon.
Pi-hahiroth, 100.
Pithom, 6, 76.

Pitru : see Pethor.
Pliny, 78, 90, 94, 206.
Plutarch, 186.
Pompey, 204.

R

Raamses, 76.
Rabbah, 184.
Rachel, 159, 167.
Rahab, 35, 124, 125.
Ramah, 51, 159, 167.
Ramoth-gilead, 224, 225, 233.
Red Sea, 17, 98, 99.
Rehob, 112.
Rehoboam, 197, 210, 211, 214, 215.
Rephidim, 118, 123.
Reuben, 33, 114, 119, 140.
Reuel : see Jethro.
Rezon, 208, 209.
Rimmon : see Hadad.
Rizpah, 190, 192.
Robertson, J., 59.
Robinson, Edward, 125.
Robinson, T. H., 61, 71.
Romans, 40, 82, 155, 156, 206, 237.
Romulus, 78.

S

SA.GAZ, 15.
Samaria, 212, 213, 216, 222, 223,
  225, 230-2.
Samson, 37, 53, 151-9.
Samuel, 36-8, 51-3, 65, 159-77.
Sargon, 78.
Saul, 27, 38-41, 52, 64, 65, 125,
  166-79, 192, 233.
Saxons, 49, 82.
Sayce, A. H., 4, 40, 58, 88, 99, 135.
Seir, 140.
Sell, E., 172.
Sellin, 62, 63, 127, 145.
Semites, 45, 49, 152, 155, 159, 172.
Seti I, 4, 16.
Shakespeare, 178, 222, 223.
Shalmaneser I, 21, 24.
Shalmaneser III, 12, 26, 69, 138,
  223, 240, 241, 242.
Shamgar, 140.
Sheba, 189, 190.
Sheba, Queen of, 206.
Shechem, 134, 144-6, 159, 210, 211.
Shiloh, 36, 51, 159, 161, 196, 209,
  213.

Shimei, 194, 195, 196.
Shishak, 10, 11, 12, 209, 214.
Shittim, 35, 125.
Shunam, 177, 194, 229.
Shur, 102, 103, 170, 177.
Sihon, 33, 119, 147.
Simeon, 114, 134, 139.
Simpson, D. C., 62.
Sinai, 31, 32, 33, 48, 61, 101, 109, 140.
Sinuhe, 80, 173.
Sisera, 64, 139, 140.
Skinner, J., 202, 210, 224, 226, 229, 236.
Smendes : see Nesubenebdad.
Smith, G. A., 150, 188.
Smith, Sydney, 26, 27.
Smith, W. Robertson, 97, 173, 175, 178, 220, 229.
Solomon, 11, 42-4, 53, 135, 159, 183, 193-209, 217.
Sophocles, 147.
Sorek, 158.
Stade, 235.
Stanley, Dean, 132.
Strabo, 156, 206.
Strahan, J., 146.
Stubbs, Bishop, 58, 190.
Succoth, 98, 143, 144, 203.
Syrians : see Arameans.

T

Taanach, 13, 135, 140.
Tabor, Mount, 139, 140, 144.
Tacitus, 120, 204.
Talmud, 60.
Tanis : see Zoan.
Tarshish, 208.
Telaim, 170.
Tell el-Amarna Tablets, 4, 13-16, 75, 82, 112.
Tell el-Ḥesy, 13, 131.
Tell el-Mutesellim, 13.
Tennyson, 147.
Thebes, 3, 4, 6, 8, 10, 12, 93.
Thebez, 145, 146, 185.
Thomson, W. M., 94.
Thucydides, 64.
Thutmose III, 2, 12, 68, 147.

Thutmose IV, 2.
Tiglath-pilesar I, 22, 146.
Tiglath-pilesar III, 27.
Tigris, 136.
Timnah, 153, 154.
Trench, Archbishop, 117.
Turks, 40, 76.
Tutankhamen, 99.
Tylor, E. B., 188.
Tyre, 26, 192, 202, 216, 219.

U

Uratu, 24, 26, 27.
Uriah, 184.
Uzzah, 183, 184.

V

Van, Lake, 24.
Virgil, 46, 83, 97, 154.

W

Wade, G. W., 30, 48.
Warren, Charles, 131.
Wellhausen, 61, 212.
Wenamon, 10.
Wiener, H. M., 113.

Z

Zadok, 54, 161, 186, 189, 194, 196.
Zagros Range, 24.
Zakkala, 177.
Zalmunna, 143, 144.
Zarephath, 218.
Zarethan, 126, 203.
Zebah, 143, 144.
Zebulun, 139, 143.
Zeeb, 143.
Zerah, 12.
Zeruah, 209.
Zidon, 26, 132, 198, 218, 219.
Ziklag, 176.
Zimri, 216, 234.
Zion, 182, 204.
Ziph, 175, 176.
Zipporah, 86, 110.
Zoan, 10, 112.
Zorah, 149, 153, 156, 158.
Zuph, 159, 167.

THE OLD TESTAMENT

CHRONOLOGICALLY ARRANGED

by EVELYN W. HIPPISLEY, S.Th.

*Licensed Teacher in Theology, Tutor to Women Theological
Students, King's College, London.*

N.B.—The dates of the Kings of Israel and Judah are taken from
the article 'Chronology of the Old Testament' in the *Encyclopaedia Biblica*; and the articles in Peake's commentary and in
Hastings' *Dictionary of the Bible* on the separate books have
been consulted. Other books which have been used are the
International Critical Commentary, the *Westminster Commentaries*, the *Expositors' Bible*, the *Century Bible*, Dr. Driver's
Introduction to the Literature of the Old Testament, Dr. Oesterley's
Books of the Apocrypha, and Dr. Charles' *Apocrypha and Pseud-
epigrapha*.

Principal Foreign Power = the principal foreign power with which
Israel was in contact at the time.

Inscriptions = inscriptions, chiefly on Babylonian and Assyrian
monuments which refer to events in the history of Israel. These
are mostly translated in the Appendix to Dr. Foakes-Jackson's
Biblical History of the Hebrews. The Code of Ḥammurabi,
Selections from the Tell el-Amarna letters, and the Babylonian
Flood Stories are published by S.P.C.K. (1s., 4d., and 6d. each).

The Book of Genesis, divided into sources by Dr. T. H. Robinson,
is published by the National Adult School Union (1s.).

Book.	Contents.	Origin.
The Hexateuch	Genesis to Joshua—contains four strands of narrative : (i) Jahvistic, Judaean in origin, *circ.* 850 B.C. ; (ii) Elohistic, Ephraimitic in origin, *circ.* 750 B.C., both written from a prophetic standpoint ; (JE combined *circ.* 650 B.C.). (iii) D Deuteronomic revision, 7th century B.C. ; (JED combined early in Exile). (iv) P Priestly author and editor, 5th century B.C. ; (JEDP combined and re-edited before 3rd century B.C.).	

N.B.—*No analysis of sources is given, but large portions belonging to the Priestly writer are indicated, as it is important to recognize the later standpoint.*

Book.	Contents.	Origin.
Genesis	i–xi. Prehistoric Narratives. xii–xlix. Stories of the Patriarchs.	JEP.
Exodus	The Exodus and Wanderings.	JEP (xxv–xxxi, xxxv–xl P).
Numbers	The Story of Wanderings.	JEDP (i–x. 28, xvii–xix, xxvi–xxxi, xxxiii–xxxvi P).
Joshua	The Conquest of Canaan.	JEDP (xv–xix P).
Judges	The Conquest of Canaan and Settlement of Tribes.	Compiled from old material (perhaps JE) by a Deuteronomic editor, 6th century B.C.
1 and 2 Samuel	History of Establishment of Monarchy, and Early Kings.	Two strands of narrative of 9th and 8th centuries B.C. woven together by a Deuteronomic editor, 6th century B.C.
1 and 2 Kings	History of Kings of Israel and Judah from Solomon to Fall of Jerusalem.	Compiled from Court and Temple records and biographies of prophets by a Deuteronomic editor, and re-edited during the Exile.

Important Events.	Date B. C.	Principal Foreign Power.	Inscriptions.
		First Babylonian Empire, 2050–732 B.C.	
Ḥammurabi's Code of Laws, based on an older Sumerian Code.	circ. 1950		Code of Ḥammurabi.
			Tell el - Amarna Letters (1450–1370).
			Stele of Raamses (Rameses) !I (1300–1234) found at Beth-shan, showing that Semites had built city of Raamses.
	circ. 1230	Egypt.	Stele of Merneptah (1234–1225 B.C.).
Crossing of Jordan.	circ. 1196		
Philistines settling in Canaan, circ. 1200 B.C.			
SAUL	1025		
DAVID	1000		
SOLOMON	970		
Division of Kingdom.	933		
Kings of Judah. *Kings of Israel.*			
REHOBOAM JEROBOAM	933		
ABIJAM	916		
ASA	914		
NADAB	912		
BAASHA	911		

Book.	Contents.	Origin.
Amos	Warning to Israel by a Judaean.	Prophecies delivered in the reign of Jeroboam II (2 Kings xiv. 23–9), 760–746 B.C.
Hosea	Warning to Israel by an Israelite.	Prophecies delivered in reign of Jeroboam II, and later (2 Kings xiv. 23–xv), 746–734 B.C.
Micah	Denunciations of Israel and Judah by a Man of the People.	Chapters i–iii—prophecies delivered in reigns of Jotham, Ahaz, and Hezekiah (2 Kings xv. 32, xvi, xviii-xx)—739–693 B.C. Chapters iv–vi anonymous prophecies, added later.
Isaiah i–xxxix	The Statesman - Prophet's Warnings to Jerusalem.	Prophecies delivered in reigns of Uzziah, Jotham, Ahaz, and Hezekiah (2 Kings xix. 20, xx), 739–701 B.C. (omit xiii–xiv. 23, xxi, xxiv–xxvii, xxxiv, xxxv, and possibly other passages which are post-exilic).

(5)

Important Events.	Date B.C.	Principal Foreign Power.	Inscriptions.
Kings of Judah. Kings of Israel.			
ELAH	888		
ZIMRI	887		
OMRI	887		
AHAB	876		
JEHOSHAPHAT	873	Assyria	
Battle of Ḳarḳar	853	(Shalmaneser	Moabite Stone.
AHAZIAH	853	III. 859).	Ḳarḳar Inscription.
JORAM	853		
Completion of Jahvistic narrative.	850		
JEHORAM	849		
AHAZIAH	842		
ATHALIAH JEHU	841		
Jehu pays tribute to Shalmaneser.	841		Black Obelisk of
JOASH	835		Shalmaneser.
JEHOAHAZ	814		
JOASH	797		
*AMAZIAH	795		
AZARIAH or UZZIAH	789		
JEROBOAM II.	782		
JOTHAM (regent)			
Compilation of Elohistic narrative	750		Tiglath-Pileser III
ZECHARIAH	743		reduces Hamath.
SHALLUM	743		
MENAHEM	743		
JOTHAM	739		
Menahem pays tribute to Tiglath-Pileser III.	738		Tribute of Menahem.
PEKAHIAH	736		
AHAZ PEKAH	735		
Ahaz pays tribute to Tiglath-Pileser III.	734		
HOSHEA	730		Hoshea placed on throne by Tiglath-Pileser III.

* The Biblical Chronology here obviously needs reconstruction. The dates given here are those of Marti in *Encycl. Biblica* ; cf. Steuernagel, *Einleitung*, and Box, *Isaiah.*

Book.	Contents.	Origin.
Jeremiah	Warnings and Pleadings to Jerusalem.	Prophecies uttered in reigns of Josiah, Jehoiakim, Jehoiachin, and Zedekiah (2 Kings xxii–xxv). Earlier prophecies written down by Baruch ; later prophecies, especially xlvi–li, added by a compiler during or after the Exile—626-500 B.C.
Zephaniah	Doom of Wicked Nations.	Prophecy uttered *circ.* 626 B.C., when the Scythians were threatening Jerusalem, and edited in post-exilic times.
Deuteronomy	The Law-Book (with additions) found in the Temple, on which Josiah based his reform.	A revision of the earlier laws, compiled *circ.* 640 B.C.
Nahum	Doom of Nineveh.	Chapters ii and iii written *circ.* 612 B.C. ; chapter i a post-exilic acrostic poem.
Habakkuk	Moral Problem raised by God's use of Chaldaeans.	Chapters i and ii written *circ.* 600–550 B.C., when Chaldaea, i.e. New Babylon, was becoming powerful ; chapter iii a lyric ode of post-exilic date.
Ezekiel i–xxxii	Prophecies of Doom, and Denunciations of Jerusalem and foreign nations.	Written in Babylon before the Fall of Jerusalem by an exile banished in 596 B.C.
Ezekiel xxxiii–xxxix	Picture of the Restitution of Israel.	Written in Babylon after the Fall of Jerusalem—584-572 B.C.

Important Events.	Date B. C.	Principal Foreign Power.	Inscriptions.
Kings of Judah. Kings of Israel. Fall of Samaria *End of Kingdom of Israel*	721		Capture of Samaria by Sargon II.
*HEZEKIAH Invasion of Sennacherib MANASSEH AMON JOSIAH	{ 720? { 715? 700 692 638 637		Siloam Inscription. Invasion of Sennacherib.
	625	New Babylonian Empire founded by Nabopolassar.	
Finding of Law-Book (2 Kings xxii) Reform of Josiah Fall of Nineveh Battle of Megiddo JEHOAHAZ JEHOIAKIM Battle of Carchemish JEHOIACHIN First deportation to Babylon ZEDEKIAH	621 621 612 608 608 607 605 597 596 596	Nebuchadrezzar King of Babylon 604–561.	
Fall of Jerusalem *Exile.*	586		

* See Dr. Robinson's note, p. 232.   If the view is accepted that Hezekiah was associated with Ahaz for a time, this would dispose of part of the discrepancy.

Book.	Contents.	Origin.
Ezekiel xl–xlviii	A Vision of the Ideal Theocracy.	Written after 572 B.C.
Lamentations	A Book of Dirges.	These poems, arranged as acrostics (except ch. v), are of exilic date.
Isaiah xl–lv	The Promise of Return.	Prophecies delivered by an unknown author at the close of the Exile, probably between 549 and 538 B.C. The Servant-Songs are possibly later.
Obadiah	Doom of Edom.	Verses 1–14 belong to an exilic prophecy; the rest is probably post-exilic.
Leviticus xvii–xxvi	The Law of Holiness.	Old Laws of Priestly character grouped together towards the close of the Exile.
Haggai *Zechariah* i–viii	Call to rebuild the Temple.	Prophecies delivered 520 B.C. (Ezra v, vi). Prophecies delivered 520, 518 B.C.
Isaiah lvi–lxvi	The Restored Community: its Faults and its Blessings.	Prophecies delivered by an unknown author in Palestine *circ.* 450 B.C.
Malachi	Rebuke of the Moral and Religious Condition of the Jews.	Probably delivered *circ.* 450 B.C.
Ruth	A Pastoral Idyll.	Probably used as a Tract for the Times about Foreign Marriages in Nehemiah's day.
Job	A Wisdom-Book, treating of the Problem of the Innocent Sufferer.	Probably based on an older story by a post-exilic author.
Leviticus	The Priestly Code of Laws.	Compiled during the Exile, and possibly published by Ezra.
Joel	The Day of the Lord.	The date is probably early in the fourth century B.C.

Important Events.	Date B.C.	Principal Foreign Power.	Inscriptions.
Cyrus overthrows the Medes.	549	Persian Empire.	
Capture of Babylon by Cyrus.	538		
Edict of Cyrus.	538		
The Return. Return of Zerubbabel and Joshua (Ezra i, ii).	537		
Building of Temple.	520–516		
Dedication of Second Temple (Ezra vi. 16).	516		
		Artaxerxes I.	
Return of Nehemiah (Neh. ii).	445		
Nehemiah's second visit (Neh. xiii. 7).	433		
		Artaxerxes II.	
Ezra's Return.	? 397		
		Artaxerxes III (Ochus).	
Jaddua, High Priest (Neh. xii. 11).	351		
Samaritan Schism.	335		

Book.	Contents.	Origin.
Zechariah ix–xiv	An Apocalyptic Vision.	The work of a post-exilic prophet or prophets, *circ.* 320 B.C. or later.
Jonah	An Evangelical Allegory.	Written *circ.* 300 B.C., and probably based on an old tradition.
1 and 2 Chronicles	History re-edited from an ecclesiastical standpoint.	Compiled, with additions, from previously existing sources by a Temple Levite, *circ.* 300–250 B.C.
Ezra \ *Nehemiah* /	Narrative of the Return and Rebuilding of the Temple.	Compiled by the Chronicler, *circ.* 300 B.C., from City and Temple records, Aramaic documents, and memoirs.
Proverbs	One of the Wisdom-Books of the Hebrews, containing Moral Maxims.	Several collections of Proverbs of various dates combined by an editor, *circ.* 250 B.C.
Song of Songs	A Marriage Drama, showing the triumph of faithful love.	Probably written in Jerusalem during the Greek period.
Esther	A Didactic Romance.	Written, perhaps on an historical basis, *circ.* third century B.C., to defend the keeping of the Feast of Purim.
Ecclesiastes	A Wisdom-Book, containing the Meditations of an Unsatisfied Man.	Written *circ.* 200 B.C.
Psalms	The Hymns Ancient and Modern of the Second Temple.	Five books of gradual growth, containing 'Praise-Songs' dating probably from the time of David to the second century B.C.
Daniel	An Apocalypse of Encouragement.	Probably founded on an older story, and written *circ.* 168 B.C. to encourage the Maccabaean party.

Important Events.	Date B.C.	Principal Foreign Power.	Inscriptions.
Alexander the Great becomes ruler of the world.	331	Macedonian Empire.	
Conquest of Palestine by Alexander.	331		
Death of Alexander and division of his Empire.	323		
		Ptolemaic and Seleucid Empires.	
Palestine under the Ptolemies of Egypt.	311		
Antiochus III conquers Palestine.	198		
Persecution of Jews by Antiochus IV (Epiphanes).	169		
Maccabaean Revolt against Antiochus Epiphanes.	167		

A list, chronological as far as possible, is appended of the principal
in the Alexandrian Canon (the Septuagint), but not in the
were never included in either Canon, but are important as greatly

Book.		Contents.	Origin.
APOCRYPHA.	APOCALYPTIC.		
Ecclesiasticus (Wisdom of Jesus, son of Sirach.)		A Wisdom-Book, containing counsels for daily life.	Written in Hebrew, probably circ. 180 B.C., and translated into Greek by the author's grandson, circ. 130 B.C.
Tobit		An Idyll of Home-Life.	Written probably in Aramaic, circ. 190–175 B.C.
	Book of Enoch	A series of Apocalyptic Visions.	Written in Palestine by several Hebrew authors belonging to the party of the Ḥasidim, between 170 and 64 B.C.
Prayer of Azariah			An addition to the Greek text of Daniel, probably written in Hebrew, circ. 170 B.C.
Song of the Three Children.		The Thanksgiving of the Three for Deliverance (Benedicite).	Dating from the Maccabaean triumph, circ. 165 B.C.
1 Esdras		History of the Jews from the reign of Josiah to the Proclamation of the Law (639–? 400 B.C.).	Written probably at Alexandria between 170 and 100 B.C.
Rest of Esther		Contains additional details as to Esther, probably imaginary.	A Greek interpolation in the Hebrew text, circ. 150 to 100 B.C.
Judith		A story of the Deliverance of Israel from Assyria by a Jewess.	Written circ. 150 B.C. and edited circ. 60 B.C.
Baruch		A work in four divisions, containing prayers of Exiles and messages to Exiles.	Written by three authors, probably between 2nd century B.C. and 2nd century A.D.
	Testaments of the XII Patriarchs.	The Dying Commands of Jacob's Twelve Sons.	Written, probably in Hebrew, by Ḥasidim, circ. 130-10 B.C. (contains later Christian interpolations).
2 Maccabees		History from the reign of Seleucus IV to the death of Nicator (176–161 B.C.). (Parallel with part of 1 Maccabees, but not so trustworthy.)	Probably abridged circ. 40 A.D. from a larger work by an Alexandrian Jew, written circ. 120 B.C.

Apocryphal and Apocalyptic Books. The *Apocrypha* were included
Palestinian Canon (Massoretic Text).   The *Apocalyptic* writings
influencing New Testament thought and phraseology.

Important Events.	Date B. C.	Principal Foreign Power.	Inscriptions.
		Seleucid Empire.	
Maccabaean Revolt.	167		
Re-dedication of Temple.	165		
Death of Judas Maccabaeus.	160		
Jonathan, High-Priest.	160		
Simon, High-Priest, and Ethnarch	142		
Independence of the Jews.	142		
John Hyrcanus.	135		
Rise of Pharisees and Sadducees.			
John Hyrcanus, King of Judaea (Hasmonean Dynasty).	107		

Book.		Contents.	Origin.
APOCRYPHA.	APOCALYPTIC.		
1 Maccabees		History of the Jews from the accession of Antiochus Epiphanes to the death of Simon (175–135 B.C.).	Compiled from existing sources in Hebrew by a devout Jew, between 1co and 90 B.C.
Story of Susanna		A Story in praise of the wisdom of Daniel.	Probably written to support new laws as to witnesses, *circ.* 100 B.C. An addition to the Greek text of Daniel.
Story of Bel and the Dragon			Perhaps written originally in Aramaic ; an addition to the Greek text of Daniel, *circ.* 100 B.C.
Wisdom of Solomon		A Wisdom-Book inculcating the beauty of Divine Wisdom.	Written by an orthodox Alexandrian Jew, *circ.* 100–50 B.C.
Prayer of Manasses.		A Jewish Penitential Psalm.	Perhaps written in Greek —date uncertain.
	Psalms of Solomon or *Psalms of the Pharisees.*	Eighteen Psalms, containing important Messianic teaching.	Written in Hebrew by a Pharisee, 70–40 B.C., probably for use in synagogues.
	Book of Jubilees	The narrative of Genesis, rewritten from a later standpoint.	Written in Hebrew by a Palestinian Jew, *circ.* 40–10 B.C. or later.
	Secrets of Enoch	An Account of the Creation.	Written in Greek by an orthodox Alexandrian Jew between 30 B.C. and 50 A.D.
2 Esdras		An Apocalypse, containing Visions of Ezra at Babylon.	A Jewish work, probably belonging to 1st century A.D., with later Christian interpolations.

Important Events.	Date B.C.	Principal Foreign Power.	Inscriptions.
ARISTOBULUS I.	105		
ALEXANDER JANNAEUS.	104		
ALEXANDRA.	78		
HYRCANUS II and ARISTOBULUS II dispute the throne.	69		
Rise of the House of Antipater.		Roman Empire.	
Pompey enters Syria and conquers Jerusalem.	65		
Judaea divided into five districts.	57		
Antipater becomes Procurator of Judaea.	47		
HEROD, King of Judaea.	37		
Herod marries Mariamne, the last of the Hasmoneans.	35		
Herod's Temple begun.	20		
Death of Herod.	4		

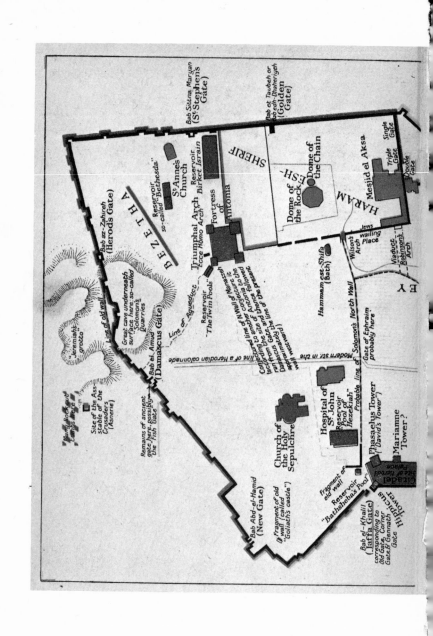